WILLIAM HAGUE

In His Own

Right

WILLIAM HAGUE

In His Own

Right

Jo-Anne Nadler

First published in Great Britain 2000
Published by Politico's Publishing
8 Artillery Row
Westminster
London
SW1P 1RZ

Tel 020 7931 0090
Fax 020 7828 8111
Email publishing@politicos.co.uk
Website http://www.politicos.co.uk/publishing

First published in hardback 2000

A catalogue record of this book is available from the British Library.

ISBN 1 902301 65 X

Printed and bound in Great Britain by St Edmundsbury Press.

Contents

For my mother, Hilary Nadler and
in memory of my father,
James Nadler

Preface

In a Yorkshire room studded with family mementoes and a framed photograph of Ffion on top of the television I sat down to watch Prime Minister's Questions. It was April 2000, shortly after I had started this project. Although this is not an authorised biography, William Hague and his family have been extremely courteous and helpful from the start. Stella and Nigel Hague had already entertained me to a sandwich lunch before inviting me to watch their son take on the Prime Minister. Fittingly for a proud father, Nigel Hague turned the television sound down when his son was not on the screen.

I am indebted to William Hague and his office for their patient and efficient dealings throughout this process. The genesis of this book has been a lengthy one, beginning in a London restaurant shortly after the last general election and eventually confirmed on the Florida gulf coast. I had travelled to America where Hague was addressing a conference to produce a live interview for the BBC. It was the first time I had had any lengthy conversation with him and the first chance I had to let him know that I would be writing this book. He seemed quite relaxed at the prospect of a stranger examining his whole life, and I trust that he will consider this a fair account.

Researching and writing a biography in less than six months is an intense experience. Inevitably I have noticed my own friends and family glaze over as I have begun yet another conversation about William Hague. In looking for a guide as to how to work,

I realised Hague himself had given me the best clue. Its part of a biographer's role to reach inside her subject's psyche. I decided I should 'be in Hague's head, but not run by it'!

I would like to thank the very many people who have been so generous with their time. There are far too many to mention here, but along with Stella and Nigel Hague, Pat and Ray Swift deserve special mention. Alicia Collinson, Brooks Newmark, Gary Jackson and Guy Hands made time for me in their busy schedules. Numerous MPs and Conservative Party officials have helped and I am particularly grateful to the offices of Baroness Thatcher and John Major for their assistance. Lords Parkinson, Hodgson, Cranborne, and Baroness Young were all extremely helpful. Of the current and former Shadow Cabinet particular thanks goes to Archie Norman, Ann Widdecombe and Michael Howard. Alan Duncan has been faultlessly generous with his time and an invaluable source.

On a personal level I would like to thank Stephen Pollard for suggesting, when I mentioned over dinner that someone should write a biography of the man set to be the next Conservative leader, that it should be me. Thanks to Mike Shaw and Jonathan Pegg at Curtis Brown for taking me under their wing. Thanks to Politicos: Iain Dale, Sean Magee and John Berry for giving me the opportunity to do this and for not interfering. For crucial research back up enormous thanks to John Parks. For taking a keen interest and offering encouragement, thanks particularly to John Spiers, Bruce Anderson, Martin Summers, Michael Crick, Paul Franklin and Guy Strafford. And for all that and very much more, Nick Green.

Jo-Anne Nadler

September 2000

Chapter One

FROM MAJOR TO MINOR

The champagne was already flowing and the smoked salmon being handed around as the victor arrived to join the celebrations. William Hague had left his campaign offices earlier that June day a backbench MP; he arrived back in the evening as leader of the Conservative Party. In the end his victory, secured by a lead of twenty-two votes, was more decisive than he had dared contemplate and more than enough reason to invite all sections of his Party to put aside their recent bitter differences and join the toast to a fresh start.

To an outside observer the fizz of a fine celebration could have appeared a vulgar indulgence for a party that had so recently suffered a humiliating national defeat. Although the leadership battle, resolved on 19 June 1997, was a direct result of the previous month's election disaster, it had been a psychological boost for the party, offering its participants and their supporters the opportunity to politic just as intensely as they had done in government. Now, with the result confirmed, the joyful relief of Hague's campaign workers was tempered by the realisation that the celebration marked only the beginning of an uphill struggle.

Not everyone at the event was convinced that this struggle would be any easier with Hague at the helm, although this was no time for disloyal whisperings. One MP, who in different circumstances would have been among the most ardent of Michael Portillo's supporters, appeared not to recall the last time he had been drinking champagne with William Hague. At a private garden party in Westminster three weeks previously he had told friends that Hague was 'no more than another Major'. Short of labelling Hague the rightful heir to Edward Heath, this was as damning a criticism as a Thatcherite Conservative could muster, but conveniently that evening his doubts seemed to disperse as quickly as the bubbles, making this young gun of the right among the last revellers to leave. Along with many of Hague's more public campaign doubters he was soon appointed a shadow post and is now in the shadow cabinet.

If judged by the most high profile party-goers, however, the right had no need to worry about their new leader's credentials. Lady Thatcher and Michael Portillo were truly guests of honour. Both had played a crucial last-minute role in turning the momentum away from Kenneth Clarke towards Hague, their latterly appointed torch bearer. Michael Portillo had remained neutral through most of the campaign, but following the bizarre coupling of Clarke and John Redwood, the right's most cherished son had thrown his weight behind Hague. Portillo personally canvassed friends of his in the Commons who were considering backing the Clarke/Redwood axis as a union of heavyweights. In a round of telephone calls the man who would have been leader pulled in votes for the man who eventually beat him to the job.

Clinking glasses alongside Lord Parkinson and a coterie of sympathetic journalists, former cabinet ministers and failed leadership contenders Michael Howard and Peter Lilley added to the impression that the right had triumphed. Even when Ken Clarke turned up in the spirit of a good loser, his preference for beer over bubbly indicated that his was a different brand of Conservatism – he hadn't beaten them and it seemed he wasn't going to join them. Earlier William Hague had joked that neither he nor Ken were bitter men – in anything but their drinking habits.

The only apparently bitter men were those who refused to join the party. John Redwood and a few of his remaining troops chose instead to mark the end of the leadership race in his offices a few steps down the road.

Anxious not to seem smug or triumphal, Hague was among the first to leave his own victory party. Despite the temptation to give in to revelry, his early departure with friend and aide Alan Duncan, and campaign manager James Arbuthnot MP sent a deliberate message that there was no time to lose for the sombre reflection necessary in planning his new team and their task.

This eagerness to get on with the job was typical of the new leader's political career. Twenty years previously his teenage speech to the Conservative Party Conference had branded him the ultimate 'Tory Boy'. In the decades that followed, Hague's rise through youth, student and then Westminster politics had been swift and efficient. The irony for this supreme career politician was that the highest realisation of his ambitions, to lead the party that had constantly fascinated and obsessed him, had come as a result of that party's own failure.

Looking back over his life he had seen the Conservative Party transform Britain only to make itself redundant in the process. Now it was his task to reform and renew the party as it had done the British economy and the aspirations of British people.

Looking back only six weeks, Hague might have reflected on an alternative conclusion for the leadership battle to which he had so nearly committed himself over a better vintage of champagne . . .

It was May Bank Holiday Monday. A pleasant evening and a bottle of Bollinger left over from dinner was ready to put the seal on a deal which would create a powerful right-wing ticket for the leadership. Michael Howard, until recently Home Secretary, had correctly spotted Hague's winning potential and in telephone conversations over the weekend following John Major's announced intention to resign, had sought to secure William's support as running mate. In return Hague would become deputy leader and party chairman were Howard to be elected leader. William and his fiancée, Ffion Jenkins, were expected to join the Howards to discuss the details of the deal when they returned from Hague's Yorkshire constituency and after the Howards' early evening guests had departed.

The Howards were hosting an informal supper party for close political friends, effectively the preliminary meeting of Michael's leadership campaign. Although talk was very much of the imminent contest to which Ken Clarke and Peter Lilley had already declared their candidacy, only three around the table knew of the meeting planned for later that evening. As far as Michael Howard, his wife Sandra and campaign manager Sir Michael Spicer MP were concerned, William and Ffion were joining them later not for a big celebration but to sort out the business of a deal which had been already agreed. In earlier conversations with Howard, Hague had agreed that they should keep the arrangement strictly to themselves to avoid news leaking out so that it could have maximum news impact at a press conference planned for Tuesday.

It would have made a potent partnership, combining Howard's particular brand of right-wing conviction with Hague's management and communication skills. Although William Hague coveted the party leadership, not only for its own reward but as a vital step toward his ultimate ambition of leading the country, he was seriously contemplating Howard's proposal. In the months running up to the general election various 'wannabe' leaders had been jostling for position so that their campaigns would be up and running once John Major had fired the starting pistol. For as long as he could remember it had been Hague's goal to lead the party, but for the chance to have come so quickly had not seemed likely in the months before the general election. No one could have predicted that two of the front runners,

Michael Heseltine and Michael Portillo, would not be joining the race.

Certainly Hague had been tipped as a future leader, but his backers had spoken of him in terms of the next leader but one; for those less enthusiastic, the next but two. For the right the next leader, of course, was supposed to have been Michael Portillo, and if he had been able to stand Hague would have backed him had he not made it to the final round himself. The battle to succeed John Major was so overt that press speculation had been rife for many months. In retrospect the Hagues say they found it hilarious that the announcement of their engagement in the spring of 1997 prompted an improvement in William's odds to becoming the next leader. Amusing though it may have been, Hague certainly had considered running in the leadership race that would inevitably follow the election, not so much with a view to winning but to register his intention for a future battle. Towards the end of 1996, in conversations with Norman Lamont, Hague had made it clear he was thinking about standing.

His considerations were also clear to the Third Term Group, a discreet dining club of MPs who had been meeting regularly since the late 1980s. The meetings of about twelve people provided the most frank environment in which Hague, especially when promoted to the Cabinet, could talk freely about politics. Each member is committed to total discretion. From his earliest contributions it was clear that Hague had strong convictions, particularly about the family and nationhood. In 1995 Hague had campaigned for John Major in the 'put up or shut up' leadership campaign against John Redwood. When the result failed to quell the sniping against Major, it became clear to Hague's fellow diners that he was now discussing policy in terms of the things he wanted to do as party leader, and that in his mind such a possibility seemed less distant. However, without being able to predict the severity of the 1997 result, Hague's post-election priorities would have been to take a holiday in the United States with Ffion and to organise their wedding.

The new reality had begun to set in overnight on 1 May, and really took root following John Major's concession of defeat. William Hague had been the only cabinet minister on duty at Conservative Central Office over the night of the general election. Richmond, his constituency, traditionally counted its votes on the Friday after an election, leaving Hague free to join the party's press operation in Smith Square. As the night drew on he found it increasingly difficult to summon up any sort of positive interpretation of the results coming in from around the country. He had expected the Tories to do badly, but not that badly. When the result from Enfield Southgate came through, television sets sizzled with the pictures of a beaten Michael Portillo in an image that immediately entered the iconography of election defeat. The conference room in Central Office was full of staff and senior party managers. Hague, immaculately groomed for his media interviews, stood among his colleagues with Ffion. In the moment that people began to absorb the implications of the news the atmosphere, thick with forced bonhomie, intensified as many sensed an almost tangible transfer of attention to Hague.

Elsewhere John Major, quietly taking in the news of his party's defeat, turned to two senior party colleagues and said: 'I suppose it will be William.'

At around 5.30 on Friday morning John Major returned to Central Office from Huntingdon. Hague was very keen to get away to Yorkshire but he was anxious to talk to Major before he left. His aim was to persuade Major to stay on as party leader for at least a few months. Hague felt that the party had been battered and would need time to take stock before being able to make a measured decision as to who should be the next leader. He was also keen to give himself as much time as possible to consider whether or not to stand. In the longer term a caretaker leadership would have given Hague the opportunity to raise his profile. He would almost certainly have played a big role in the shadow cabinet, giving him the chance to shine in the House. John Major, however, was not to be moved. He told Hague that he would stand down as soon as possible. He was adamant that he could not continue as leader, that it would be bad for the party because his authority for leading a shadow cabinet had been irreparably undermined.

After working through the night at the end of what had been a gruelling election campaign, Hague took the first morning plane out of City Airport and flew back to face his count. He was unsettled about the impending leadership race and his mind was too full of the recent events to want to think it through. There was some relief at the Richmond count, where he had been able to keep the Conservative majority in five figures (10, 051), but the press questions were all about the leadership race. The amnesty he had suggested to John Major was already irrelevant. Ken Clarke declared his intention to run for leader while William's count was still going on. At the conclusion of the count Hague went to his Richmond home to sleep, and to put burdensome decision-making out of his mind.

Hague woke the next day not much clearer and with a constituency meeting to attend. The managers of a sports centre that he was due to open had taken for granted that Hague would still be their MP. However, they hadn't bargained for the interest of the national press, who had arrived to ask Hague about his intentions for the leadership race. By the end of the morning news had broken that, for health reasons, Michael Heseltine would not stand for leader. Freed from constituency duties, William set off for an afternoon walk with Ffion. Her advice to him was simply 'follow your instincts.' The problem for Hague was that he still was not sure what his instincts were telling him, even though he was absolutely sure of one thing: if he were to stand he would win.

He believed he was the only candidate who could take sufficient votes from across the parliamentary party. He was also sure, as he had been for as long as he could remember, that he would one day lead the party. What he doubted was whether this was the right time for him to do it. It was the job he had always wanted, but he did not want it then. The timing did not fit his plans. The chance had come too soon.

When William and Ffion returned home matters were complicated further by the advice of friends. The display on the telephone answering machine was flashing 32. While he had been out there had been many callers, friends and colleagues, nearly all suggesting he should stand. His university friends Alan Duncan and Brooks Newmark were insistent. Party figures including Baroness Miller, a stalwart of the grass roots, pledged her support.

More significant in terms of the specific electorate involved, there were calls from MPs who also held party offices. Michael Trend was the party's deputy chairman and Andrew Mackay a deputy whip. If Hague were to enter the race such people would be an invaluable resource as their positions required public neutrality. When he eventually decided to run he was able to count on the support of around eight or nine people who could justifiably tell other candidates they weren't revealing their choice. It would give his team the edge in terms of calculating real support.

Another Oxford chum, Guy Hands, a close friend and political ally, took the opposite view. He believed it was the wrong time for William to stand, not least because he had some real living to do before he could really qualify for such a role. Hands told him to forget about the leadership for at least five years. In blunt but persuasive terms he told William to enjoy time with his new fiancée. His message said: 'Fuck your brains out for a few years'. It must have seemed an attractive option because despite the preponderance of encouraging messages, Hague's instincts were still confused. His mother, Stella, must have added to his quandary. She said: 'Why would you want such a thankless job when you're just about to get married?'

One caller seemed to offer him a way out. A proposal from Michael Howard was an apparent solution to his dilemma.

A deal with Howard offered Hague a great launch pad on which to position himself as a leader in the making. This was more than an aspiration on his behalf; it was an understanding between both men. Michael Howard had never endeared himself to the wider public but among many Conservatives he is admired and respected as a man with a keen sense of honour and duty. In the aftermath of a cataclysmic defeat he considered it his responsibility, as the most senior figure on the right, to run for the leadership. Privately many Conservatives already believed that whoever was to win, the party had little chance of denying Tony Blair a second term. The arrangement with William Hague would ensure that the right had a lineage. Hague would assume the role of apprentice, being groomed to take over the leadership after the Tories' second election defeat. Hague felt a natural empathy with Michael Howard, although their recent political friendship had developed only since he had joined the cabinet in 1995 as Secretary of State of Wales. He had strongly supported Howard's crusade against the liberal consensus on home affairs. Outside their ministerial responsibilities the two shared a common line on Europe.

Hague continued to take soundings over the next day, although he remained non-committal. Alan Duncan joined him for lunch in the constituency but was unable to convince his friend to stand. Hague did not discuss the Howard proposal with Duncan. Later he telephoned the former Scottish Secretary

Michael Forsyth, who had just lost his seat in Stirling. Like Howard, Forsyth, renowned for his consistent advocacy of unadulterated Thatcherism, had only become friendly with William during their time together in cabinet. With a common political agenda the two had forged a successful working relationship while holding cabinet office for Scotland and Wales. Following Michael Howard's proposal, Hague sought his advice. Forsyth told him what would happen, rather than what he should do. He confirmed what Hague already believed: 'If you decide to stand, you will win.' He advised Hague to consider that the party was in for a very rough ride and that accepting the role of party chairman wouldn't necessarily make for an easier job than being party leader. Nevertheless Forsyth counselled caution, saying William should think very carefully about his next move. The cautious approach was in marked contrast to their last meeting. At an election rally in Stirling the Scottish Secretary had dreamed up a publicity stunt to allude to the uncompromising right-wing credentials of himself and his guest, William Hague.

Throughout the election the main parties had called on animal imagery to spice up their campaigns. New Labour had sported a bulldog, albeit an emasculated one, to communicate its own brand of patriotism. The Conservatives had illustrated their attacks on devolution with a weeping lion, representing an ailing Britain. Michael Forsyth wanted to harness the picture power of the real thing, and organised a photo-call at a local safari park. He and Hague took photographers into a cage of lion cubs. Once inside the cage the lions proved a lot more ferocious than they looked, but apparently William remained calm and unflustered.

If not completely fearless, Hague was certainly bold, as his political career had already suggested, although this was undoubtedly the most difficult decision he had yet had to take.

In the hours before a resolution Hague remained concerned but characteristically calm. He knew that his only real problem was the matter of timing. He considered the strategic and personal advantages of Howard's proposal and came to a decision. On the Bank Holiday Monday, as he set off to catch his plane to London, Hague spoke to Howard on his mobile phone. The conversation was short and to Howard the message seemed unambiguous: 'I've made up my mind, I'm coming with you,' Hague said.

That was the deal that had been confirmed by the time that the Howards, William and Ffion and Sir Michael Spicer had begun the bottle of champagne. The tone of the meeting was not celebratory, however, rather a nuts-and-bolts discussion of arrangements for a press conference the following day. Together they would announce that William Hague would back Michael Howard and that they would combine forces as the dream ticket of the right.

The deal fell flat almost as quickly as the uncorked champagne. As William and Ffion walked back to Dolphin Square in Pimlico, they again discussed the options. In the few days since the general election disaster, Hague had already begun to feature prominently in the frantic search for immediate solutions to the Tories' long-term problems. The *Sunday Telegraph* and BBC's *On the Record* programme had both conducted surveys among constituency chairmen and in both Hague had come out as the favourite choice to take over from Mr Major. On reflection, Hague wondered if he was selling himself short.

After strolling through the elegant streets of SW1 the couple returned home, but although it was late William was in no mood to sleep. According to legend this was the moment they found a string of answering machine messages urging Hague to stand. That was certainly the story that his supporters were keen to communicate to help explain a change of heart.

Mischievous rumours have since suggested that callers that evening had found the answer machine turned off. In fact apart from sleeping there Hague was so rarely at the Dolphin Square flat, which he shared with veteran MP Sir Donald Thompson, that some of his friends did not have the telephone number. Certainly Hague's closest friends had been frantically calling each other, anxious to agree on a combined assault to convince him to go for it. The key persuader was old friend Brooks Newmark. Newmark had recently fought an unwinnable Conservative seat at the general election. An American, he had become a close friend of William and of Alan Duncan when he studied for his MA at Oxford. Together the three had gone on a debating tour around the USA and forged a close social and political alliance. Hague had spoken to Newmark over the weekend, alluding to the proposal from Michael Howard. Newmark was against the deal from the start and urged Hague not to accept. He wasn't convinced that Hague had taken his advice and called Alan Duncan in his constituency, Rutland, to step up the pressure.

It was already late evening on Monday when Duncan spoke to Newmark. As neither man had Hague's telephone number, Duncan urged Newmark to get in his car and drive to Dolphin Square. He arrived some time after 10 p.m., still wearing the pyjamas he had donned for an early night. Dolphin Square is a vast complex of apartments. With many MPs and peers living there it acts as hall of residence to the Westminster village. Newmark's mission to lobby Hague was nearly set off-course by his ignorance of the precise address of his friend's new home. He called Duncan, who eventually guided him to the right flat by tracking down the address from a call to Donald Thompson's other home. Late in the evening Newmark eventually found the right door and fulfilled his mission. 'You would be crazy not to take this chance,' he urged.

After meeting his friend Hague spent a sleepless night. Even without the benefit of a premonition about the extraordinary attack that was primed and ready for Michael Howard in the shape of Ann Widdecombe, he had concluded that Howard could not win. He could not guarantee that his own supporters would automatically back Howard merely because he had. Hague felt his supporters wanted him for leader, but not necessarily for a lesser role in someone else's premiership. It was the rationale he later used to explain his decision to Sir Michael Spicer. A week after becoming party leader Hague found himself the guest of Sir Michael at a long-standing engagement to speak in his Worcestershire constituency. It was an uncomfortable situation for both men. Choosing to confront the awkwardness, Hague told Spicer that he had become convinced his partnership with Howard could not have beaten Ken Clarke.

There were other things to consider as he mulled over the decision he had made. There is the historical context that no chairman of the Conservative Party has ever become its leader. The general election result had just highlighted the most obvious cautionary tale of a hailed – but then seemingly failed – leader of the right. Michael Portillo's ambitions had been dashed conclusively by his defeat in May, but they had already been undermined by his decision not to rise to John Major's 'Put up or shut up' leadership challenge two years before.

The example that really effected a change of heart was the career of Michael Heseltine. Like Hague, Heseltine had famously decided in youth that he would lead the Conservatives. Like Heseltine, Hague had mapped out his intended career and life plan. But even with all that planning Heseltine had not achieved his ultimate aim, and it was a precedent that Hague did not intend to repeat. He realised that plans sometimes have to make way for the adventure which life offers unexpectedly. With time to reflect Hague had been putting his thoughts to an intellectual test. It was characteristic of his approach to problem solving. Sometimes in order to reach a decision he feels it is necessary to make the opposite decision and put that to the test. As he analysed the reasons for backing Michael Howard he concluded that not standing himself was the opposite of what he really wanted. He was at last following his instincts, as Ffion had advised. He also concluded that apart from a likely disagreement with Michael Howard, he had nothing to lose. If he stood and lost, he could stand again later. That was the thought that kept him composed, at times some suggested complacent, throughout his campaign.

It was a reassuring thought but not one that he needed to rely on, being confident that he would in fact win. At the first possible opportunity he telephoned Michael Howard. It was about 6 o'clock in the morning when he told Howard: 'I just have to stand.' With adrenalin already flowing, Hague went for an early-morning workout in the Dolphin Square gym. When he returned some time after 7 a.m. Michael Howard called him back and tried to dissuade him from his decision. Hague's mind was now made up. He called Alan Duncan to tell him the news. 'Are you still with me?' he asked. 'Of course I'm fucking with you,' came the reply. It was a good omen. Duncan had been a key organiser in John Major's successful leadership bid in 1990. The campaign had been run out of his Westminster home, where William had lodged as a new MP.

Howard's team were angry and saw a way to score points against their self-appointed competitor. The previous night they had discussed the content of a joint press release with Hague. Now they were looking at a very different message to take to the press. Alan Duncan's opposite number in Howard's team, Tim Collins MP, quickly made it known that they considered Hague's decision not so much a reasonable change of heart but a serious breach of faith. In the battle of the spin Howard's team scored an early hit. Although Hague maintained that he had not agreed to anything more than a commitment to think the deal over, the leak from Howard's camp made Hague look at best indecisive, at worst untrustworthy. Privately Hague knew that whatever leeway he thought he had left himself in earlier discussions with Howard, his erstwhile running mate certainly had been entitled to believe that he had made a firm commitment. Later that day, in the oak-panelled splendour of the Institute of Civil Engineers, Howard held a press conference to launch his solo campaign. Had there been a deal with Hague, demanded the press, and had Hague reneged on it? Howard fashioned a temperate response with his rather unique brand of charm, but his answer was clear: 'Yes and Yes'.

In backing away from the deal Hague had fatally undermined Howard's chance of winning anything but a short-term propaganda coup. A breach of loyalty and a lack of respect for seniority were, and are, 'not quite cricket' in terms of Tory etiquette. Hence the start of the leadership campaign did not reflect well on William Hague.

Ironically for an otherwise uncontentious career, Hague had scored his first black mark at the start of his leadership bid. Although Hague had been infamous from the age of sixteen for his pint-sized proselytising at the Conservative Party conference, he had never courted controversy. His time in the House of Commons had been marked by his quiet application to the job. He had avoided joining party factions and was diplomatic to the point that he was vulnerable to the charge of being merely a career politician.

The image problems associated with his youth and relative inexperience were reinforced by the inauspicious start to his campaign, but it was a start none the less and there was no time to waste in making up for the opening hesitations. A couple of hours after Howard's launch the fledgling Hague campaign held its first meeting in the offices in which they were to remain holed up for the next six weeks.

The first meeting was convened by Hague's then PPS Nigel Evans, and brought together MPs James Arbuthnot, who was to become the campaign manager, long-time friend Alan Duncan, and Jonathan Sayeed in whose offices at 24 Stafford Place they were meeting. It was an informal round-table discussion to which all contributed, including Ffion Jenkins. The campaign themes were in their infancy, but all agreed the central message was William's freshness and his commitment to renew the party, even if the substance of that promise had yet to be thought out. Mark Fulbrook, a former Central Office agent, was the first person to suggest that reforming the party machine should become a key point in Hague's platform. Fulbrook was a veteran campaigner who had cut his teeth on countless election campaigns. Since 1992 he had been running his own political campaigning business, to which many Conservative MPs subscribe as a backup to the service offered by Central Office. His company went on to produce Hague's literature, but as the campaign took shape Alan Duncan ensured that he emerged as the key media manager, leaving less of a role for others including Fulbrook and Evans. While still 'in the loop' Fulbrook designed a leaflet knocking Ken Clarke. The caption read, 'If you vote for Ken Clarke you'll make one man very happy', revealing a picture of Peter Mandelson. The leaflet was vetoed by Duncan who, though not averse to negative campaigning, preferred to employ his techniques in a more subtle way.

There were many details still to decide, but even on that first day Hague and Arbuthnot had a confident sense of direction. They could already count on the votes of fifteen MPs. Hague told Arbuthnot that if they won forty or more votes in the first ballot (the date of which was still to be set) he would become the Conservative leader.

On Wednesday morning Hague told his team, 'I was a bit shell-shocked yesterday, but now I'm ready for battle.' He fired the opening shot by launching the campaign in a press conference that was a marked contrast to the traditional Westminster settings favoured by his competitors. The 'Fresh Start' theme was echoed by a professional, contemporary styled set of various shades of blue and purple. The sleek look of the campaign launch, held in the Westminster media centre's Atrium restaurant, was as important as its content.

Throughout the six weeks of the leadership battle Hague was to have his political credentials constantly questioned. With so short a record he was criticised as inexperienced. With so few policy initiatives to point to he was accused of standing for nothing, of being 'another Major' because of his efforts to build a team from all sections of the party. The common jibe was that he was Hague the Vague. It was largely as a result of having chosen to make the culture of the Tory party, rather than its philosophy, central to his campaign. At the risk of appearing overly concerned with the packaging and not the content, Hague's decision to give his campaign a modern branding was to symbolise his unique approach. The emphasis on presentation was far from merely frivolous, as some critics suggested. It was a sign that Hague was open to learning from New Labour's skilful use of the media. 'I'm not planning on doing a Peter Mandelson,' Hague told reporters, 'but I am planning to modernise our approach to communicating with the country.'

Unfortunately things were not looking quite so slick behind the scenes. Ever since over-enthusiastic friends of Michael Portillo had revealed their leadership plans for him by booking extra lines from British Telecom in the immediate aftermath of John Major's resignation as party leader in 1995, the company seems to have played a jinx on similar operations. Attempts to fit extra lines into Stafford Place were getting nowhere. William Hague's teams were being denied their immediate order for ten new lines because they would have to have been routed through the system serving Buckingham Palace. Hague's leadership bid had become a national security problem. Embarrassment and inefficiency were eventually curtailed when a way was found to route the lines through from Victoria.

Whilst always avoiding the term 'new', Hague's central theme of a fresh start was given greater emphasis by his use of modern graphics. This symbolised Hague's pledge to 'make over' the party as an inclusive, open, refreshed party which welcomed newcomers as well as the old guard. At the core was also an explicit commitment to exorcise the 'sleaze' and misbehaviour that had tarnished the party name. As long as the party looked and seemed outdated and corrupt it was likely to put off those to whom New Labour had recently appealed. In the first days of the campaign Hague wrote to the Parliamentary Commissioner for Standards to ask about the conventions of funding such a campaign. Soon afterwards he published a list of his campaign donors, chief of whom was the carpet millionaire Lord Harris. At the close of the campaign all monies received were declared. Hague believed that the Conservatives had managed to disguise and confuse their message because of their inability to communicate it efficiently or attractively. Although that was largely due to the splits of the Major years when it seemed there was no clear message, it was also because the party machine had not caught up with modern marketing techniques. The marketing mantra was as much in evidence at the coal face, as at the public face of the campaign. Reminders of Hague's 'unique selling points' were pasted up in the campaign bunker, the principal one being that he represented a Fresh Start.

As political plotting is a subversive activity, the subterranean offices supplied by Jonathan Sayeed at 24 Stafford Place were appropriate headquarters. A stone's throw from St James's Park and few minutes' walk to the Commons, the mock Georgian town house opens up into a rabbit warren of offices. Sayeed had just come back into Parliament, having used the time since losing his seat in 1992 to run a political lobbying firm, giving him a breadth of experience in the arts of quiet persuasion essential to the Hague campaign. The offices, which run below Buckingham Gate, were soon filled with a team of eager volunteers. Predominantly male, the bright young things drawn from the Central Office election team, management consultancy, public relations and lobbying related to Hague and, in some cases, hoped to emulate his career trajectory. On the whole the team worked well, but there were some tantrums as the campaign grew more intense.

The age and gender of Hague's team also became the subject of smears from advisers to John Redwood's campaign. The phrase 'bachelor boys' was coined to imply that the Hague team somehow lacked the red-blooded credentials needed in a winning team. In politics, and in the Conservative Party particularly, speculation about an opponent's sexuality has become a favourite sport. Then it was a sign of just how introspective and self-obsessed the parliamentary party had become, and it was also the age-old stuff of political rumour that oils the wheels of the Westminster press machine. If the Conservative Party was generally more relaxed about talking about homosexuality, as it is gradually becoming, such rumours would lose their intended sting.

Hague found to his cost that experimenting with a more liberal tone rebounded on him. Before the first ballot he told a newspaper that he approved of the idea of gay marriage, or rather that he did not disapprove of it. The *Daily Telegraph* argued this was questionable judgement in a Conservative and the story also contributed to the speculation about his own orientation. (It was an issue about which he remained nervous once elected leader, issuing a statement shortly after the 1997 conference to correct a BBC story that stated he supported gay marriage.) The *Mail* ran a piece in its diary column alleging that Hague had proposed to another girlfriend only months before his engagement to Ffion. The suggestion was that neither relationship was serious.

Alan Duncan was furious and phoned the paper's managing director, threatening to sue. Duncan told the paper he was sure of his facts: he had checked with Jane Hardman, the unnamed PR executive who was the subject of the rumours, and said she immediately denied that there had been a marriage proposal. Nevertheless these rumours were potentially damaging.

As Hague was a relative newcomer to Westminster compared with the other leadership contenders, the big guns of the Tory establishment knew little about him. Behind closed doors enquiries were made about his private life. Quite early in the campaign a heavyweight right-wing columnist made discreet investigations on behalf of potential endorsers. On Tuesday 13 May MPs met at the Carlton Club for a team meeting on the eve of the new parliament. John Major spoke of 'grasping the silver lining', whilst gossip of the leadership election was less high-minded. A former whip and senior aide to the Clarke camp admitted to Hague's investigator that there was nothing in the whips' 'little black book' that compromised William. The next day Alan Duncan quashed an enquiry from the press gallery. The *Telegraph* wanted to know whether it was true that William had an injunction out against the *News of the World* and the *Evening Standard*. It wasn't. It was a mark of Hague's own relative sophistication that when asked by journalists during the campaign if he was gay, he dismissed the suggestions in good humour. As no skeletons were ever revealed, Hague was able to go on and build a team which included key players from the party's establishment.

At the start of the campaign, however, the team was marked by the absence of well-known figures. The key speech writer was George Osborne (now Conservative Prospective Parliamentary Candidate for Tatton), who had earned his spurs advising

Douglas Hogg, the former Minister for Agriculture, throughout the unfolding of the BSE disaster. In a move worthy of Hague, Osborne astutely judged that William was a winner and offered his services early to play a part in shaping that victory. Other of his policy-adviser contemporaries had vacated their neutral Central Office roles to join Peter Lilley's camp, which came to resemble a Portillo by proxy campaign. Anthony Gordon-Lennox, a former BBC producer and Central Office media manager, was very much involved in the sharp image of the Hague campaign.

If short of big names, the tone of the Hague campaign was young, energetic and generally professional. After the initial excitement of joining the contest there was a lull. In mid May James Arbuthnot warned Alan Duncan that 'the wonks were in mutiny'. Post-election weariness and complacency were setting in. Already one opponent had been holed beneath the water. Michael Howard's campaign was effectively stymied by Ann Widdecombe's accusations about his role in the sacking of prison chief Derek Lewis. However, rather than celebrating the misfortune of a rival, senior members of Hague's team hoped Michael Howard was still a runner. They worried that if his support collapsed completely his votes might go straight to John Redwood, before, as they believed, Howard would endorse William.

With so many chiefs, Arbuthnot, Duncan, and recently defeated MPs Charles Hendry and Sebastian Coe, plus Hague himself, the line of command had become confused. Duncan didn't share the taste for conciliatory management techniques. When on 20 May there was news to announce – former Treasury minister John Maples was joining the campaign – Duncan found the Stafford Place press operation empty. He was furious and bawled out volunteers Barnaby Towns, Hague's former special adviser, Sean Williams and Ceri Evans.

Although the leadership race was under way within hours of the Conservative defeat, the initial days and weeks after 1 May were only a phoney war for the contenders. According to party rules the formal timetable of the contest had to be set by the 1922 Committee, which had still to pull itself together from the much depleted ranks of Conservatives in the new parliament. Added to the practical difficulties of adapting to opposition, there were further complications in the growing protest of Conservative grass roots members. The mood of the party workers was angry. Many who had given their loyal support and hard work felt betrayed by Members of Parliament whose indiscipline was considered a significant factor in the party's massive defeat. Members felt they had been taken for granted and began to lobby their representative body, the National Union, for a voice in this new leadership election.

Until the 1960s Conservative Party leaders had not been chosen so much as ordained. Their succession was managed by senior party figures as one set of elder statesmen decided among themselves who to appoint according to conventions of seniority and continuity. Since the selection of Edward Heath as leader, the franchise had passed to all Conservative MPs. Many party members never forgave their MPs for deposing Margaret Thatcher. Others had had their patience constantly tested by the tiresome leadership challenges and rumours of challenges that haunted the Major years.

Sensing this bitterness, the National Union Chairman, Robin Hodgson (now Lord Hodgson), decided to push for a change in the election rules which would give members a proportion of the votes. The proposal met with thorough disapproval from the 1922 executive and its new Chairman, Sir Archie Hamilton. Hodgson had approached the remnants of the executive even before the parliamentary party had elected Hamilton on 21 May. Apart from defending the principle of investing MPs with the sole right to vote for their leader, Hamilton was keen to get the election under way for political reasons. There was talk of a plan by the Tory left to install a caretaker leader. Tristan Garel-Jones, a most Machiavellian Euro-enthusiast, had suggested that the former Defence Secretary, Tom King, might be a sensible interim leader while the party adopted new rules. When Hamilton asked King how long he might hold such a post, King suggested around eighteen months. It was all that Hamilton, a classic right-winger, needed to hear to convince him that the election should be held soon, and that there must be no thoughts of a caretaker leader. Within eighteen months there could well be a by-election, which might allow for the return to the House of the left's long awaited leader to be, Chris Patten. Even if such thoughts were fanciful, they were also destabilising. Hamilton was determined to proceed with the election and that meant no reform in the short term.

Hodgson's case was not advanced by party chairman Brian Mawhinney either. Although Mawhinney gradually began to appreciate the groundswell of opinion building in the party membership, his conversion came too late to force the pace of change. If nothing more could be achieved Hodgson decided at least to formalise the existing requirement that members be consulted during a leadership contest. He arranged for the Electoral Reform Society to poll all constituency chairmen. The results, along with a survey of peers and MEPs, were revealed at each stage of the formal proceedings. Although they were no more binding than a consultation, the publication was a graphic reminder that the grass roots would increasingly agitate for a change in the rules.

Early national opinion polls indicated that Hague, relatively untainted by the squabbles of the Major years, was a popular choice among activists. Buoyed by these results, the Hague campaign realised the potential of appealing directly to party members – and of course in the first couple of weeks of the campaign it was still possible that a rule change might have given the members a role in a new electoral college. To Hague's detriment, the profile-raising campaign tour on which he embarked in May meant that he missed some Westminster meetings, most notably a meeting of the Thatcherite backbench 92 Group which was addressed by the other candidates of the right.

Apart from high profile events, however, much of the daily grind of the campaign did take place quietly in Westminster. Hague spent days meeting MPs for one-to-one chats in his Commons office. Although the Conservatives had done very badly in the election there were forty newcomers (including some returning) on their benches. Hague had to meet all of them as well as those colleagues who just wanted to know more about him.

The decision to take the public face of the campaign out of the impressive Westminster headquarters and on the road was part tactical and part symbolic. It was an early suggestion from Alan Duncan who argued that the tactic would distance Hague from the perceived arrogance of the Tory establishment, distinguish his campaign from the others and create a momentum in his favour that would influence his electors in Westminster through their constituencies. In the early days it was also a practical necessity, giving the campaign an identity that it was failing to win through the association of heavyweight backers. It gave Hague one of his campaign slogans, that there should be 'no no-go areas' for the party. Hague used the line at his launch press conference on 7 May and put it into action by addressing rallies in places where the Conservatives had fared particularly badly in the general election. He travelled to Manchester, to Scotland and Wales, to Yorkshire and to Bristol.

Hague's appeal to the party membership was also a way of highlighting his own election programme which came to concentrate on reforming the party structure and modernising the professional machine. Although the theme was taken up by other candidates, particularly Stephen Dorrell, whose 'campaign *interruptus*' didn't even make it to the first ballot, Hague had left himself open to accusations of concentrating too much on management and not enough on articulating a policy agenda to compete with New Labour.

Appropriately, Hague began his national tour in Yorkshire where on 16 May he told activists in Barnsley that, if elected, he would ballot party members, and convene a special conference of all sections of the party to secure their endorsement. He had been unsure of the tactic almost until the last moment and was still writing his speech in the car from London. He had been preoccupied with his proper job. Earlier that day Hague had had to appear in the House answering on the Government's devolution debate. It was one area of policy which he had no intention of modernising. The party was determined to oppose the government's plans, as Hague had personally for twenty years. Even before appearing at the 1977 conference proclaiming the cause of liberty, Hague had won a Yorkshire Television public speaking contest talking about devolution. He was sure he had scored points in the House as well, though not all of his own devising. The new Scottish Secretary, Donald Dewar, proposing for the government, had been distracted by his pager going off in the chamber.

Hague's second speech on the opening day of the tour was a success. On home soil, an audience of 150 people had packed the hall. The television pictures were successful and the commitment to the party ballot made headlines. Later in the month, on 23 May, Hague made a similarly bold announcement when he told Bristol Tories that he intended to double the party membership within two years. His aim was that half the members would be younger than he. It fulfilled a short-term aim, to make news over the weekend, although it was seldom referred to again and three and a half years on the aim is nowhere near realised.

Championing the cause of party reform brought Hague one his more influential backers. Newly elected MP Archie Norman was already a national figure because of his excellent business reputation earned by reviving the fortunes of the Asda super-market chain. Norman's election as member for Tunbridge Wells was a much needed boost to the Tories. A canny operator, Norman was slow in endorsing Hague even though in a previous role he had poached William from his first job at Shell to join the management consultants McKinsey and Co. As a business expert Norman wrote a paper on reforming the professional side of the party which later became the basis of Hague's reforms. During the leadership campaign Norman sent the paper to Hague and to Clarke. He waited until the beginning of June to come out for Hague, convinced, he said, by William's 'winnability'.

Archie Norman's endorsement was part of a programme which Hague made a priority as May turned to June and the campaign was intensifying. Towards the end of May Hague had taken a surreptitious break from Westminster. By then the relent-less effort of the general election campaign and the four weeks since was turning to fatigue. The US holiday that he had promised Ffion turned into a two-day break in Brussels. However justified, it would not have looked good to be seen to be deserting his post, although the destination may have raised his credibility with the Tory left. Some in his team were unimpressed about this mini-break, wondering if he was really committed to winning. But Hague had also made a personal commitment to his fiancée and knew that, as he was bound to win, it would be some time before they could take a proper holiday. Instead the couple spent two days sitting in the sun-flecked squares of Brussels with William's old friend Nick Levy and his wife Caroline. Nick has been a close friend since the two met through mutual Oxford acquaintances. In the past they had been on several active adventure holidays but this was just a chance to relax with some Belgian beer and good food.

When Hague returned to duty he sensed that some momentum had gone from his campaign. He set about a more vigorous effort to recruit and unveil endorsements on a daily basis. Along with Archie Norman, Hague also announced that Michael Forsyth, Michael Ancram and Lord Parkinson were joining his campaign.

Parkinson had not known Hague but felt a natural affinity with him when he went to meet him earlier in May. They shared a similar business background and a common political agenda, although Hague had never joined Parkinson's right-wing Conservative Way Forward group. As a prominent member of the Thatcher government and a past party chairman, Parkinson was to prove a valuable link with the Conservative establishment.

On 5 June nominations formally closed with five candidates ready to join battle: Hague, Howard, Lilley, Redwood and Clarke. Hague's signatories were David Heathcoat-Amory and Sir Peter Tapsell. Tapsell, a veteran parliamentarian of some forty years' standing, hadn't known Hague but favoured him right from the start of the campaign, convinced that Hague's youth and debating skills would be vital in opposition. Although Hague said he was trying to remodel the party along modern meritocratic lines, the influence of the old college tie still made a difference. Tapsell, an Oxford alumnus and trustee of the Union, recognised a kindred spirit in the similarly qualified Hague. His was, however, primarily a pragmatic decision based on what was best for the party. The last time he had signed nomination papers it was to propose Michael Heseltine in his bid to wrest the leadership from Margaret Thatcher.

For many established figures in the party this was a difficult time. Their loyalties were torn. Norman Lamont had committed himself to his long-time friend and colleague Michael Howard, but he also felt an obligation to Hague who had served as his Treasury PPS during the Exchange Rate Mechanism debacle in 1992. As the Howard campaign faltered, Lamont told Duncan he was keen to hear a pitch from William. He was also considering his own future and whether he should forsake a possible by-election return to the Commons by taking a place in the House of Lords. Gordon Brown had told him he would facilitate the move because he was grateful for his support on Labour's first announcement in government, giving a measure of independence to the Bank of England.

The alliance of support across all sections of the party which William was building reminded some of John Major's leadership campaign. For many this was not a positive comparison, suggesting that Hague would also take too consensual an approach to leadership. Suggestions that Hague was not fighting a heavyweight political campaign did hit home. As the contest heated up Hague found himself vulnerable on the key political issue: Europe. Although a consistent sceptic, Hague did not want to leave himself open to the charge of being 'Europhobic'. Labour had convincingly portrayed the Tories as isolationist and anti-European. Hague wanted to communicate his severe doubts about the Single Currency without associating himself with the small but vocal section of the party that favours withdrawal from the European Union. At the start of his campaign he had told the press that he was against the Single Currency 'in principle', but he had stressed he did not want to make it the defining issue of his campaign. Opposing the currency in principle sounded clear enough, but it did not hold up to the forensic scrutiny inevitable in a contest pitting Conservative against Conservative. It was the issue which came to dominate the closing days of the campaign, when ironically Hague's own position became less the point at issue than the machinations of his competitors.

On Wednesday 21 May Hague made a high-profile and controversial speech in Westminster to answer criticisms that he was John Major 'mark II' and had no clear agenda. He told the audience of four hundred party members in Methodist Central Hall that he had spent twenty years arguing the case for rolling back the frontiers of the state, a reference to his first speech on such a platform during the 1977 Conservative Party Conference. 'These were my beliefs before Mrs Thatcher took office. These were the beliefs we saw the great Conservative government put into effect in the late 1980s and 1990s smaller state. These are the beliefs I still hold today.'

In drawing together the themes of his campaign Hague criticised his own party's record. 'The free and prosperous society that we had championed became tainted with the image of sleaze, greed, self indulgence and division.' The real impact of the speech, however, was not its criticisms of the whole team, but the personal attack on Major that was implied by the description of his period in office as a 'constantly shifting fudge'.

As the ongoing leader of his party, John Major had to maintain a diplomatic silence and neutral stance. Amidst the pantomime of the leadership contest the real business of Westminster had to go on. Major had still to head his now heavily diminished team in the House and oppose the Prime Minister. In exchange there developed an unwritten understanding among MPs that to criticise Major's stewardship at Number 10 was not acceptable, and that it would only further undermine their position. It was a code that Hague broke in the Central Hall speech, an attempt to give 'edge' both to his message and to his campaign.

As chief spinner for the Hague team, Duncan realised the speech would be seen as an attack on Major, even if that was not its intention. On first reading he had found the speech rather lacklustre when looking over Hague's draft but his attention was caught by the 'shifting fudge' phrase. Hague told him, 'It's true so we should keep it in.' Borrowing a tactic from New Labour, whose media skills the Hague team particularly admired, Duncan gave an exclusive preview of the speech to the London *Evening Standard*. When the second editions arrived later that morning the headline read: 'Now Hague Stabs Major'. A flood of excited media calls followed. The storm was worse than Duncan or Hague had expected and a damage limitation exercise was soon underway. When Duncan telephoned Major's office to attempt a conciliation he found the news had gone down very badly. Major was furious: he took the comment personally and believed Hague was as guilty as anyone of contributing to the 'fudge' he now sought to demonise.

Hague agreed not to make any comment in advance of the actual speech that evening and not to issue any further press releases to the other newspapers until later that afternoon. He hoped that Prime Minister's Questions would distract lobby journalists and give his team time to rewrite sections of the speech. By the time Hague delivered the speech that evening the text had been changed to put greater emphasis on cabinet responsibility, and thereafter Hague was always at pains to stress that his intention had never been to mount a personal attack on Major. For many his defence seemed unconvincing and it has left a lasting and negative impression with Major.

The move was criticised by Hague's right-wing competitors Michael Howard and Peter Lilley. It also raised speculation about which candidate the former Prime Minister would eventually support: at that stage Ken Clarke seemed the most likely recipient of his vote. Given the crowded field of competition on the right, speculation was rife about the likely recipients of other high-profile endorsements, most notably which candidate would win the backing of Lady Thatcher and Michael Portillo.

The twice yearly parties of Robbie Gibb have become a fixed point in the calendars of the young movers and shakers of the right. A long-time supporter of Michael Portillo, Gibb had sealed his reputation as a political fixer *par excellence* through his party activism from student days. As a BBC political producer he had been well placed to build up his contacts book into a *Who's Who* of the Eurosceptic right. The summer party in his Pimlico basement flat was always packed with political fellow travellers, including MPs, prospective MPs, journalists and advisers. After the initial shock of losing Michael Portillo from the race, Gibb quickly transferred his allegiance to William Hague. As a fellow thirtysomething Yorkshireman, Gibb related to the political journey that had shaped Hague's agenda.

Gibb persuaded Alan Duncan that it was in William's interests to attend the party on the first weekend in June. Superficially a pleasant distraction from high politics, the canapés and white wine were actually the fuel for a lobbying effort to deliver the votes of MPs whose first choice would have been Portillo. Hague went straight to the party from a lunchtime interview for the BBC, declining a Corporation driver in favour of a lift from an old friend.

Throughout the campaign each camp held frequent parties and receptions to enable prospective backers to mingle with their candidate. The Gibb party was an informal event on neutral territory allowing the various camps a chance to mix. Hague chatted to MPs including Bernard Jenkin, Robert Syms and David Ruffley – and when he moved into a discreet conversation with Michael Portillo observers were keen to look for any signs that this would lead to an overt backing.

It was an endorsement that would have satisfied some doubters that Hague really was one of them. Partly by design, but also by default, Hague's right-wing credentials were unproven. His reluctance to be drawn into making ideological pronouncements had added to the impression that his campaign was of the centre, leaving Howard, Lilley and Redwood to compete for the right. For anything but shorthand convenience the labels 'left' and 'right' had long been an inadequate way of characterising the various shades of opinion in the Conservative Party. Europe, however, remained the one issue that still divided MPs along distinct lines and would inevitably decide the outcome of the leadership contest. In the afternoon sunshine Hague and Portillo chatted about the endgame: how to stop Clarke, and hence how to keep the party sceptical about the Single Currency. If their agreement on that point was not in itself an endorsement from Portillo it would later become one, but only in the final hours of the campaign.

The next day, 2 June, Hague went on a pilgrimage to the Thatcher Foundation. The good disciple was looking for an opportunity to reacquaint himself with his political heroine. Earlier in the campaign rumours had circulated that Lady Thatcher was preparing to back John Redwood, but her office denied that. In fact close advisers knew that privately she had already told Michael Howard that he was her preferred candidate.

According to a Thatcher confidante: 'Margaret told Michael early in the campaign that he had her support. She knew him the best and thought he was a strong and stable candidate for the right. This was a private understanding, however, as she did not want to undermine the chances of the other right-wing candidates. Apart from his early conference speech, she did not really know Hague. She did not know what his politics were.'

Indeed, Hague knew she could not take for granted that he was a right-wing candidate – hence his desire to update their relationship. Hague and Thatcher talked about Europe. 'Europe,' she told him, 'is responsible for all those important *isms*, Communism, Fascism and Bolshevism. The only good *ism* in Europe is Thatcherism.'

The conclusion of the campaign took the Conservatives through a series of public spectacles which were bizarre even by their own recent standards. On the evening of Monday 9 June the party which had just been trounced in the general election still had the stomach to hold five drinks receptions, one hosted by each of the leadership contenders. Surprisingly for the candidate offering a fresh start, Hague's happy hour was held in the bastion of establishment Toryism, the Carlton Club. MPs arriving for some last-minute arm-twisting were met by a delegation of self-styled Mexican bandits, 'the Portillistas', courtesy of a Channel 4 satirical programme. Hague was thrown by them, not sure whether to acknowledge the pranksters or to ignore them completely.

When the camps assembled the next day for media interviews following the announcement of the first result, the bandits were back. But amidst the madness which is College Green on such an occasion, with television crews fighting for interviews and competing MPs in a state of high excitement, practical jokers couldn't make much of an impact. The real impact was the shock of an unexpected result. Commentators had differed in their predicted outcome to the poll, but only by a few votes here and there. On two points there had been agreement: that Ken Clarke would come top of the ballot and that John Redwood would come last.

Clarke also decisively topped surveys of constituency chairmen, MEPs and peers, but his result in the ballot itself was not as strong as his team had hoped: some had confidently predicted he could gain more than 60 votes. Most people had rightly predicted that William Hague would come second, and he had gone past the figure of 40 which he had believed from the start would lead him to eventual victory.

In the event the result of the first ballot was:

Kenneth Clarke	49
William Hague	41
John Redwood	27
Peter Lilley	24
Michael Howard	23

The real story of the vote was the relative victory of John Redwood, who beat both his right-wing competitors to the third place. Earlier in the campaign the three had set out their stalls to parliamentary colleagues at a special meeting of the 92 Group. Hague's non-attendance due to his absence on his campaign tour did not reflect well on him and was added to the perception among MPs that he was spending too much time away from Westminster, too little time clarifying his policy position. Peter Lilley had taken the general election result very badly and suffered a tangible loss of confidence. Colleagues were dismayed by his lacklustre performance to the 92. Michael Howard performed well but had had his chances diminished by Ann Widdecombe's personal attack that he had 'something of the night about him'. The man with a distinct something of the right about him, John Redwood, delivered a self-deprecating and polished performance helping him to his first round success.

Since responding to John Major's leadership challenge two years previously Redwood had worked assiduously to establish himself as a serious contender and shake off his 'Vulcan' tendencies. But try as he had to woo the party at large and win the confidence of the nation's opinion formers with ideas from his Conservative 2000 foundation, Redwood had been unable to overturn his distinctively user-unfriendly image. No one doubted his conviction and application, but in the comment leading up to the vote the press echoed what most Westminster observers thought: that this highly serious man just couldn't be taken seriously. For a few moments at least the first round result gave Redwood the last laugh and, he thought, should have given him the opportunity to form an alliance with Peter Lilley and Michael Howard, bringing with them some of their 48 votes.

Hague believed that was highly unlikely, and for him the first round result was almost a perfect distribution of votes. He did not share the view of commentators who automatically grouped Redwood, Howard and Lilley together as allied right-wingers. He knew that in cabinet he had been far closer than John Redwood to the Home Secretary and the Social Security Secretary. Nevertheless, Redwood had formed the impression that there would be discussions between himself, Howard and Lilley after the first ballot. Although he had reservations about Michael Howard, due to an unhappy period serving as his junior in the Department of the Environment, he respected the like-minded Peter Lilley and felt particularly disappointed at being excluded from his post-ballot calculations. Redwood called Lilley immediately after the result, but the call was never returned. As Hague had expected, Lilley and Howard chose to endorse his campaign, effectively shoring up his position as the only candidate who could beat Ken Clarke. Hague did not offer either a role in the shadow cabinet but as many expected Lilley and Howard later joined Hague's front bench as shadow chancellor and shadow foreign secretary.

Almost since the moment he won the leadership Hague has been criticised for taking the party on a 'lurch' to the right, but during the campaign detractors were keen to suggest that he was no conviction politician. The philosophical purity test is a peculiar sport of the political class, particularly for those members of it whose own contribution is played out mainly on the sidelines. The core themes that had motivated Hague from youth, including freedom, national independence, self reliance, responsibility and enterprise, had remained a consistent feature of his career and were repeated often during the leadership campaign. Hague's voting record as an MP should also have met the approval of Tory traditionalists, supporting as he had the rights of unborn children and opposing Conservative proposals to make divorce easier. Hague had also taken a consistently sceptical line on Europe, but in the fevered point-scoring atmosphere of the campaign, he came under great pressure to clarify his precise position. The catchphrase 'In Europe but not run by Europe' was considered a selling point to the public, but for the purists to whom Hague was trying to appeal it was meaningless. Explaining the position as a commitment to oppose the Single Currency for the lifetime of Blair's first parliament and to stand by that policy for the next election was vulnerable to misrepresentation. In shorthand, Hague's team said it meant staying out of the currency for ten years, the duration of two parliaments. The figure came to be seen by detractors on different wings of the party either as a compromise or as ideological.

The line was mocked at a meeting of the Positive European group of Tory MPs. Hague was asked: if ten years, why not nine and a half? Advocates of the Single Currency said Hague was playing with ideology to score electoral points, but for the party's committed sceptics the line was actually too pragmatic. Hague had not satisfied them that he was opposed to the Single Currency in principle.

Early in the campaign the veteran Eurosceptic Bill Cash had asked all the candidates to write an article on the Single Currency for his publication, the *European Review*. As Europe was to be the key issue on which candidates would be judged and his magazine went to all MPs, he was surprised that the Hague team took their time in supplying him with an article. When he eventually received it he was pleased to read that William had again declared himself against the currency in principle: 'I am opposed to a Single Currency in principle but I do not believe it is in Britain's interests to withdraw from Europe.'

Cash felt it was particularly important that MPs had a chance to question the candidates in a formal meeting, and through the 1922 Committee arranged a hustings for Monday 16 June. It was the eve of the second ballot, in which a candidate would have to win an overall majority plus 15 per cent over his nearest rival to win outright. The weekend's press had been mixed but Hague had received an important endorsement from the *Sunday Times*. Under the headline 'William the First' the leader comment encouraged Tory MPs to back Hague as 'an authentic advocate of the centre right . . . who offers a way out of the quagmire the Tories are in built on . . . an overwhelming determination to fight Labour on the new ground.' In more guarded tones the *Sunday Telegraph* advised that Hague was the most sensible risk. It was a risk taken that day by former Education Secretary Gillian Shephard and six other former ministers who joined the Hague camp.

At the Monday night meeting Hague did not measure up to the line he espoused in the *European Review*, and played into the hands of the Redwood supporters by refusing to say he would 'never' take Britain into a Single Currency. More damagingly, he also infuriated the left with a controversial line on shadow cabinet discipline. In the battle of briefings that ensued later that night Hague's line was spun by Tim Yeo and deconstructed by Shaun Woodward from the Clarke camp. Hague had insisted that all members of his shadow cabinet would have to agree to his policy line, on Europe as with everything else. Experienced moderates were incensed as Hague's position amounted to a loyalty pledge and seemed to turn on its head the idea that policy should be arrived at through discussions within the shadow cabinet.

What appeared a clumsy mistake had been a deliberate move. So convinced had Hague remained of his ability to win, that he had spent the previous afternoon discussing initial thoughts for his victory speech with George Osborne. Hague's tactic at the Monday hustings was straight out of the Thatcher divide-and-rule style of management. He understood that he had to take on the Single Currency supporters and in so doing would establish a policy which was in tune with most of the party. He expected that it would lose him some votes but he was determined to win on his own terms. He told his team that he could not offer the left a deal which would repeat the 'constantly shifting fudge' of the Major years, although once elected he was not so resolute.

Ahead of the result of Tuesday's second ballot, James Arbuthnot and Alan Duncan exchanged predictions. Duncan expected Clarke would lead by ten votes. Arbuthnot, though confident of his maths, was worried by Redwood. 'I'll never believe Redwood has hit the ceiling until there is a stake through his heart,' he told Duncan. For Hague there were also some positive results from the National Union poll. In all sections, constituency, MEPs and the Lords, Clarke was still in the lead but Hague had strengthened his position. The real result was not so clear cut. Ken Clarke had a narrow lead over Hague with 64 votes to 62. John Redwood had 38.

Hague had expected to beat Clarke by a couple of votes and realised he had sacrificed some support as a result of his performance at the hustings.

Redwood's supporters knew that he held the key to deciding the future leader of the party, but they were irreparably split. Iain Duncan Smith wanted Redwood to meet Hague so that they could at least discuss what they might have in common. Hywel Williams, Redwood's press coordinator, was dismissive of Hague and had already initiated a meeting with Ken Clarke.

The early evening meeting was arranged by Shaun Woodward, MP for Witney, at the Vincent Square home of his father-in-law, Tim Sainsbury. Woodward was then a newly elected Tory MP hoping to play a senior role in an opposition led by Ken Clarke. Williams was convinced that Redwood would best be served by an alliance with a big hitter, regardless of how great the differences between Clarke and Redwood. As if to emphasise Clarke's big hitter status, Michael Heseltine acted as his key negotiator. Redwood remained relatively quiet throughout the meeting, deferring to Hywel Williams, who had established a rapport with Heseltine. With the assurance that MPs would be allowed a free vote on Europe, the deal was effectively concluded. Redwood had made up his mind to transfer his support to Ken Clarke, with the qualification that he needed to bring his supporters on board for the arrangement.

In the meantime Iain Duncan Smith had succeeded in arranging a meeting with William Hague at the Chapel Street home of Barry Legg. Legg had just left Parliament but as a consistent right-winger had played a senior role in Redwood's campaign. The meeting proved brief and ineffective. Neither Hague nor Redwood seemed to know what to discuss, although Hague suggested that the logical move for Redwood would be to support him. Hague was constrained by his public commitment against offering shadow cabinet posts for votes, and Redwood had told supporters he could not sign up to a policy which left open the possibility of joining the Euro – unlike the deal with Clarke which allowed him a free vote. In reality Redwood had already committed himself to a deal with Clarke, and he was not minded to look for an alternative with Hague. When Redwood later convened a meeting of his supporters, many were dismayed and angry at being presented with a *fait accompli*. Bill Cash and John Townend told him immediately they could not back the deal. Whatever their previous doubts about William Hague, he was discernibly more of their way of thinking than was Kenneth Clarke.

Early the next day Cash received a call from the Hague camp. Rumours of an extraordinary deal were reaching Hague's office.

Unsure of how Redwood's supporters would divide up, Hague's team was seriously worried about their chances in a final ballot. It was time to deploy their ultimate weapon: Lady Thatcher. Cash was asked to apply his impeccable sceptical credentials to the efforts to recruit Lady Thatcher. Others joined the assault on the Thatcher Foundation's telephone lines. Sir Tim Bell, Michael Howard and Lord Archer all called to persuade her of the need to back William. On hearing the rumours Lord Parkinson called and spoke to Thatcher. She had no problem dismissing the rumours, refusing to countenance the thought that John Redwood was capable of such a deal. Although her first choice candidate, Michael Howard, had already put his weight behind Hague, Thatcher still remained reluctant to endorse one right-wing candidate at the expense of the other. Duncan knew, if proved true, that the rumours would convince Thatcher to offer her explicit help. He called her aide Mark Worthington and advised him to urge the Thatcher Foundation to turn their television sets to Sky News. Soon the news was being confirmed. The sight of Redwood and Clarke outlining their version of the Ribbentrop-Molotov pact at their morning press conference was enough to have the Iron Lady firing up her handbag. In her eyes Redwood's actions were a defection to the left and a particularly deep betrayal coming from the man she had trusted to be head of the Downing Street policy unit.

Hague had already made a significant move towards harnessing the expertise and influence of the Thatcher period, by asking Lord Parkinson on the Tuesday of that week if he would consider once again taking up the role of party chairman. At first Lady Parkinson was against the idea, but Wednesday's news of the Clarke-Redwood pact acted as a spur to step up efforts on William's behalf. Along with the rest of Hague's team, Parkinson was fearful that Clarke's experience would sway even those who disagreed with his position on Europe. The deal, described by

Hague as an 'instability pact', galvanised arrangements with Lady Thatcher and proved a potent lobbying point, raising the temperature of the final day's push. It had genuinely infuriated many on the right who felt Redwood had debased his principles with a careerist capitulation. Although he tried to reassure supporters that he had Clarke's word, many worried that Clarke's commitment to entering the Single Currency would negate any arrangement with Redwood. Some were reminded of a time before Margaret Thatcher, when the right had been excluded. David Heathcoat-Amory had resigned from the Major government over the 'wait and see' approach to Europe. Attracted by Hague's feeling for business, he had been a prestigious, early backer of his leadership bid. Faced with the prospect of a Clarke leadership Heathcoat-Amory joined the last-minute effort to convince waverers that a vote for Clarke would hand the party over to the 'Heathites'.

Lady Thatcher agreed to issue a statement attacking Clarke and Redwood, but she was circumspect about taking a more public role. At the Hague headquarters frantic efforts were being made to organise a high-impact press conference, to be the last of the campaign, for later in the day. Sets were being booked and the location confirmed for a return to the Atrium, where the Fresh Start had had its first airing. As the afternoon wore on, the calls to Lady Thatcher's office continued. Hague himself phoned but was not able to speak to her directly. Soon after three o'clock, as the final arrangements for the press conference were being concluded, a call to Alan Duncan confirmed that Lady Thatcher had agreed to a photo-call with William outside the House of Commons. Duncan paged Hague with the news, 'Phone Thatcher, Super Urgent'.

The Baroness told Hague that she would appear in a photo-call with him, but she did not intend to make a statement. She was in the House of Lords that afternoon and would meet him shortly before five. In terms of news management it was a great coup, allowing pictures to get back to newsrooms in time for the evening news programmes. Concluding the business of the formal press conference, Hague told journalists to meet him outside the St Stephen's entrance to the Commons in a few minutes. He and Alan Duncan walked the short distance from the Atrium at 4 Millbank to the peers' lobby in the House of Lords. There they met Lady Thatcher and walked with her through the Lords to Central Lobby. She was resolute in her commitment not to say anything at the photo-call. In the few moments they stood in Central Lobby preparing to face the snappers at St Stephen's, Duncan delivered the decisive blow. 'You do know what Clarke's supporters are saying about you?' he asked Thatcher. 'They are saying a vote for them is revenge for 1975.' This time it was personal. Her demeanour changed in a split second. As she and Hague walked into the waiting glare of the media spotlight, Lady Thatcher walked straight to camera and announced in an authoritative tone: 'It's William Hague. Have you got the name? Vote for William Hague to follow the same kind of government I did. William Hague, have you got the message?'

The sight of the former Prime Minister lined up with prominent members of the Major government gave Hague the picture he wanted, but only served to underline how far the Conservatives had fallen since her departure. As Tony Blair was enjoying a particularly sweet post-election honeymoon, the country's former leaders were still divided about how to lead themselves.

Cheerleading for Hague proved thirsty work. As she turned away from the cameras Lady Thatcher told Hague she rather fancied a cup of tea. Alan Duncan suggested that Gillian Shephard, an important late arrival in the Hague camp, accompany them to the Commons tea room. Enlivened by the fight for her legacy, Lady Thatcher exuded authority as she glided past the rows of new Labour MPs. She asked Hague to point out the Redwood supporters who still needed converting. The pit-stop turned into another lobbying opportunity in which she was joined by many of the Hague campaigners searching out the remaining waverers.

The tea provided necessary refreshment before the last round of telephone calls to MPs who hadn't been in the tea room. Michael Portillo and Lord Lamont joined the effort. John Bercow, a newly elected MP, had backed Redwood after Peter Lilley dropped out in the first round, and was infuriating colleagues by keeping his final decision to himself (as he has done ever since). These first weeks in the House were proving a baptism of fire for the new MP: his support for Redwood had already provoked a letter from Lord Parkinson advising him to 'take a water can with you as you march into the wilderness'. Bercow avoided a direct appeal from Lady Thatcher because his answering machine wasn't working. Later there was a blazing row with Alan Duncan. Bercow was furious that Duncan seemed to be threatening him: 'You know you're a new MP. A vote for Clarke might not play well in your constituency,' Duncan said.

The propaganda victory of the Thatcher endorsement had raised spirits in the Hague team, but having won the battle of the press conferences some were very unsure that they would win the war. Obviously flawed though the Redwood-Clarke pact was, it had confused the arithmetic. Inside the Hague camp there were at least two sets of predictions. The most gloomy, that saw the result hanging on two votes, was shared with campaign workers. As the eve of the poll drew to a close, Hague hand-wrote a note to all Conservative MPs and sent it with copies of helpful leader articles from the first editions. Charles Moore, editor of the *Daily Telegraph*, which had harried John Major's government for its lack of direction, warned that Ken Clarke would introduce the most left-wing policies he could get away with. *The Times* shone an inquisitor's bare bulb on six named Thatcherites who were considering standing by their commitment to John Redwood by voting for Clarke. The column asked if MPs wanted their party to become a 'credible opposition or a theatre of the absurd'. Before leaving his HQ for the night Hague and Arbuthnot discussed their private prediction for the result which saw them winning by seven votes. The next day's announcement of a victory by 22 votes – 92 to 70 – was far better than expected and saved Hague from appearing to have won by default.

At the party's headquarters later there was palpable relief at the conclusion of what had been an emotional ordeal compounding the fatigue of the general election campaign. Central Office sent a car to the Commons to bring the new leader to his first commitment as party leader. Immediately after the result had been announced Clarke had gone to Hague's Commons office to offer congratulations. Clarke told him then that he did not want to join the shadow cabinet. Hague was grateful to him for offering him such a convenient solution to a potential problem. He offered Clarke a lift over to Central Office and they travelled the few yards together.

The press conference to welcome the new leader became a free-for-all as journalists were joined by party officials, friends and elected colleagues. Ffion looked flushed and excited as she hurried through the scrum to join William in the formal setting of the press conference room. Alan Duncan, her chaperone, was beaming with 'I told you so' pride and Brooks Newmark was enjoining people to 'drink the atmosphere'. In a corner a press huddle had formed around Ken Clarke who was telling journalists that he intended to rejoin the back benches.

Although a press conference, the meeting also fulfilled party rules which required all sections of the party to approve the appointment of a new leader. In a move exemplifying the need to modernise, Brian Mawhinney asked the meeting to pledge its support for Hague. The 300-capacity room was filled to overflowing and there were representatives of all sections of the party there along with the press. A murmur broke out, rising to a roar. It was an unscientific test but was read as the necessary endorsement. One voice spoke out in protest, not at Hague but at the method of his confirmation. Eric Chalker had been a long-time thorn in the side of party officials with his dogged campaign for democratising reforms. As the old guard handed over to the new, Hague promised that change was on its way and it would start with a special conference to seek the endorsement of his leadership from the whole of the party.

John Major made an eloquent testimony to his successor's qualities, calling Hague the 'most outstanding young political talent in the country today'. In a dig at his own predecessor he promised always to give Hague his public support. In a role he had been perfecting for seven years, Major made a polished warm-up act. In return Hague paid tribute to Major and to Ken Clarke, accepting he now had the responsibility to 'lead and to heal'. He warned that the party should be prepared for change, that there would be an end to the 'school debating society' culture, but it should also be proud of its achievements. Restating the themes of his campaign, he promised to create a party which was fresh, clear, open and united and would double its membership within two years. In more traditional mode he invoked the spirit of General Montgomery. A supporter had written to him during the leadership race with some advice from the General. Hague quoted Montgomery's resolve to 'brook no bellyaching'. It was a discordant reference in a speech otherwise concerned with the future.

In a party so steeped in history, however, reminders of its traditional values were close by. In an upstairs meeting room Lord Whitelaw was waiting for an audience with the new leader.

While William was delayed en route, Ffion was first to the meeting. In a grandfatherly manner befitting the party's most senior grandee, Lord Whitelaw's first words to her were: 'Now you must get married as soon as possible.'

William Jefferson Hague had become the Conservatives' youngest leader since William Pitt two hundred years previously. At thirty-six, Hague had spent twenty years banging the Tory drum, and at this, his proudest moment, he reminded the audience why. He wanted to lead the party because the state spends too much, because he wanted to promote freedom and responsibility, self-reliance and less government, and to defend the nation. It was a faith he had been practising since childhood.

Chapter Two

A YORKSHIRE LAD

Half of you may not be here in thirty or forty years' time, but I will be and I want to be free.

William Hague, Conservative Party Conference,
Blackpool, 1977

At sixteen William Hague officially launched his political career. His short speech to the Conservative Party Conference in 1977 brought him more than fifteen minutes of fame and a reputation that has preceded him ever since.

But for all the display of ultimate 'Tory Boy' credentials, the young William had not been born with a silver spoon in his mouth. A steel spoon would have been more appropriate for a boy who grew up in the midst of industrial South Yorkshire. Although there were already signs of the conflicts that would devastate those communities in the 1980s, it was a stable and relatively buoyant area throughout the period of national economic decline which was the backdrop to Hague's childhood. It was, and is, a traditional Labour-supporting area at parliamentary and borough council level, although the county-wide West Riding authority (disbanded in 1974) sometimes had Conservative majorities, largely reflecting the views of the rural communities. As a political landscape in which to grow up this offered a diverse and subtle blend of influences. Although the conurbations that surrounded the Dearne and Rother valleys – Rotherham, Barnsley and Sheffield – have an industrial heritage, Hague's immediate environment was green and agricultural. The scenery remains rich and varied. In the 1960s of Hague's childhood, the same soil was offering up the fruits of farming and mining as coal was dug from the seams below the fields. Where the soft hills recline the boundaries between urban and agrarian merge. The suburbs of Rotherham and Barnsley are spread in neat, grey rows on the outer rings of the valleys which surround the villages of Greasbrough and Wentworth, home to the Hague family. These days Greasbrough has expanded to include satellite estates serving Rotherham. When William Hague was a small child it was still a tight knit community where families had lived for generations . . .

Although it was not completely dark, the light was on in Stella Jefferson's window at Manor Farm. In 1944 the farmhouse stood, as it still does, on the junction of Church Street and Main Street in Greasbrough village. Teenager Stella's bedroom window faced southwest towards the village green. The other side of the house overlooked Wentworth Park towards the ancient estate village of Wentworth, a couple of miles away. The Jeffersons were an established farming family: Stella shared the home with her parents and her two sisters, Mary and Marjorie. Stella was sorting through some of her things when the peace of the evening was abruptly broken. A shot coming from Main Street shattered the window. The light had made her a target, but thankfully only for the village pranksters.

Best friends Jack Willey and Nigel Hague had found a new way to attract the attentions of the opposite sex. The Willey family had been butchers in Greasbrough since the eighteenth century: their business in Main Street had been there for over a hundred years. From his room above the shop young Jack Willey could see Stella Jefferson's window at the farm. Nigel, his partner in crime, lived a minute's walk away in a mid-Victorian house, Rossiter Villa, facing the stream running through the village green. In the absence of a Cupid's arrow the spirited teenagers decided to convey their interest in Stella with an air rifle. They calculated the air pellet would do no more than rattle the window and hadn't counted on the resulting fuss. Within minutes of the impact Mr Jefferson came storming round to the butcher's to reprimand Jack and Nigel. Himself a keen shot, Mr Jefferson was secretly rather impressed with the skilful aim, but he was on a mission to deliver the boys to his wife who would administer the scolding. As the wife of the village farmer and an organiser for the local Conservative Association, Hilda Jefferson was a respected Greasbrough figure. It seems her admonishment had no long-term effects because the families remained close friends, and before too long Nigel Hague and Stella Jefferson were courting.

It was a worthwhile match, since the Hagues were a big name in Greasbrough. Nigel's father Bert ran the firm established by his father in 1870. Charles Hague had set up the soda water company in Park Gate, a mile or so from the village. His father before him was almost literally a Greasbrough founding father, having been the builder who constructed most of the village, including the family house in Rossiter Road. The Hague men were robust characters, known for their tradition of story telling to an *ad hoc* audience gathered in local hostelries. Bert Hague would tell jokes and recite funny rhymes while refreshing his performance with a good supply of bitter. Like his son, he had had his share of teenage kicks and one story is the stuff of village legend. When walking the fields very early one morning he impressed the local builder Arthur Cooper. Cooper told his own son to follow the example of Bert Hague, who obviously couldn't wait to get up and prepare for a day's work. In reality the reason for the dawn constitutional did not warrant such a charitable interpretation. Bert was only just returning across the fields from neighbouring Wentworth, after a whole night at the bar at the George and Dragon, the pub which was to become a regular for his son and his son's son.

The tradition of hospitality was second nature in so close a community. It was a calling that had always appealed to Hilda Jefferson. She had considered playing a bigger role in the community by becoming a Conservative councillor, but was closely beaten by the Labour candidate when she stood in 1946. Post-war Manor Farm was not quite what it had been. The landlords, the Fitzwilliam family which owned much of the surrounding area, were turning many of the fields over to opencast mining. By the end of the Forties she had persuaded her husband to leave Manor Farm and set off for Scarborough. There she took over and ran a guest house, the Delverne Hotel, Granville Road. Hilda had taken her husband out of the farm, but she had not taken the farm out of her husband. He missed agriculture so much that he took up a job on a farm near the guest house. Initially her daughters moved with her but soon Marjorie and Stella became engaged to be married. Mary stayed on to help her run the hotel. Stella Jefferson returned to Greasbrough, where in 1949 she became Mrs Nigel Hague and moved round the corner from the farm where she had grown up into the villa in Rossiter Road. The new Mrs Hague, aged twenty-one, wanted a large family. Nigel was happy for her to have as many children as she liked; after all she was to be a traditional mother giving her full-time attention to raising the family.

Within a year the first Hague child arrived. Within four years there were three daughters: Jane, Veronica and Sally. When the girls were old enough they all went to the Greasbrough junior and infants' school which, like most of the village, had been built by their great-grandfather. Now long since demolished, it was a bastion of traditional teaching values and a happy school. In terms of teaching methods the school was run as a grammar school and was considered old-fashioned, increasingly so as the Fifties turned into the Sixties and the quest to reinvent the educational wheel was gaining influence. Days began with a formal assembly, which was always Bible based, and pupils would take a turn to read a passage from the Bible and related prayer. In the classrooms children sat in neat rows at individual desks with ink wells filled by ink monitors. The class teacher would sit at a high desk teaching with 'chalk and talk'. It was considered a good posting for a teacher wanting to learn their craft. The curriculum was basic and the discipline taken for granted. A cane hung on the back of the Headmaster's door but it was more for show than practice. It certainly wasn't required for any of the Hague sisters who were all well behaved, conscientious if not brilliant, pupils. Greasbrough junior school was the perfect training ground for the eleven-plus and admission to a grammar school. The eldest sister Jane was preparing for that change, moving to Rotherham High School, as the family itself was about to change.

Nigel and Stella Hague had taken their three daughters on a trip to Southport. Most family breaks were spent visiting Stella's family at the Delverne Hotel, but on this outing the girls wanted to visit the model village over on the west coast. As it was a family occasion the sisters were encouraged to make a wish. One wanted a pony, another a piano, but six-year-old Sally said she wanted a brother. Of the three wishes, hers was granted sooner than she expected, as Stella Hague was already pregnant with her fourth child. Stella enjoyed being a mother and, with all her daughters in full time education, was keen to have another child. On 26 March 1961, in a nursing home in Rotherham, Stella gave birth to a baby boy with a shock of white blond hair. The boy was named William Jefferson Hague. The name was not popular with his sisters but William had been a long-standing name in Stella's family; thus he inherited both his forenames from his mother's relatives. Nigel's old friend Jack Willey and his wife Anne were made godparents to the baby. In the Hague family this was a tradition based on the ties of friendship rather than the call of the church. Nigel Hague has always had disdain for organised religion and Stella prefers a low key, personal approach. God, she says, is in the garden. So William Jefferson Hague was brought home to join the family in Rossiter Villa, where he would spend the first ten years of his childhood.

Life in the Hague household was comfortable though not indulgent. Nigel Hague's business was flourishing after expanding into wines and beers, but the proceeds were shared with his brother, the partner in the company, and Nigel's share had to support his wife and four growing children. The family house, which they now fully occupied, looked handsome, but with three bedrooms it was a tight squeeze. The eldest daughter Jane had a room to herself. William grew up sharing a room with Sally and Veronica, until Jane left home and Veronica was allowed to move into the room she had vacated.

It was a lively home with the three girls keen to make the most of the novelty of having a baby brother. The family was a close one, keen on playing games. The living room floor was often strewn with the remnants of an afternoon playing board games or cards: Monopoly and draughts were particular favourites. Prodigious though William proved to be, as a toddler he was a little young for such pursuits. Instead he would try to amuse his sisters by occupying the middle of the room and squealing with laughter. As he grew older he picked up his grandfather's skill of recounting limericks, which he would find hilarious even if the rest of the family didn't. The game-playing was also a feature of family holidays in Scarborough, particularly when the weather was bad. A rented beach hut was shelter cum games room for wet summer days. On better days Mrs Hague would dress William up to be recorded for posterity on the family cine-camera. His sisters sometimes felt that their young brother was a little spoilt. Sally, although much bigger than the toddler, didn't think it was fair when her father restrained her from defending herself against a mini but aggressive combatant. Jane, eleven years his senior, thought William could wrap their mother round his little finger.

Stella Hague was particularly ambitious for her son. The household was not an intellectual one but valued good education. The two eldest girls went to Rotherham High School and Sally to Oakwood Comprehensive, also in Rotherham. All three went on to study secretarial skills at the North of England Secretarial College in Leeds.

William's education was to have more of an academic emphasis than his sisters'. It started with his introduction to the local library before he could walk. While the three girls were in school Stella would take William in his push-chair round to look at the books. He certainly took to books with great zeal. When his Aunt Mary read to him to entertain him during one of those drizzly days in Scarborough, she was amazed that at the age of four he was able to read the story back to her. He was not allowed, however, to register for a library card until he started at school, so the first day William went to Greasbrough Junior his mother had to go back to the library to sign him up.

William's start in school was not as seamless as his sisters' had been. As a local authority school Greasbrough was open to the whole community. The year William joined, his year teacher, Joan Brothwell (then Marsland), already had 49 pupils registered. William was number 50. The Hague sisters had sat in classes of around thirty and Mrs Hague was not pleased at the difference. William too seemed unimpressed. After two days at the school he registered his protest at the start of the third day by refusing to take his coat off. His early introduction to books must have paid off as he told his mother he didn't want to stay there: it was too easy for him. Stella Hague contemplated keeping William at home and after a few occasions of keeping him away from school was told off by Joan Brothwell. She was warned the place would go to someone else on the waiting list if William did not take it up properly. After that he knuckled down to his school career, quickly making a good impression. It was a working-class village and many of his contemporaries were the children of miners. Coming from a small business background young Hague was not typical but in so small a place notions of class distinction were less an issue than where you came from. So William was very much just an ordinary member of the class, except that is for his particularly bright intellect.

The class size did not hamper William's academic development, although he became used to occupying himself when the lessons became too easy for him. Before long he was put up a year. The headmaster, Mr Williams, reputedly told other staff that he expected great things from the Hague boy. He was good at all the academic subjects, though he was easily bored by art and sport. William tended to be a quiet, conscientious pupil, although he was prone to the odd bout of tomfoolery. When he was about eight Stella received a call from the school to say that William had somehow hurt his hand. She turned up to collect him to find that he was indeed unable to move his fingers. Much poking and prodding proved that yes, William had a damaged hand. The hand however made a remarkably quick recovery when William returned home, missing the art class. Despite his antipathy towards drawing and painting, William did prove himself a keen little performer. At Greasbrough he started his school dramatic career as a goblin. He wasn't the most gifted singer or dancer in the class but he loved being on the stage, with an audience of more than his sisters to entertain. It was a hobby, which lasted through to his A-levels.

Outside school hours William was expanding his other interests as well. As his sisters grew older he had to find more ways of amusing himself. By the time he was eight his eldest sister had left for college, with the next soon to follow. Sometimes he would walk home from school past Willey's butchers and find himself under attack from their dogs. Jack thought it amusing to set the dogs to chase the boy into the backyard of the Harrisons, who acted as occasional babysitters for the Hague children. There William could spend hours being amused by Mr Harrison building things with rubber bricks. It was an interest which he translated at home with Lego, and gradually from Lego castles emerged Lego forts and Lego battlefields, the perfect foil for Action Man soldiers.

At around the same time towards the end of the 1960s Stella's mother Hilda suffered a heart attack and was ill for many months. Nigel, Stella and William used to try to visit her each weekend. It was then that game-playing William was really introduced to cards. Hilda Jefferson was not well enough to leave her bed but could manage a game of cards. Sometimes William's Aunt Mary would join in. Later, after her mother's death in 1971, Mary became William's regular opponent in 'Wot', a game with a particularly complicated scoring system. In the early days Aunt Mary was the clear winner, but as their contests were to go on for many years, William made sure he had a chance to beat her at her own game.

Expanding Charles Hague and Company into wines and beers had been a successful move for William's parents. The number of pubs and working men's clubs in the area secured a successful trade, and in time the family aspired to something more desirable than the Greasbrough house that they had inherited. The chance to move came just as William was turning ten and thinking about changing schools. The Hagues were offered the opportunity to move the two miles down the road to the historic village of Wentworth.

Unfairly, South Yorkshire has not shared the rest of Yorkshire's reputation for picturesque villages and unspoilt countryside. The current parliamentary constituency of Wentworth is large, encompassing several other villages and parts of Rotherham. The village of Wentworth, however, is an idyll to compare with the best of the Dales or the Cotswolds. The immaculately preserved stone cottages and neatly preened gardens on the estate of Wentworth Wood House, with the longest façade of any British stately home, make the village the obvious place to aspire to for South Yorkshire's well-to-do. It is a place which draws visitors to its parkland and olde worlde pubs. Despite its manicured appearance, however, Wentworth's character is more complex than a typical Tory shire: indeed, Labour have traditionally won around fifty per cent of the village vote in parliamentary elections. It would be a crude interpretation which suggested that the Hagues moved from working-class Greasbrough to middle-class Wentworth, although a first glance can give that impression. Unusual tenure agreements add to the village's exclusivity as it is a listed village and even now, it is almost impossible to buy a property there. All houses are tithe properties owned by the Fitzwilliam Estate. Including the several working farms there were about 300 people living there when William and his family were told there was a house available to rent. Recently there has been some modern development on the outskirts of the village, out of sight of the centre, but even now villagers talk of 'letting outsiders in'. Ironically the young Hague who became so enthralled by Margaret Thatcher's project and its refocusing of the Conservative manifesto around the emblematic policy of council house sales was to develop his political convictions in a house that his parents had chosen to rent after leaving the one they owned.

Cortworth Cottage is about half a mile away from the village church and the centre around Main Street. A few shops are bordered by the two vital engines of village life, The Rockingham Arms and the George and Dragon. The cottage, which became home to ten-year-old William and his sister Sally before she went to college had no immediate neighbours. Originally a cottage, the name stayed even though a larger house was built on in the eighteenth century. Whereas Rossiter Villa had a small garden, the six-bedroomed 'cottage' was surrounded by open fields and had an acre and a half of its own land. The view was broken only by the surrounding woods. If Mrs Hague thought God was in the garden, this was certainly an inspiring playground. As William became older he loved to play in the fields, particularly to go on long walks with his golden retriever, Caesar. His enjoyment of walking was learnt from his father who had regularly made the five-mile walk across country from Barnsley to Greasbrough. The dog was another perk of moving 'to the country'. William was just a normal – if unusually self-sufficient – child who took his country walks for fun, but the history and the influences of the area were there to absorb.

The view from the crest of Coaley Lane, running up from Main Street, looks north towards Corton Wood, the mining village which took the brunt of the worst disruption of the 1984–5 strike. Looking south towards Wentworth village the swathe of fields gives way to woods, hiding the grandeur of Wentworth Wood House. The house, with enough rooms for each day of the year, was the family home of the second Marquis of Rockingham, twice Whig prime minister in the second half of the eighteenth century. The estate is still run on behalf of his descendent, by marriage, the Earl of Fitzwilliam. From Wentworth the panorama includes the industrial landmarks that affirm the area's working heritage – cooling towers, chimneys, the blackened steel paraphernalia of mining – and the monuments built to mark its aristocratic history. The landscape is studded with follies. The Hoober Stand, the Keppels Column and the mysterious Needle's Eye are eye catching reminders of the land's ancestry.

The Fitzwilliam family mausoleum, on the same road out of the village as Hague's house, contains a bust of Conservative founding father Edmund Burke, who was private secretary to Prime Minister Rockingham. Burke's philosophy articulated the quiet, practical, common-sense Conservatism born out of ordinary people's experience of the world rather than the ideological theorising of political élites. Students of history would also read in Burke an early advocate for checking the advance of the state, a challenge to the prevailing intellectual consensus that accepted the case for increasing regulation.

Wentworth's architectural remnants would set an enquiring mind racing, while its land and the history of its cultivation also convey a particular political message. Local historians, including the former Labour MP Lord Hardy, recognise the responsible stewardship of the Fitzwilliam family. Apart from leasing out farming land, the Fitzwilliams later built the collieries that powered the industrial revolution. The relationship between the owners and the workers was good; the family was respected, as thoughtful employers with a sense of *noblesse oblige*. Although the Earls were not keen on the rise of trade unions during the age of the Chartists, unusually every miner had guaranteed rights including a pension. This was a Whig family, which administered the area with benevolent paternalism. In a more modern setting that culture fed into an organic shire Conservatism, and until the 1980s imbued political debate in South Yorkshire with a courteous respect for other opinions.

Although Wentworth was to nurture the seeds of the young politician in William Hague, he had other concerns when he first moved to Cortworth Cottage. The move had taken him into a different education authority and gave him the right to sit for a scholarship to the prestigious grammar school at Ripon. William was duly awarded a scholarship, and at the age of eleven set off for an adventure fifty miles away from his new home. It was not a success. As an out-of-towner William had to board, but the school was a day school, and so only a minority of pupils was in residence. He disliked it right from the start. In Greasbrough he had been used to a busy household within a close knit community. The new school seemed impersonal. Although he had been a conscientious pupil, William now started to play up. On coming home for breaks from school, he perfected a disappearing act just as he was due to return to Ripon. Once he was found in the woods above his house with his dog and a survival kit he had put together in the kitchen. The next time the clue was in the missing cupboard key. Halfway up the staircase at the back of the house there was a large cupboard. In earlier times it had been an apple store. In William's home time it became a perfect hideaway. When his family had been unable to find him anywhere his father suddenly noticed that the key, always kept on the outside of the door, was missing. After much knocking and shouting, William eventually unlocked the door from the inside. He was sent back to Ripon again, only to run away from the school. He phoned his mother from the telephone box outside the Cathedral but he had not gone far enough to evade discovery by canny teachers. The Hagues realised that, scholarship or no scholarship, William had taken against the school. Reluctantly they agreed to let him come home. Nigel Hague told Stella that no son of theirs should be unhappy at school.

Had William stayed at Ripon Grammar his prodigious political career might have seemed rather less distinctive. With the Conservatives keen to broaden their base, Hague has proclaimed his comprehensive schooling, but the character of his new school, Wath Comprehensive, was not so different from the one he had left behind in North Yorkshire. Although Wath had technically made the decision to go comprehensive, in tune with the educa-

tional vogue of the 1960s and the reforms of the Wilson
Government, it was still in spirit a grammar school. The year that
William was admitted the school was still called Wath Upon
Dearne Grammar school, only losing the selective name when the
West Riding authority was disbanded in 1974. William was able
to take up a place for the Spring term because he had won the
scholarship to Ripon. That qualified him for entry, where other
pupils had still to pass an eleven-plus exam. Universal admission
had not yet been introduced, and partly as a result teachers
remember his year as particularly gifted. William would have been
unaware of the local debate over comprehensivisation which had
taken place during the early 1960s. The resolution in the case of
Wath meant that the school decided to preserve many of the
traditional customs and teaching methods of its grammar school
heritage. In the early 1970s Wath was predominantly a mining
village although its history was agricultural and the character of
the town reflected this mix of interests. Some of the nearby
villages that sent children to Wath school were more occupied
with the Sheffield steel industry. In that respect William had
certainly joined a school which had more of a diverse social mix
than Ripon. Within that mix he would have been considered a
middle-class boy in a working-class school, but it was a distinction of which he was unaware and it did not influence his group
of friends.

If anything, geography was the common factor in William's
gang. His closest friends all came from villages like Wentworth on
the outskirts of Wath, and their friendship grew out of the camaraderie of the school bus. Just before William was due for his first
day in the school, teachers told David Rusby, a Wath farmer's
son, that he should look out for the new boy on the bus. David's
home, Coaley Lane Farm, is a mile or so away from Cortworth
Cottage, but as there are only fields separating the two, the boys
were neighbours. David had had a term's head start on making

friends, but over time the school run confirmed a firm friendship between the two which lasts to this day. When William returned from school his dog, Caesar, would be sitting at the front gate and the two would go and play up at the farm. As he became settled at Wath a circle developed, including miners' sons David Limb and Keith Washington, and Nigel Parry, whose parents ran a small shop. The friendships strengthened as the boys grew older and, at the first possible opportunity, learnt to drive. However, the progression to driving was not trouble free. By the time William was eighteen he had been involved in three accidents that resulted in 'write offs'.

The first, when he was fifteen, was the most serious. David Rusby had just left the school bus when William, sitting near the front, was one of the first children to notice a car lurching dangerously towards them. It was snaking down a hill, clearly out of control, apparently slipping on ice. The car was involved in a head-on collision with the bus, killing its driver. It was bloody and brutal and William was the best placed witness. He had to relive the accident in detail when he appeared as a witness at the court hearing some weeks later. In a comfortable and secure family life it was the closest William had come to childhood trauma.

Later Rusby was the driver when he and William took two girlfriends, Jane and Alison, out for an evening. It was certainly an evening they would remember. Ice was once again the cause of the accident from which remarkably all four emerged unscathed, although the car was left wrapped around a lamp post. In the final accident William was the driver when he was hit by another car. The other driver was drunk. He had another lucky escape but the car was beyond hope.

The move to Wath gave William to chance to pursue outdoor hobbies, even if he was to disappoint his father with his lack of interest in cricket and football. Although William did not enjoy team sports his keen interest in walking later developed into running, a habit that has become a way of life in adulthood. The countryside was a bit of an adventure for young William, giving him plenty of opportunities to entertain himself. While his youngest sister Sally was still living at home, he would climb up into the barn opposite her window and fire water pistols into her room. When she moved away to study William was still only eleven but he was a resourceful child absorbed in his own company as much as that of others. The household had a new guest in Nigel's mother, who by now had been widowed and was too elderly to live alone, but she did not spend much time with the boy. So he was free to indulge the passion for Lego he had developed in Greasbrough. Characteristically if William was going to do something, he was going to do it well, and his games with toy soldiers were no casual affair. Now that he had his own bedroom he was able to devote the whole of it to restaging the Napoleonic wars in *papier-mâché* and tin. The entire floor was covered by his home-made battlefields and troops of soldiers whose precise moves were re-enacted with strict attention to historical detail. He guarded the war room closely. On one occasion his cousins, children of Stella's sister Marjorie, came to visit and playfully disrupted a battle in progress. Thereafter he would lock his bedroom door whenever they came to the house. He applied the same methodical focus to card games. The games he had been playing with his Aunt Mary became more competitive.

In 1975 his parents realised a lifetime's ambition by taking a holiday to America. (It sparked an abiding interest in the USA: since then they have visited every state.) Aunt Mary came to look after William, and she did not realise that the hours they spent playing cards were no casual entertainment. When William later left for university she found that he had been keeping a running score of all the games they had played over many years.

William approached his schoolwork with the same degree of single-mindedness and determination. School was an environment in which, knowing he was clever, he was able to flourish. Academically Wath was a strong school, retaining the traditional teaching practices of its grammar school background, but keen to develop pupils' other interests. The grammar school inheritance was still at its strongest during the first years that William attended, and the school did better by its brighter pupils than by the less able. It had yet to develop an approach appropriate to its new comprehensive status. Pupils were called by their surnames (though not always the girls) and teachers, some of whom wore gowns, were addressed as 'Sir'. There was a strong house system, each house with a classical name, which gradually became less significant as more emphasis was put on the horizontal year groups. With around 250 pupils in each year, the year groups would fully reflect the academic range of all the pupils although lessons were streamed. As in Greasbrough, William's intellectual potential was soon spotted, but although a bookish boy he was not considered a swat.

Confirming his father's disappointment at William's lack of interest in team games, his extracurricular activities were musical. He and David Rusby were keen, if not gifted, members of the school choir: his music teacher Barbara Senior considered him a very reliable bass. He was part of the choir which sang at Fountains Abbey for the television programme *Songs of Praise*, and he regularly made it to the chorus for the school's annual Gilbert and Sullivan performance. As he moved up the school he became particularly keen on the cross-country walking group and taking school trips. Even when having fun there was always a competitive edge. When swimming with friends William would insist on setting a target for lengths, and then try to beat it. When he joined the Rusby family on holiday in Maplethorpe fourteen-year-old William insisted that the boys could justify building a sandcastle only if it was the biggest. David and William set off for the beach with a full sized garden trowel.

Although they were instinctive Conservatives, Nigel and Stella Hague had never been politically active. Nigel Hague has strong opinions but his favourite forum for expressing them was – and is – over a pint with a few friends. Both he and his brother Charles were considered by friends as further to the right than Attila the Hun, each branded a 'hanger and a flogger'. On moving to Wentworth the pro-active branch of the local Conservative association spotted new recruits and canvassed their support. Stella paid her dues and attended occasional branch receptions as a way of being involved with village life. When William was twelve she noticed his passion in toy soldiers was waning. The studied fascination with historic battles had naturally progressed to an interest in more recent conflicts and was evolving into political enquiry. Stella was a little embarrassed to admit to the Conservative branch secretary, Pat Swift, that her son was interested in politics but was undecided as to whether he was a Liberal or a Conservative.

Pat Swift spotted a challenge and a potential new member. The first move was to encourage William's interest in the Conservative Party with personal deliveries of the party newspaper. It was an appropriate way to capture the attention of a boy who loved reading and was showing a precocious interest in current affairs, absorbed by the early evening news on television as he ate his dinner.

It certainly was a riveting period to become absorbed in the news. Nationally the constant drip-drip effect of economic problems politicised the lives of those who would otherwise have been uninterested, and internationally the continuing repercussions of the Cold War made tangible the threat to national security.

William's interest in military history led him to a growing fascination with the Second World War and with Churchill. From there it was just a short leap to wanting to know more about Parliament, and the obvious reading matter – albeit unlikely for a now thirteen-year-old boy – was *Hansard*. Not surprisingly, the official record of the parliamentary debates was not regular stock in Wentworth's newsagents. Stella Hague, keen as always to satisfy her son's enquiring mind, placed a special order. Before long William was hooked. The formal debates of *Hansard* appealed to the tactician who had studied winning moves on the battlefield and was adding chess to his games repertoire. For a boy who devoured information and delighted himself by collecting facts, politics offered a whole new world of detail and statistics to master. Imagine – all those strange constituency names, the lists of majorities, the dates of elections! It was a cornucopia of facts and figures. The passion and the conviction were to develop as his interest grew and his appreciation became more sophisticated.

Pat Swift's next move was to involve him actively in the local party. The perfect opportunity presented itself in May 1974 when she herself stood for Rotherham council in Rawmarsh: she recruited William to join her on the campaign trail. His first experience of canvassing for the Conservative Party was in the mining villages of Brampton Bierlow and Corton Wood. These were working villages with none of the manicured lawns of Wentworth. For a young Tory it was a challenging environment in which to cut his campaigning teeth, particularly as it was a low point for the Conservatives nationally. In March of that year Edward Heath had resigned as Prime Minister following an inconclusive general election result. February's election had followed the second miners' strike of that administration. The first in 1972, about pay, was resolved fairly quickly in favour of the miners, whose case was largely supported by the government's own inquiry into pay under Lord Wilberforce. The 1974 strike, also on pay, heightened the effects of the international oil crisis and emphasised the extent to which Heath had departed from his manifesto commitment to break the post-war corporatist consensus. Although the atmosphere of the 1974 strike was hardly more militant than the previous one, there was an appreciable difference. Arthur Scargill, not yet president of the NUM, was on his way up and was gaining media attention as a result of the emergence of picketing. Heath's inability to contain the miners' demands within his incomes policy became emblematic of the Tory defeat. The battle lines between old left and new right were gradually emerging for a collision yet to come.

When Hague later developed his own platform he was as critical of this period of Tory rule as he was about Labour administrations. But these were early days and William's role as canvasser was not to persuade but to enquire about voting intentions. If people had any questions he would fetch Pat to answer them. The area was strongly old Labour, but the industrial disputes, although increasingly political, were not as bitter or confrontational as those under Thatcher. The reorganisation of local government had entrenched Labour dominance of the area, so that the new region of South Yorkshire earned the epithet 'The Socialist Republic'. On the whole the Liberals and Conservatives were the only canvassers, particularly in local elections. The issue for Labour was not so much if they would win, but by how much. Conservatives were regarded more as a novelty than as a threat, and young William particularly so. Despite the overwhelming opposition to Tories, he did not encounter any bitter doorstep dressing-downs. Political activity was still well behaved and the worst that happened to William was his leaflets being torn up.

William's friends were becoming aware of his growing interest in politics, although they thought it very odd. At thirteen he told David Limb that he had a life plan. He intended to study PPE at Oxford, becoming involved with the Union and become an MP by the time he was thirty. By the time he was fourteen he had memorised the names and majorities of all the constituencies and was become more opinionated. Putting the world to rights at the edge of the games field earned him a strict rebuke from the PE teacher, who called him a 'useless lump of lard' for discussing politics and disrupting the game. It was, however, the only one of his school subjects that suffered. After a year of physics he had chosen to study mainly arts subjects and languages, including Greek and Latin which were a staple of the Wath curriculum.

Alongside lunchtime choir practices William added membership of the school's new debating society. William's geography teacher and head of year, Derek Hinchliffe, was concerned at the decreasing importance which universities were placing on the tradition of the formal debate. Hinchliffe, a Labour councillor in Barnsley, felt it was his responsibility to encourage interested students before they reached further education. The son of a miner and a firm believer in the inspiration of a good education, Hinchliffe was the president of the Barnsley Debating Society. The group he established at the school was initially a forum for debate, and Hinchliffe would introduce subjects for discussion – commonly politics, religion or relationships. Heady stuff for teenagers, though William was at first a studied listener. As interest in the project grew the debates became more formal in tone and Hinchliffe noticed William playing a greater role. Among a predominance of Labour sympathisers it was obvious that William took a different view. An emerging theme was the need to rein back the unions.

When Hinchliffe left the school at the end of William's fourth year to pursue a calling in the Methodist Church, William was chosen by his peers to make the presentation. The Parker pen set presented that day has since gone on to register many marriages conducted by the Reverend Hinchliffe, and he and William still correspond.

The debating society, which after Hinchliffe's departure was handed over to the politics master Robert Godber, fuelled William's interest in Parliament. When he was fifteen Stella wrote to the local Labour MP, Peter Hardy (now Lord Hardy of Wath), asking if they could visit him at the House of Commons. Hardy, a governor of Wath school, was pleased to entertain them although he knew would not be able to recruit William to his cause. William's introduction to the Commons, complete with tea on the terrace, confirmed his ambition to be an MP, although even he had not thought that he was likely to be standing against Peter Hardy, as he later did in Wentworth at the 1987 general election.

William was now an active Young Conservative, but between elections this was as much a vehicle for a social life as for any serious politicking. Although his close friends teased him about the politics he took it in good part and did not let his passion dominate all of his free time. Much of that was spent helping out with his father's business. Lest he get too grand, William had a down-to-earth holiday job as a driver's mate, helping with drinks deliveries to the local working men's clubs. It was hands-on experience of the sheer hard graft of running a successful small business. The company employed around fifty people and although it was too small to be hit by a strike, the prevailing climate of industrial relations was a constant worry to Nigel Hague. William was in no doubt about his father's irritation at the tendency of successive governments to interfere with business in general, and the increasing regulations that affected his own working life.

By this time the Hagues had expanded into part ownership of several pubs, including The Rockingham Arms in Wentworth. The 'Rock', as locals know it, was frequently the venue for a meet of the area's hunt, and Stella Hague used to prepare the punch for the Hague stirrup cup. The cup itself commemorated the original Charles Hague who had established the drinks business. William did not inherit his father's interest in shooting, but as he grew older he certainly inherited the family penchant for the pub and appreciation of good beer. In his 'O' level year he took a school trip to Luxembourg and wrote to his parents: 'On the ferry I had too much lager, but I could still stand up.'

The fifteen-year-old's taste for beer and politics did not disrupt his studies. At 'O' level he achieved eight grade A results and one B, for Greek. His only comment to the headmaster afterwards was, 'I was never very good at Greek.'

It wasn't his only achievement of the year. William had been taking a more active role in the debating society and was developing a real taste for public speaking. At home he had taken to listening to recordings of great orators, particularly Iain Macleod, whose death in office in July 1970 during the early days of the Heath administration had denied the Tories one of their most charismatic figures, and Winston Churchill. William's head of year was now Robert Godber, who went on to teach him politics at 'A' level and lent him some of his own records. William told him that when it came to Churchill's oratory, 'no one else should be mentioned in the same breath'. Godber was very much a mentor, a highly civilised man who felt duty bound to encourage William's talent. As a Tory who had stood for election in Barnsley, home of the National Union of Mineworkers, Godber empathised with William's willingness to wave the flag for Conservatism in a school which was overwhelmingly Labour supporting. He was keen to pass on his own sense of place and respect for the different strands of influence, from the countryside and the industrialised urban development, which could give depth to William's developing views. It was clear that being the son of a businessman, particularly running a small enterprise, was significant. William was concerned about the state of the economy, the government's paralysis in the face of rising inflation and lack of teeth in the face of the unions. Yet he also sympathised with the efforts of hard-working people, regardless of class. Godber observed that William related to some of the values of the area's Labour traditionalists. After all it was partly his heritage and the background of many of his friends. He also noted that William took a less accommodating view of intellectual, middle-class Labour.

Under Godber's tutorship William entered and won a youth public speaking competition organised by Yorkshire Television. At the final in Hull the host, Richard Whiteley, was as surprised as other observers by William's choice of subject. His peers stuck to fairly anodyne issues like their pets or a local landmark. William had chosen the rather dry and mature subject of devolution. When it came to the question-and-answer session however, William lapsed into a more tribal response. He told the audience his hobby was 'socialist bashing'. It was a hobby he had been practising, if only verbally, at the Rotherham by-election in June 1976. William ratcheted up his credentials as a Young Conservative activist by heckling the Labour candidate during the public meeting at Greasbrough town hall. The mainly Labour audience was more surprised than offended at the teenage Tory rant.

Later that year William attended his first Conservative Party Conference. The 1976 conference in Brighton saw the party launch 'The Right Approach', its main policy programme since Margaret Thatcher had beaten Edward Heath in the leadership contest the previous year. Thatcher had been careful to maintain a range of opinion in the shadow cabinet but the tone of the Conservative message was moving to the radical right. It was an exciting time to be involved with a party in transition, as the state of the country increasingly demanded a change to the politics practised since the war. William was fast becoming a Thatcher disciple; her image bedecked his bedroom walls. Stella Hague asked Pat Swift if she would take William down to the conference. Had she been less strict William might have launched his career a year earlier. Buoyed by his public speaking success, he was very keen to speak at the conference, but Pat was adamant that he did not place a request to do so. He had not had permission from school to go and his appearance on the television would reveal her role in encouraging him to go AWOL. William found consolation in noticing that a seventeen-year boy had spoken that year. It gave him a record to beat, as he would still be only sixteen the following year.

The next autumn William took the precaution of requesting time off from his 'A' Level studies (Economics, Politics, History and General Studies) to go to the Blackpool conference, again chaperoned by Pat Swift and her husband Ray. Robert Godber equated the week off to work experience and recommended he be allowed to go.

Godber knew William could afford the time off. His essays were thoughtful and stylish, although Godber sometimes wondered how hard William had worked. His ability to construct an argument came instinctively rather than through much preparation. And so it was with the speech.

The speech at the 1977 conference that has coloured the perception of William Hague, boy and man, was prepared quickly the night before he delivered it. Unusually, William had prepared a draft speech over the previous weekend, thinking he might try to speak on the first day in the Trade and Industry debate. On arriving he decided to hang fire until he had had a chance to see more of the other speakers. Having studied the form he was ready, and made adjustments to his draft the night before the economy debate. After an early fish dinner, William told Pat and Ray that he wanted to go back to the hotel to prepare his speech and asked permission to attend the Young Conservative disco later the same night. On the way to the dance he submitted his request to speak and hoped that a touch of self-promotion would influence the conference organisers in his favour. On his entry form he had added 'William Hague, aged 16 and winner of the Yorkshire Television public speaking competition'.

The next day Derek Hinchliffe, the man who had introduced William to the art of public speaking, pinched himself. The star of the evening news was his protégé, the boy whose talents he had spotted only a couple of years before. The voice and the message were unmistakable, even if the delivery and the conviction had developed apace.

For a short speech it has had a lasting effect, as much because of its delivery as its content. When William heard his name called he felt nervous, as he mounted the platform really anxious, but as he began to speak his natural love of performance took over. He had never spoken into a microphone before, but it helped. Once he realised that his voice could fill the whole hall he really let go. Sixteen-year-old William had the authoritative tone of a seasoned politician, powerful but rather disarming in a teenager. The tweed jacket and tie added to the impression that this was a youngster impersonating the weighty oratory of a more experienced person. Its credibility was redeemed, however, by William's winning formula of making his age the central theme. It made his performance genuinely compelling and lifted it above the act of a brainy show-off. In front of an audience of thousands in the hall, the shadow cabinet, party leader Margaret Thatcher and television cameras, William warned them his might be the last generation for the Conservative Party. He spoke with conviction, challenging the party to save itself and the country by taking radical measures. Rather than maintain the prevailing economic and social order, the Conservatives had to 'roll back the frontiers of the state' and 'create a capital owning, home owning democracy for the young people'.

William repeated this message in his first published article that appeared in the northern edition of the *Daily Mail* the following week. He described himself and his friends as a

'Generation in Doubt'. He wrote of a loss of confidence in the political system as even the last Conservative government had completely failed to reverse 'the grinding inefficiency of the corporate state'. In order to win the support of his generation the Conservative Party had to become 'the party of radicalism and change'. In a message which still seemed pertinent during his own leadership campaign twenty years later, he warned the party against chasing the middle ground 'in a futile attempt to beat the left at its own game'.

These were weighty themes for a schoolboy. Freedom is at the core of Conservative philosophy, but it could have seemed an abstract concept for a boy whose own liberty was then most obviously constrained by homework. It was hardly enslavement, but William acutely believed that tangible freedoms were at risk, both domestically and abroad. These were heady times as the libertarians and *laissez faire* economists were stepping up the fight against the *dirigiste* tendency to put freedom back at the centre of the party's philosophy. Mrs Thatcher's ascent to the leadership brought with it a quest for new ideas. The arguments for economic liberalism were being made by newly formed think tanks, the Adam Smith Institute and Sir Keith Joseph's Centre for Policy Studies. William read the work of the free market Institute for Economic Affairs and absorbed the ideas of Sir Keith Joseph who had distinguished between the common ground, ideas with the potential for popular support and the Macmillanite middle way, an unworkable compromise between left and right, socialism and the market. Such tensions had always existed in Conservatism but had become more urgent set against the obvious failure of the governing consensus.

In both his speech and his article, William made greater freedom an attainable goal by taking up the cause of liberal economics and urging Thatcher's party to reduce government interference in people's lives. It was an agenda to lower taxes, to reduce regulation, to eliminate the union stranglehold to allow ordinary people more choice in education and health. In the context of the late Seventies with an incomes and prices policy, top rates of income tax at 83 per cent, capital gains tax reaching 97 per cent, moves to restrict the development of private medicine, the demonising of private education, inflation, unemployment and the beer and sandwiches culture of Number 10, Hague's message was far from academic, as freedom was discernibly under threat. In an analogy to which William would particularly relate, Margaret Thatcher had described Britain as the 'pocket money society', in which people were only left with pocket money after the state had spent the rest of it on centralised provision of pensions, welfare, education and health. In return the pocket money kid told Thatcher to stick to her guns for his generation that 'above all wanted to be free, free from government, the government that they think should get out of their way'.

In the conference hall, the immediate effect of the speech was to bring the shadow cabinet to its feet and put the media in a frenzy as a new political star shone. He seemed to shine more brightly as the day continued with national television appearances including *News at Ten* and *Nationwide*, on which he made an uncompromising appeal to Geoffrey Howe to take up his message. The next day Pat Swift told William not to enter the conference through the side door as he had done previously: 'You'll never go through the side door again,' she told him. His entry to any door that day was greeted with lines of press and cameras. He was dubbed 'William the Conqueror' by the *Daily Express* and 'Maggie's Bionic Babe' by *The Sun*. Amidst all the flurry and accolades, a word of caution from Sir Keith Joseph set the tone for William's response. Taking the boy to one side to have a quick word in his ear, Joseph told him that what he needed was 'a period of obscurity'.

As his school bus drew up outside Wath Comprehensive the following Monday, that obscurity seemed some way off. A crowd of journalists and photographers had gathered to greet his arrival. William returned their interest with courtesy and composure but had taken Sir Keith Joseph's advice to heart. He agreed to repeat his walk into school three times for the sake of the cameras, but after the third he told them his economics class had to take precedence. Apart from the article for the *Daily Mail* and a later appearance on Radio Four's *Any Questions?*, William turned down many other similar requests.

He did appear on a local broadcast but only with his mother's help. While William was out doing his father's deliveries one day during the holidays, Stella received a call asking whether he would do a short interview later that evening. When he returned home, Stella found him in poor repair. William had developed the driver's mate habit of having a few pints along the way, perhaps a drink at every stop. Hauling crates was heavy, sweaty work and bitter seemed like appropriate refreshment for the beer delivery boys. The trouble was that on this occasion William had been promised to the local radio station, so Stella had to sober him up quickly to avoid embarrassment. On another occasion his friends stepped in. Sometimes, fuelled by beer, his passion for proclaiming would reassert itself. On Christmas Eve the boys were celebrating in the George before the midnight service in the village church next door. Full of seasonal spirit, William told friends he wanted to give his own sermon during the service. He seemed so determined that David Rusby and his other friends felt the only way to avoid ruining the service was wrestling him to the ground to keep him out of the church.

After a period of ribbing from school friends, which mainly consisted of chanting his speech at him on the school bus (one recited the whole speech in the bar at Wath's George and Dragon) William settled down to A-levels and enjoying the enhanced social life which learning to drive offered. His close friends took it in turns to hold a Saturday night party every few weeks. They were typical teenage parties with unisex flared jeans, too much lager, Genesis, Meatloaf and girls. William and David would take girls out to pubs in neighbouring villages. One attempt to impress nearly turned to disaster as William, having lost his way somewhere outside Sheffield, decided the logical way back was to retrace the exact route he had taken. This took him, David and their two dates straight into the oncoming traffic of a one-way slip road. On that occasion a very fast U-turn was the only solution.

Much to his delight and the envy of many of his peers, William's celebrity helped him to win the attentions of his first steady girlfriend.

Kim Birch was a school friend from a neighbouring village who was happy to be drawn into William's Young Conservative branch along with a bunch of his other friends. With curly blonde hair and a flawless complexion she was the envy of her school girl friends, and the object of desire for the boys. William was unusually excited when she agreed to go out with him, telling Stella that he had found it hard to concentrate on his exams because of it. Kim and William became an item and their relationship lasted sporadically through and beyond his time at university. Later, after he left Oxford, the romance was rekindled for a while and a friendship survives to this day. However infatuated William initially was with Kim, his long-term aims did not allow for too much distraction. At the wedding reception of his eldest sister Jane, held in a marquee in the garden of Cortworth Cottage, William told Pat Swift the plan for his own love life. He had already told friends that he intended to fight an unwinnable Tory seat in his twenties, enter Parliament by the time he was thirty and become a minister shortly afterwards. He filled in the rest of his life by announcing his intention not to get too serious about a girl until he was an MP, and not to marry before becoming a minister. The pinnacle of his ambition was revealed to friends after the school's annual Gilbert and Sullivan performance. William had a part in the chorus of *Princess Ida*. During the after-show party in the Creswell Arms in Swinton, he told his music teacher of his ultimate role.

'You know, Mrs Senior,' he said, 'one day I'm going to be Prime Minister.'

Although friends and teachers teased him about his lofty aspirations, they did not dismiss them. Even as a youngster Hague had the composure of a far more experienced person. His determination was clear, his approach to all things focused and precise and his self-confidence undented. His family roots and small-town background gave him a sense of place, his intellect and political heritage a sense of purpose. His speech had brought him some detractors, so much so that even twenty years after it was made young William was still the inspiration for mocking parodies. The comedian Harry Enfield created his most odious character, Tory Boy, based on the young Hague. Tory Boy is the spotty youth who lectures his own parents over dinner. Just a year after he made the conference speech the *Guardian* was already asking if Hague was the youngest ever has-been in politics. In fact Hague was biding his time and developing his philosophy. In winter 1978 – the 'Winter of Discontent' – Hague published his Manifesto for Britain. The ten-point plan was written for the *Free Nation* newspaper, the paper of the National Association for Freedom (later the Freedom Association). The NAFF was then a new, radical pressure group pushing the Conservatives to put liberty at the centre of their economic and social agenda. By involving themselves with high profile disputes like the 1977 strike at the Grunwick film processing factory, a *cause célèbre* of the left, NAFF were helping to give the new right the excitement of being on the intellectual front line. Associating with NAFF was the stuff of grown-up politics, more sophisticated than the fundraising, party-holding activities of most Young Conservatives. By writing for *Free Nation* Hague was associating himself with the new guard. The agenda he described is still an accurate summary of his own philosophy, combining the traditional conservative instincts of his background with a personal taste for meritocratic reforms and the rational, dry approach of a liberal economist.

As leader of the Conservative Party, Hague will fight the next general election under the banner of the Common Sense Revolution, a theme he launched at the 1999 Conservative Party Conference. Commentators have rightly observed that this is a formula Hague discussed with Canadian Conservatives during a fact-finding tour of North America early in his leadership. After a devastating defeat in 1993, Canadian Conservatives found the Common Sense approach helped in their revival.

In fact, the roots of Hague's Common Sense Revolution go back much further than his trip to Canada. His 1978 Manifesto for Britain starts with a call for common sense change. Although Hague increasingly relished the excitement of involving himself in a movement to radicalise the Conservative Party, he also respected the 'small c' conservatism of his beliefs, recognising that change should accord with the reasonable instincts of people. At seventeen Hague had produced a broad agenda, both intrinsically Conservative and radical. He called for stronger defence and law and order (suggesting the return of corporal punishment), but beyond that a diminution in the role of the state through tax cuts, denationalisation and council house sales. The strong streak of meritocrat and Poujadist is reflected in the call for greater employee participation, improving core teaching skills in comprehensive schools, and a completely new upper house, ending the hereditary principle.

The first step on William's ladder to the top was Oxford. He had decided his route to political success would be hastened by a degree in PPE at Oxford, and given that the university had provided five of the Tories' seven leaders since 1945 (now six of the eight) such a course augured well for William. Balliol College had had the most success at producing leaders but William applied to Magdalen, not because it had become the centre of the Oxford right, but because Wath had had some past success in sending pupils there. In the summer of 1979 William achieved the 4 As at 'A' level needed to secure his entry.

With his reputation before him, William was off to Oxford to prove the Tory boy had credibility.

Chapter Three

THE RIGHT GENERATION

The distinctive mark of a Tory is a love of variety, a belief that the good things in life flow from originality and individuality and that the policies that have been pursued in this country in recent years have tended to elevate the state above the individual and to expand and enhance the role of government.

William Hague to the Oxford Union, 23 May 1980

While Hague's teenage visits to the Conservative Party Conference had been appropriate work experience for a budding politician, his time at Oxford was to prove the real training ground. Although he graduated with a first in PPE, academia took second place to student politics throughout all but the final weeks of his undergraduate years. In a deliberate strategy, he fitted both his studies and his social life around the demands of the never-ending round of elections in which he quickly became involved. Hague's first-class degree was matched by his political supremacy, reaching presidency of both the Oxford University Conservative Association (OUCA) and the Oxford Union Society with relative ease.

Contemporaries regarded him as the ultimate political hack and yet he was never despised as many machine politicians are. Oxford offered William the most fertile territory in which to nurture his political skills: the opportunity to fight and win elections, a high profile platform on which to sharpen his debating talents and a network of talented contemporaries and well connected alumni.

As an ambitious Young Conservative, William had astutely identified Oxford as a necessary addition to his political CV. In recent years the prominence of Cambridge graduates in the Major cabinet gave the impression that a so-called Cambridge Mafia dominated the Conservative hierarchy. In reality Oxford has been the pre-eminent engine of the Tory high command. For a 'wannabe' Tory leader, graduating from Oxford, particularly from its University Conservative Association, was a sensible move. Having secured his place and its attendant career advantages, Hague was also blessed with luck. He was lucky to arrive at Oxford at a time when Conservatism was very much in vogue among the students, and when his own brand of Conservatism was on the rise within OUCA.

The Oxford Union Society, founded in 1823, had long been the focus for aspirant politicians and has launched the career of many. Despite its name, it is not a students' union allied to the National Union of Students. There is a branch of the NUS in Oxford but without its own facilities it does not play the central role in students' lives that its allied branches do in campus universities. Instead the Union, with its central location and gentlemen's club ambience, has become the *de facto* students' union and the *de rigeur* social centre, although in Hague's day it mainly attracted that minority of students for whom politics was a driving force.

The official business of the Union is as a debating society, but throughout the 1970s the range of these debates narrowed and moved to the right. During the previous decade's idealised romance with egalitarianism and student radicalism, the left had increasingly come to view the Union as élitist and establishment. Over time they came to boycott it and, in some cases, to disrupt its events: for example, the Revolutionary Socialists shouted down a meeting with the then Labour Foreign Secretary, Michael Stewart, over his stance on the Vietnam War. By the time that Hague arrived at Oxford some years later the formal boycott of the Union had passed but it had left a lasting impression, many Labour students feeling ill at ease with an institution from which they had excluded themselves. Thus formal debates at Oxford were dominated by the right and, reflecting national politics, student opinion had also moved rightwards. A poll of students carried out by the Oxford University magazine *Isis* just after the 1979 election showed that 40 per cent of students polled were Conservatives, only 31 per cent Labour. The magazine confirmed that the centre of gravity in student politics had been moving to the right for some time, and more so in Oxford than elsewhere. It concluded that the shift was partly due to disillusion with the Callaghan government, and partly to a general cynicism about politics.

If Hague was lucky in arriving at Oxford during a resurgence of the right, he was even more fortunate in the choice of college that had been determined by his school. Magdalen had produced one of William's political gurus, Sir Keith Joseph, but even that accolade was insignificant compared with its leading position as an engine of electoral success for the right wing of OUCA. When Hague went up more than half of the students at Magdalen were members of the Conservative Association. OUCA had a membership of around 1500 students throughout the university, but in true student style the association was deeply split. The reasons for conflicting allegiances were complex – partly political, partly collegiate, partly social and partly to do with the background of students. Hague found himself slap bang in the middle of the so-called Magdalen machine, a campaigning vehicle for the right of the party which had succeeded the Mansfield machine as the most effective organisation for the coalition of the right. These electoral alliances were a necessary consequence of the sheer amount of political activity generated by the practice of termly elections, in which Seventh Week polls determined a complete change in officers for both OUCA and the Union for the following term. Hague had already planned to get involved with OUCA and was aiming to hold office. His choice of friends ensured that once on the electoral bandwagon, he quickly established a momentum that made the whole process of running for and holding office the central motivation of his student life.

Other than books, William was not one for possessions. He arrived at Magdalen with a few bits and pieces, and his girlfriend to help him move in. Kim and William eventually found their way to his relatively inaccessible room, high up in the New Building at the back of the college. Although the location was not considered the most salubrious, the New Building is actually an early eighteenth-century Palladian hall with wisteria tickling the south wall. The view from the back looks over a historic mulberry tree to the Deer Park, and to the meadow beyond the Holywell Mill Stream. It was a picturesque setting in which to bid farewell to Kim, at least until the end of the Michaelmas term. She was to remain his girlfriend throughout the first year of his Oxford career, but their friendship continued during his vacations in Yorkshire.

For some, arriving at university is an opportunity to indulge in sex, drugs and rock 'n' roll. Indeed, William's time at Oxford coincided with a particular resurgence of student excess among a determined group of privileged youngsters keen to evoke the spirit of Evelyn Waugh. Wine, women and song were not William's priority, though, and having a girlfriend at home was more than enough of an excuse to prevent sex from distracting him from the all-consuming world of Oxford politics. His first introduction to that world, and to the Magdalen machine, came on his first day.

Guy Hands, a Mansfield undergraduate and enterprising OUCA hack of a year's standing, was on a mission. The rivalry between his camp and their opponents, the Tory left in their latest incarnation, the Tory Reform Group, was intense. Guy knew he had to recruit the fresh blood before they did.

With conservatism in the ascendancy within the Oxford student body throughout the late Seventies the motivation to fight socialism had been waning. Student Tories were far more concerned with fighting each other and the OUCA elections had become synonymous with factionalism and questionable practices. A rule change in 1974 had attempted to clean up a system that had been characterised by blatant abuse, with colleges promoting certain 'tickets', or slates, almost in the manner of a union block vote and disproportionate influence being exerted through lavish drinks parties. The enmity between warring camps is illustrated in David Blair's history of the Association by the incident in 1975 that saw the thorough soaking of a prominent 'wet'. Damian Green (now a front bench member of Hague's Westminster team) was a key member of the Oxford TRG. By the time William went up the story of Damian's dunking was already the stuff of OUCA legend. Green had been on his way to dine at Magdalen when he was waylaid and thrown over the bridge into the Cherwell. College members who were also allied to the Magdalen machine had taken exception to the prospect of their HQ playing host to such a key opponent.

At that time the Magdalen machine had been in control, but the competition between different factions was not wholly a fight between the left and right of the party. Broadly, the TRG represented the left and Magdalen the right. Certainly by the time William had arrived the TRG was primarily associated with the 'Heathites' and Magdalen increasingly with the rising free marketeers, or Thatcherites. But even within these camps there were unlikely bedfellows. The TRG attracted its share of meritocratic, metropolitan and grammar school Conservatives whose economics would have allied them with the right, but whose liberal social views inclined them against the more extreme, traditional, public school elements of the Magdalen machine. Similarly some privileged Tory wets felt culturally more at home in the alliance of the right which included elements of establishment Conservatism, albeit authoritarian. In some cases individual colleges could exert considerable influence in favour of particular candidates and so alliances were often based on college loyalties and friendships as much as political conviction. The year before William joined OUCA, Magdalen had made a crucial tactical error in agreeing a joint ticket with the TRG. It allowed in a TRG president, whose incumbency enabled him to assist his own candidates. William arrived just as Magdalen was gearing up for the fightback.

Guy Hands had determined that William would play a crucial part in that fightback. His visit to William's room on his first day in Oxford was no random drop in to a potential new recruit. William's arrival had been keenly anticipated for some time. His appearance at the 1977 party conference and consequent media attention had already made him a celebrity, the key target for both political camps. Although his views were known to be on the right, particularly on law and order and the economy, his background might have inclined him towards the party's left. Hands was determined that Magdalen would make him their own. Like Hague, Hands did not come from privileged Tory stock and was inspired by Margaret Thatcher's resolve to dismantle vested interests. Like Hague he had little sympathy with the authoritarian branch of his party, and indeed on many social issues he was considerably more liberal than William. Like Hague Hands was also extraordinarily driven, for him success was a way of proving wrong his early teachers who had dismissed him because of dyslexia. In Oxford, Hands had already made a name for himself as a successful entrepreneur who managed two businesses

– an art gallery, and selling art door-to-door – alongside his studies. In Conservative circles he had also established a reputation. With so many party figures themselves Oxbridge graduates the Oxford and Cambridge associations receive disproportionate attention from the senior party. In anticipation of William's arrival a senior party official had a quiet word in Hands's ear. He told him to look out for William and take him under his wing. For an unknown undergraduate the occasional excess of student life would go unnoticed but for one as high-profile as William there was the party's reputation to consider, as well as his own.

It took Hands several days to convince Hague to join the Magdalen machine. William's reservations were based on the perception of Magdalen as a bastion of public school élitism, but in Guy he found a kindred spirit utterly committed to wresting the power base for their own Thatcherite creed. Guy enjoyed the fact that his commercial flair and lower-middle-class background jarred with many of his OUCA contemporaries. He knew his own strength was as a supreme strategist who thrived on building alliances and doing whatever was necessary to get out the vote. In William he saw a real political talent, someone he had admired for his teenage radicalism and someone whom he could help to the top. Today Guy Hands is one of the most successful financiers in the City of London with a personal fortune of many millions, certainly more powerful if not more influential than Hague. Ironically, in his role with Japanese bankers Nomura Hands has been responsible for buying the ultimate symbol of 'Cool Britannia', the Millennium Dome.

Back then in Oxford he identified a common purpose with William, and a complementary set of skills, and it was not long before a firm friendship and political alliance of mutual advantage was formed. In William's early Oxford days Hands was a vital 'minder', giving him practical tips such as advising him to sign the register at OUCA meetings even if he had not attended.

When he would later stand for office the register would suggest he had loyally turned up every week.

Guy was not the only person who had heard on the grapevine about William's arrival. Indeed, it had already become a subject of some mirth that Oxford was soon to be graced with the presence of the 'boy wonder'. The tutor who had interviewed him for Magdalen, R. W. Johnson, later told colleagues that he had just offered a conditional place to the boy who had made 'that speech'. Not surprisingly, Hague's precocity had made him figure of fun: most students aware of his reputation were predisposed to dislike him. Perhaps Hague's most helpful political skill is his acute sense of self: he is able to win people over with his down-to-earth manner and self-deprecating use of humour. When he later became President of the Union he told a journalist that he had deliberately kept a low profile after 1977 because he had thought it was inappropriate for a teenager to be seen pontificating on subjects of which he had little experience. Even so his first task at Oxford was to live down the residual Tory boy image, which he did with a combination of humour, politeness and a policy of avoiding contentious arguments with friends and colleagues. He reserved debate for the formal chamber, where his stylish flair enhanced his reputation. His Oxford contemporaries the *Sunday Times* columnist Andrew Sullivan and academic Niall Ferguson have both written about the ease with which Hague's natural charm won him friends and supporters.

The best indicator of his successful makeover into a credible and popular figure was that he avoided being named 'Pushy Fresher'. Writer and broadcaster Michael Crick was Union president the term that Hague went up. Previously he had edited the student newspaper *Cherwell* and introduced the annual 'Pushy Fresher' award. As the name indicates, this was an opportunity for the paper to 'out' the most obnoxious new arrival who through naked ambition and crude hackery deserved that dubious accolade. (Later winners included upper-class fraudster Darius Guppy and BBC broadcaster Nick Robinson.) By the end of November 1979 Hague was sufficiently active to be mentioned as a contender, although he was in part reprieved by a break on his electoral ambitions brought on by a bout of chicken-pox. The illness prevented him putting his full energies into the OUCA elections so that he missed a place on the executive by four votes, although he had written about 'Labour's amnesia', defending the government's record against opposition attacks, in the OUCA magazine *Spectrum*. The *Cherwell* column noted that William Hague had arrived with a reputation but was keeping a low profile, apparently on the advice of a local party official, but it predicted a resurfacing of 'rampant ambition'. However, it clearly didn't surface enough to condemn him as he didn't win the award, even though some detractors had already named him 'Super Hack'. *Cherwell* concluded that a rival magazine's description of Hague as 'sly' was incompatible with pushiness. As open ambition is generally unappealing, Hague tactfully kept his intentions to himself, although on a trip home to Yorkshire he did tell Robert Godber that he was determined to rise to the challenge unwittingly offered by his politics tutor, Bill Johnson, who had told him that it was almost impossible to become president of OUCA and the Union and take a First. That comment during the Michaelmas term of 1979 was the spur to his eventual success in all three.

As chicken-pox had temporarily stunted his progress, Hague's efforts to get elected to OUCA's executive were stepped up in the Hilary term. The association had just been through one of its customarily bitter post election fall-outs as the TRG felt increasingly threatened by the resurgent Magdalen machine. Andrew Pelling (now a Conservative member of the new Greater London Assembly) had won the presidency for the TRG, but amidst allegations of ballot rigging an election tribunal was held. These were frequent events, called at the discretion of the outgoing president.

At their most serious a tribunal could overturn the election result, but in this case Pelling survived. OUCA's right were also held to account for allegations of electoral abuse in what became known as the Mansfield Tea Party tribunal. Hague was one who attended the November party and was later called before the tribunal. The party was a Magdalen machine affair at which elections to the Union committee had been discussed in a way that may have contradicted Union rules against overt campaigning. On that occasion, Hague and all the other tea party goers escaped sanction because the prime suspect, Nicholas Prettejohn, condemned himself in a drunken post-dinner admission and was consequently stripped of his post as Union treasurer. Such was this storm in a tea party that it didn't prevent him from later winning the Union presidency. (Prettejohn is now chief executive of Lloyd's of London.)

The left's control of OUCA served only to fire the resolve of Guy Hands to win for Magdalen next time round. His aim was vastly helped by the defection of Richard Old, from Trinity, who abandoned the left for Magdalen. Together he, Guy and William planned to hold the presidency between them for the next three terms. Guy knew that William had the flair for political success. He had seen him go down a storm at the Oriel College political debating club but he also worried that his occasional youthful exuberance, usually enhanced by an evening in the Union bar, could take the edge off their plans. On one particular occasion in the Hilary term, William amazed his friends and dismayed Guy with a clumsy prank. The ceremonial formality of Union events and its traditional clubby atmosphere hold a particular attraction for those with a pretentious leaning. Unlike many frequenters of the Union, Hague had no taste for the effete and the theatrical. It just did not chime with his bluff Yorkshire approach.

One evening William was drinking with his closest friends, Guy Hands, Gary Jackson, and Alan Duncan (now Conservative

MP for Rutland and Melton). Duncan, a former Union president with designs on Westminster, had met Hague through political circles on his return to Oxford for postgraduate research. He had been impressed with Hague's sophisticated grasp of politics and his steely composure, although that evening he might have been rather more composed. Duncan's relationship with Hague was to develop into a vital friendship running parallel to their joint ascent of the political ladder. Hague would have been aware that Duncan had an impressive reputation as an Oxford politician. He was renowned for his oratory and contemporaries believed that, of the two, Duncan had the more obvious promise, but he has not always found it easy to tailor his beliefs to fit the prevailing political climate. Jackson was a Maths student at Brasenose and like Guy a year ahead of William. Similarly motivated by the Conservatives' radical agenda, Jackson and Duncan had been actively involved in campaigning for John Patten during the previous year's general election. Although a Lancastrian, Jackson related to Hague's northern candour and the two have remained good friends, particularly coming to share a joint love of America.

The four friends were enjoying their evening in the Union when William admitted that he was irritated by the theatrical behaviour of a prominent Union member who was inexplicably sporting fancy dress. Polly Woolley was a colourful, larger-than-life figure with her own clique of camp followers. Although she was not considered a political heavyweight, Polly had a certain social standing in the Union and could command a number of votes in any election. With several pints inside him, William felt emboldened to make a stand against Polly's holding court. As part of her party gear Polly was wearing a wig. The devilish streak in Alan Duncan dared William to pull the rug from under Polly's feet by removing the rug from her head. So there, in front of a packed debating hall, William did the unthinkable and humiliated Polly by whisking off her wig and revealing to the assembled audience of Oxford's chief hacks her less than flattering, thoroughly flattened real hair.

Guy Hands was furious. This thoughtless prank could have endangered his plans for OUCA dominance – the overlap between Union and political membership was significant – as well as William's own ambitions for the Union presidency. Guy calculated that Polly's influence could have swung about thirty votes, which were not worth alienating for the sake of a moment's lack of focus. He warned William that his political career was in ruins, and he feared that William might become too susceptible to the advice of the more impulsive Duncan. In the elections themselves, however, William seemed lucky once again. If anything his mischievous display had lent him a laddish credibility which any number of beautifully crafted speeches could never have achieved. The Hilary term ended with William elected as Political Action Officer for OUCA, and Magdalen's man Richard Old triumphant against the TRG as new OUCA President. William's drunken prank seemed not to have harmed his credentials with the Union electorate either, as he was also elected to the Library Committee for the Trinity term. And after effusive apologies to Polly, William succeeded in establishing a reasonably friendly relationship with her.

Although Hague had been an ardent attender at the weekly Union debates, his first occasion as the main speaker came during Trinity term. From his first term he had contributed to debates from the floor. When he first got up to speak at a Michaelmas term debate featuring Michael Heseltine and David Owen, he was booed by some of the Tory contingent determined to do down 'Maggie's bionic babe'. The antipathy soon dissolved as his wit and easy style won people over. The skill of a Union debater is to create a convincing case, whether or not it is from personal conviction. For his first 'paper' speech Hague was only too pleased to be opposing the motion that radicalism had no place in the Conservative Party, and to offer up his sincere prescription for giving it greater radical edge. William's advocacy for radical Conservatism drew on reactionary and modernising instincts, both motivated by a distrust of élites, whether of the liberal consensus or of tradition. The backbone of his argument was that the Conservatives had to be radical in government to liberalise the economy and reduce the role of the state. Alongside his trademark thesis he also argued that radicalism encompassed a tough line on law and order, proposing that corporal punishment, particularly the birch, should be brought back. It was an early but characteristic strike against the liberal consensus. His uncompromising zeal also extended to a profound strike against tradition in his call for the Conservatives to 'recognise the need to reform the House of Lords as soon as possible and make the vast proportion of it democratically elected'. Furthermore he revisited the themes of his schoolboy 'Manifesto for Britain' in arguing for electoral reform: 'There are a growing number of us in the Tory Party who are members of Conservative Action for Electoral Reform and wish to see the introduction of the Single Transferable Vote for Westminster elections.' Although such views would seem radical in a contemporary leader of the Conservative Party, twenty years ago there was a greater audience for such ideas among forward-thinking Conservatives. Having since tempered his views to suit the prevailing culture of his party, Hague has shown that he is essentially a pragmatic politician, who is guided but not ruled by his convictions. While a minister he certainly increased his standing within the party with his staunch opposition to New Labour's proposed constitutional reforms – opportunistic perhaps, but more revealingly a sign that he practises the art of the possible.

The Union speech was particularly well reported by *Cherwell*, a paper that he had described as biased in favour of the TRG in an internal OUCA memo. Nevertheless *Cherwell* had to concede that Hague had made a 'rousing Churchillian speech' that was relevant to the motion and contained jokes which had 'convulsed the audience because they were genuinely funny'.

William was gaining an awesome reputation for his debating skills. Oriel don Jeremy Catto, then Senior Librarian at the Union and thus on the same committee as the newly elected Hague, even now considers him the best speaker he has ever heard, with a classic debating style. He admired the way in which Hague would give way to the opposite side and then incorporate their point into his own argument. Although his discussions with William were generally about Union business, Catto was impressed by Hague's mature composure and his obviously bright mind. These chats with Catto also strengthened the friendship with Alan Duncan, a former protégé.

With Richard Old in the OUCA presidency the Magdalen machine had arrived once again, but Guy Hands was only part of the way though his plan to dominate the association for several terms to come. Next on the agenda were the elections at the end of Trinity term. His plan was to succeed Old as President with William moving up as Secretary. Two decades later Hague was to talk about opening up the inner processes of the Conservative Party to greater scrutiny. At university he also announced his distaste for some of the more dubious tactics employed in the practice of the elections and later ran on a reform platform, yet he was never completely immune from employing similar methods when necessary. During the Trinity elections the Magdalen machine found itself on the receiving end of negative campaigning literature, outlawed by the association rules. Taking all these petty point-scoring issues as seriously as only students can, William doubled up as private detective to expose the misdemeanour. Somehow he was able to track down the exact typewriter which had produced the offending literature and in a triumphal tour of vindication he and Guy paraded around Oxford with the type indented ribbon that proved the skulduggery of the left.

The real scandal, if such a word is appropriate, is the patronage available to the sitting president. When Hague duly followed Hands as OUCA president for his fifth term, Hilary 1981, his own record of straight dealing came under question.

Hague's election platform for the OUCA presidency was much like his bid for the party leadership. He campaigned on a programme of internal electoral reform, pledging to clear up the conduct of elections. As early as his first few weeks in Oxford, Hague had expressed dismay at the culture of elections in which a lot of money was spent on drinks parties to sway opinion, and college block votes were secured by slates issuing paper tickets listing their designated candidates. Many bottles of champagne were sacrificed in the cause of budding Conservative careers. Whilst Hague was certainly unimpressed with the flamboyance of this behaviour, his adoption of the reform ticket on the advice of Hands was, if nothing else, a supreme tactical manoeuvre. Cleaning up elections had been the cause of the left; in associating it with Magdalen, Hague denied the TRG a distinct agenda and was successfully elected. Once President, Hague did clamp down on the practice of ticketing, so that candidates were no longer allowed to campaign by issuing what amounted to written instructions for voters who might only have been signed up as OUCA members hours before an election. To buttress that reform, Hague also introduced a system of single transferable vote, a reform that has lasted until today.

Hague's image as squeaky-clean electioneer was, however, marred by his own record in office. The election of Hague's successor and fellow Magdalenite, Peter Havey, was considered suspect enough to warrant a tribunal. Hague was accused of 'ballot box stuffing', but on that occasion there was insufficient evidence to prove his guilt and Hague maintains his innocence.

More embarrassingly, while Hague was President of the Union he was found guilty of electoral malpractice. During the Trinity term of 1981 Hague was running for Union President and acting as returning officer for the OUCA elections. In his OUCA role he failed to distribute manifestos to all colleges and he broke his own reformed rules by allowing some candidates to canvass colleges themselves. In his defence Hague said he had been distracted by the news that he had won the election to Union president. His punishment was a reprimand and ban on his being allowed to act as returning officer again (unlikely anyway as he was already in his final year). He was found guilty of 'incompetence and blatant irresponsibility'. Other than issuing a rebuke there was little the tribunal could do to an ex-OUCA president, although a tougher punishment was unlikely, given that the tribunal chairman was Guy Hands.

Hague's conduct within the tribunal was also questionable. It was customary for an academic to take up a senior role on such tribunals, or at least to be issued with a tape of the proceedings. Mysteriously, the recording of that tribunal never reached Lord Blake, its senior member, and Hague admitted that crucial parts of the tape were erased, in his words, 'while I was recording my memoirs'. The tapes would also have incriminated Guy Hands who was accused of writing the manifesto for another member of his slate in what became known as the 'Kevin Steele Affair'. In a surprisingly common practice Steele had been signed up as a member even though he described himself as a communist. As a Mansfield mate of Hands, Steele agreed to stand on the Magdalen slate but when he later thought better of it Hague, the returning officer, refused to withdraw Steele's nomination. When he went on to be elected the affair was investigated by a tribunal but there was no charge that could stick. Even if they had broken the spirit of a fair election, technically Hague and Hands had done nothing wrong. The rules at that time allowed students to be members of as many political groups as they liked.

Even for Hague there was some student fun to be had which wasn't totally about politics, although that was still the dominant theme of his year living out of college. Guy Hands's end-of-terrace house in Nelson Street had already achieved a reputation for drunken parties and student excess before William moved in as tenant. The house, a modest two-up-two-down, had hardly any furniture, making it ideal for hosting parties.

Hands was taking a break from his studies to run his business Hands Fine Art. What with Guy's liking for women, William's healthy taste for beer and a constant round of electors to impress, Nelson Street became synonymous with a good time. Guy had a steady girlfriend, Julia, who later became Mrs Hands, but while she was studying in Cambridge he occasionally gave in to the temptation of girls closer to home. For the first term of their cohabitation Guy was OUCA president, for the second it was William. Even among women who were bright enough to get into Oxford, this relative celebrity apparently raised their sexual allure. Surprisingly, some women considered it something of a coup to bed an Oxford politician. While Guy was certainly titillated by his enhanced appeal, William seemed uninterested in his. He enjoyed joining in with Guy's seduction games, but showed little interest in reaping the rewards for himself. Sometimes the notorious alcoholic concoctions, particularly the adult chocolate milkshakes, were enough to facilitate casual encounters. On other occasions Guy found himself the beneficiary of advances which had really been intended for, but not taken up by, William. Frustratingly for Guy this was not the case when on one occasion the two had succeeded in attracting a girl who was the object of many Oxford male desires back to Nelson Street.

The three had developed an unusual friendship, a sort of passive *ménage à trois* in which Guy fancied the girl, a fellow

Conservative activist, but she had her sights on William. An awkward three-way flirtation had been developing over several weeks when Guy decided to bring matters to a head. He challenged her to a bet over whether she would be elected to the standing committee of the Union. If she won the election, she would take Guy and William to dinner. If she lost they would take her. In the event, Guy and William won the bet and the three went for dinner at the popular Randolph. The food was less a feature of the dinner than the drink, fuel for more serious flirtation as Guy attempted to beat William to the eventual prize. Then back to Nelson Street and experimental cocktails to while away the early hours of the night. Guy's patience lasted beyond his sobriety, but began to run out as alcohol threatened to reduce his ability to take matters further. Eventually he challenged their guest: 'Well, which of us are you going to sleep with?' The answer was William, but when Guy surfaced the next morning there was no evidence that she had stayed and neither she nor William have ever revealed the outcome.

Friends had the impression that William wasn't particularly sexually driven. He certainly spent time alone with girls in their rooms late at night, sometimes when he had escorted them home after an evening at Nelson Street, but there was no indication that anything more intimate than conversation occurred. William just considered he had better things to do with his time and had a heightened appreciation that unguarded behaviour might later impede his political career.

If Guy had been looking to for revenge on William for attracting away some of his potential conquests, the perfect opportunity arose when the two went to a student party in North London. On an unusual trip away from the all-consuming world of Oxford they visited medical student friends of Guy's. Guy and William were fairly confident that their tolerance of alcohol was better than most students', but in these medics they had met their match. Drinking games led to dares and to several guests at the party being stripped naked and thrown out into the street. Guy escaped such humiliation, but William did not. In front of a drunken group of strangers the 'rugger bugger' hosts chose Hague as a victim for their favoured party trick, but it rebounded on one in spectacular style. Hague, cold and exposed, was saved frostbite by a neighbour who went to complain about the noise. Guy remembers: 'William was so furious that, forgetting his state of undress, he barged back in, punching the most obnoxious of my medical friends hard in the face, knocking him to the ground. It drew a cheer from the rest of us who had been dying to do the same thing for ages but lacked the nerve.' It is hard to say who would have been the more embarrassed – the naked assailant or his victim who remained laid out on the floor for twenty minutes.

The rumours that circulated about Hague during his leadership campaign of 1997 may have pointed to some University dalliance with homosexuality. Other than the fact that Hague had gay friends, and promoted a Union debate on the issue of equalising the age of consent, there seems to be no evidence to give substance to any of these rumours. University contemporaries find it hard to equate the Hague they knew, the intense political animal with a weakness for a pint, with the picture of him as a camp crusader. Guy Hands: 'Certainly in the fifteen months that William lived in my house in Nelson Street I didn't see that William's sexuality was anything but heterosexual, and indeed never have since.' Although there were pockets of gay activity that coalesced around the Union and OUCA, William was not associated with them. The male-dominated world of Oxford Conservatism certainly attracted its fair share of sexual experimentation, some furtive and some quite blatant in dining clubs such as the Piers Gaveston (named after Edward II's catamite) and the Assassins, but William did not attend either.

Although William wasn't especially interested in sex, he was not a prude. On a trip home to Wentworth he argued with his mother about Guy's right to sleep with his girlfriend Julia, while they were guests in his parents' home. Against Stella's preferences William won the argument. On that occasion Guy had at least made it to Yorkshire, complete with a set of pictures from Hands Fine Art to offer for sale to the Hagues! Another trip was equally problematic and reached the gossip columns of the student press. Travelling up to Yorkshire at the end of the Michaelmas term 1980, Guy, Gary and William were forced to abandon Guy's smoking car. Despite his entrepreneurial activities Guy was reduced to driving a wreck, which caught fire a few miles outside Sheffield.

With typical student bravado William liked to boast that he never did any work, but this was a disingenuous claim. The workload at Oxford was more demanding than at many universities, particularly in the first year when he was expected to produce two essays a week. Friends noted that he was scrupulously well organised and single-minded about each of his activities. As his studies of Philosophy, Politics and Economics coincided with his extracurricular interests, William's main hobby of reading served two purposes. He would often wake early in the morning and read for a couple of hours before breakfast. During his first year, when students are often prone to indulge other interests at the expense of studying, his tutors never noticed William slacking. With his computer-like mind he did not need to spend as much time studying as many other students: he was considered an 'information sponge'.

A common theme characterised William's academic interest in politics and his practice of it. He was less interested in philosophy and ideas than in the nuts and bolts, and he gave up the philosophy part of his course after the compulsory first year. Although remarkably bright, William was no member of the student intelligentsia who thrive on coffee-shop philosophising and analytical deconstruction. He preferred instead to focus on thoroughly researching material for the construction of coherent and consistent arguments. He was well suited to the Oxford teaching style, which favours students who can write under pressure.

Unlike some political animals, Hague was not interested in engaging in ideological discussions with tutors or other students. One of his tutors was Derek Robinson, a fellow South Yorkshireman who had been an adviser to the Labour government. Robinson taught him economics, including a particular course on Labour Economics and Industrial Relations. In tutorials William revealed his free market instincts, but did not indulge in political evangelising. If anything Robinson felt that William might have articulated his ideology more strongly. Similarly, Hague's contemporaries do not remember him discussing the big political issues with them, although it was a troubled time for the new Conservative government. He was certainly intense about university politics but perhaps surprisingly the dramatic events of Thatcher's early years hardly penetrated the febrile atmosphere of Oxford introspection. William's arguments seemed driven more by pragmatism than ideological purity. Although he revealed deep convictions about his preference for small government, he was not dogmatic or doctrinaire about the solutions. In their frequent discussion about trades unions, Robinson recognised that William wanted them reformed, but, unlike other Tories, he did not demonise them. In a Union debate on labour reform William argued against the closed shop but concluded that trades unions have 'an essential role to play in capitalist society, but there comes a point where the extension of the rights of some workers erodes the rights of others'. Robinson felt that William had a particularly sophisticated understanding of the implications of any statement. Certainly by his final year William understood better than most students how to construct an argument which was logical, coherent and persuasive.

As a politician and debater these core skills were important, but they made him successful only because of the crucial ability to entertain. The Oxford debating style is admired and criticised in almost equal measure, for while its great practitioners require intellectual agility, they also need to be able to crack a good joke. Politicians who cut their debating teeth in the Union are often accused of putting style above substance. Having the mental agility required to wound an opponent with sparkling wit doesn't necessarily make for a seasoned politician. If Hague didn't particularly enjoy philosophising, he certainly thrived in the debating chamber where he definitely did not pull any punches. In one high-profile event (Trinity 1981), debating against Shirley Williams on the future of the Social Democrats, he brought the house down with his hope that 'the Social Democrats would not degenerate into some sort of heterosexual wing of the Liberal Party', a moment of *Schadenfreude* in a reference to Jeremy Thorpe.

Hague reached the heights of Union president autumn 1981, the first term of his final year, having made himself virtually unbeatable. His long-running adversary Andrew Pelling realised that his campaign was practically hopeless in the face of William's reputation and Magdalen back-up. In the Presidential debate of June 1981, where candidates showed off their oratorical skills, Hague supported the motion that 'This House calls for Economic Sanctions against South Africa'. Hague argued that apartheid was immoral and selective sanctions were required, although he did say South Africa was not uniquely evil and he felt that, to some, oppression and exploitation are vicious and indefensible when done by whites and capitalists but moral and virtuous when done by blacks and communists. Displaying a similarly liberal tendency when President, Hague chaired debates on homosexual rights and on legalising prostitution. In this regard Hague would have distinguished his views from the reactionary right, who contributed to the coalition of views within the Magdalen machine.

Foolishly, though, he was not always so discriminating in his social life. Thanks to the intervention of Guy Hands, William avoided an embarrassing encounter with the press. He had accepted an invitation to a dinner organised by the far right, traditionalist Monday Club because some of its members would probably vote for him. The controversial reputation of the Monday Club guaranteed that this would be a high-profile event, provoking the antagonism of the left which championed the 'no platform to racists' policy. (The Monday Club had become the *bête noire* of all shades of liberal opinion after hosting an evening (before Hague's time at Oxford) with self-professed racist Lady Birdwood, during which Nazi-style salutes were allegedly made). The advertised meeting was bound to attract press attention in expectation of student protests. On the evening of the meeting a tabloid journalist who knew Hands telephoned him with a tip-off that his paper was sending a photographer. Hands knew he would have to get William out of the meeting, or his future career might be dogged by an unfair association with the Monday Club. Fortunately for Hague, Guy got him out in time.

The sheer number of elections can make the world of Oxford politics narrow and self-obsessed. During Hague's final year he was given the opportunity to perform on a broader platform and to engage in 'grown-up' politics. Together with friend Brooks Newmark and fellow Union hack Chris Wortley, Hague was selected by the English Speaking Union to go on a debating tour of American universities. Newmark, a Harvard graduate student, had met Hague through OUCA in his second year and was at Worcester College, like Magdalen a centre of machine politics. Newmark recognised in Hague a supreme political operator, and, particularly on the American tour, a skilled communicator. The tour was to take them to five different universities, at each debating a different aspect of British policy in Northern Ireland. In Boston the debaters met up with old friends Alan Duncan and Nick O'Shaughnessy, another former Union president. Duncan and O'Shaughnessy were studying at the Kennedy School of Government. The two had become close friends at Oxford, where they would discuss religion as much as politics. Duncan was then a passionate evangelical.

O'Shaughnessy had left Oxford before Hague's arrival so was particularly impressed to see for the first time his polished and remarkably confident debating skills. At first the Americans and the Brits took some time in adapting to each other's style. Unlike the Oxford emphasis on flourish, the American debating tradition put more emphasis on empiricism. At first it did not seem as though William could rise to the occasion. His first contributions were met with laughter provoked by his accent. He refused to allow it to throw him. More significant than a difference in accent or oratorical style, the atmosphere of these debates was rather more combative than the often self-congratulatory Union events. This was particularly so in Boston, the home of America's Irish republican sympathisers. A large audience turned up, including a strong contingent of Irish American militants. Hague found the charged atmosphere sharpened his performance – a talent that Hague has certainly used to his advantage in the Commons, though it does not necessarily equip him for success in the age of the television soundbite. In Boston, Hague showed that he was as adept in dealing with hecklers as he was in presenting his formal case, a forthright defence of British policy and Unionism. When a woman in the audience tried to shout him down, Hague countered by asking the room to 'allow her one last memorial outburst'.

After the debates were finished Newmark and Hague went on to a conference organised by the Bow Group, a Tory pressure group, with its American sister organisation, the Rippon Society. The conference was taking place during the early days of the Falklands crisis, and as with the Northern Ireland debates provided one of the few occasions when Hague actually found himself making a case that mattered beyond the precious world of Oxford politics. It was an exciting, vital taste of real politics, as America had yet to give Britain its unequivocal backing in the dispute. Hague and Newmark were in effect persuaders for the British case to an audience that included senators and congressmen. Newmark, an American by birth, also noticed in Hague a great enthusiasm for the States.

This was William's second trip to the USA. A year previously he had taken a holiday to New York and Washington with Gary Jackson, to visit Jackson's sister Veronica who had moved there. Jackson was amazed at the way Hague hoovered up American political facts and figures with exactly the same wide-eyed enthusiasm that marked his first schoolboy enquiries into political ephemera.

The American debating tour came after Hague's term as Union president and during the Easter break before his finals. It was a characteristically confident move to take a break from studying so close to the exams. Although friends and tutors recognised that William had studied in his first and second years, he maintains that he only really applied himself during his last two terms. He had made time for OUCA and the Union, then he made time to concentrate totally on his degree. The approach was methodical and single-minded, the strategy that had brought him success in each of his Oxford endeavours.

Friends differ in their reading of Hague the tactician. Some considered him ruthless, others merely extremely efficient. In reality his determined application seldom required him to be ruthless; he set himself distinct objectives and then worked towards them with purpose. He achieved success by charming people, rather than stabbing them in the back, although sometimes his ambition made him appear two-dimensional.

On one occasion in the run-up to the elections for Union president, Hague met an acquaintance in the street. She was not a political fellow traveller but had already decided to support him as the best candidate for president. Although blatant electioneering was against Union rules, William, ever the politician, could barely the resist the opportunity to press the flesh. He greeted his potential voter with rather more enthusiasm than she considered necessary, but when she told him that he already had her vote, he seemed thrown and he walked away as all other small talk deserted him.

Close friends certainly considered William obsessive about politics, but did not find his interest dry or calculating. They saw William approaching Oxford politics with gleeful enthusiasm. He enjoyed the frisson of conspiratorial plotting and his competitiveness drove him on to want to play the game better than the other players. He was less explicitly ambitious about his long-term plans than he had been as a teenager. After all, there was no tactic more guaranteed to irritate his fellow students than to remind them of his aim to reach Number 10. However there was no slackening of his intentions, merely an adult understanding that being a career politician does not always help a politician's career. He knew that he had to develop other interests and, as he had told friends at school, take up a job outside the Westminster machine.

Hague left Oxford with 'a good First', respected and much liked by his peers. He had won all but one of the elections in which he had stood, having occupied all the key committee posts on OUCA and the Union. His chairmanship of OUCA had brought almost automatic regional chairmanship of the national Tory Students organisation. Hague was chairman of the Wessex Area Federation of Conservative Students before the organisation had reached its most notorious period, leading to its eventual closure by the party chairman, Norman Tebbit. By the mid-1980s the FCS had become a hotbed of so called 'blue trots' outbidding each other for ever more radical incarnations of right wing machismo. In Hague's day the Thatcherites were still united in delight at having wrested the balance of power from the 'wets'. They considered Hague 'one of us', a competent, efficient organiser and right winger, but certainly not a factional player.

William had developed his skills as an operator and as a public speaker, but his own philosophy had barely changed. The almost effortless skill with which he debated was a testament to his abilities as an entertaining speaker but gave away little about his true convictions. Casual wit came more naturally to him than impassioned demagoguery.

Then as now, many suggested that he was not a conviction politician. His Oxford politics actually displayed a mature consistency based on distinct convictions. He had gone up as a convinced monetarist and economic liberaliser with traditional Tory instincts on defence and law and order – what Alan Duncan described as the 'firm smack of small government'. He left with the same core beliefs, despite the severe recession that initially worsened under Thatcher's early reforms, and had formed very specific views of what was appropriately the business of the state and what was not. He was a traditionalist only in so far as tradition had touched him, so his patriotism was shaped by his own love for Yorkshire and his belief in the family was the logical conclusion of his own happy childhood.

Yet he was no preacher of convention for its own sake: hence his willingness to consider constitutional reform and the seeds of a libertarian approach to personal morality. Essentially he is guided by what works, the politics of the possible. This has enabled him to appeal to a wider constituency than his own machine, although he was inevitably viewed as a political animal through and through.

Even his own interests outside politics such as transcendental meditation seem further evidence of his self control and relentless ambition. As Union President, Hague organised a speaker meeting about TM, a practice he had picked up from his eldest sister Jane. It was quirky enough to endear him to a mixed audience, yet it only confirmed that even his relaxation time had to be used in the most efficient way possible. In his concluding address to the Union, when standing down as President, Hague certainly went some way to play up his human qualities with a strong dose of self-parody. He proposed the evening's debate that 'This House Prefers a Blonde', certainly a populist title, without explicitly explaining it during his speech. Perhaps, he suggested, it referred to himself, yet he acknowledged the standing joke around the thinning of his own hair. He was also at pains to thank all of those who had helped his presidency, particularly friends who advised him on clothing in view of his advanced colour blindness. The self mocking was an attempt to deflect from the humiliation which was the traditional ritual of the President's farewell debate. Guy Hands certainly tried his best, and in part succeeded in embarrassing William, but also in pandering to the gossip-mongers with deliberately provocative references to their friendship. 'For six months', he said to Hague, 'you've been sharing my house and, dare I say it, my very own blow up Margaret Thatcher.' He went on to list Hague's desired qualities in a mate: 'She's got to be a good housekeeper, to have thin ankles, mustn't have any interest in politics, she's got to have blonde hair and to have something of the personality of a Scotsman and little bit of the character of a cat.' Hague was extremely relieved that no one at the meeting solved that particular riddle, although it might have done wonders for his image.

William Hague had certainly used his time at Oxford in the most efficient way possible, laying the foundations for future success. In his first debate as Union president, an examination of the Thatcher government's record over two and a half years, he was talent-spotted by Treasury minister Leon Brittan. It was another of Hague's fortunate encounters, leading to an advisory role in the Treasury and a friendship that introduced him to Richmond, the North Yorkshire seat he would inherit when Brittan stood down.

Chapter Four

THE CAREER PATH

Who lives in a house like this? A modest flat in a two-floor Victorian terrace house in pre-gentrified Clapham. Otherwise sparsely decorated, the first-floor flat is dominated by books, nearly all about history and politics. In the spare room alcohol meets the ascetic as a rowing machine competes for pride of place with the crates of fine wine. It's the home of two aspiring young politicians, William Hague and Alan Duncan.

This first London home in the early 1980s put William right on the political front line. He had graduated with his first-class degree and a place on the highly respected fast track graduate recruitment scheme at Shell UK. With London calling he needed a place to live and was offered a spare room by Duncan, already working for Shell. It was an ideal arrangement as the two friends shared common goals and had a similar sense of humour.

Number 14 Hazelbourne Road was an appropriate address for a crusading Conservative as the street marks the border between the London boroughs of Lambeth and Wandsworth, and graphically illustrated the opposing philosophies of the two authorities. The houses on the western side of the street, including Duncan's flat, were in the Conservative borough, paying a fraction of the rates charged by socialist Lambeth to the east. The appearance of the road did not suggest a significant political divide: the Lambeth and the Wandsworth sides were equally shabby. Today Clapham is one of the capital's most sought-after residential areas with property prices to match, but even now Hazelbourne Road remains one of the area's few neglected streets despite being only a stone's throw away from Clapham South underground station.

Along with the lively local political situation in late 1982, there was also a general election brewing. Hardly had Hague unpacked his rowing machine before he was off to the local Conservative office to sign up as an activist. The Battersea agent Jean Lucas was delighted to see two new recruits offer their services. Even in such a prominent Conservative borough, keen new members are hard to find and the parliamentary seat was Labour held. Lucas was sitting in her overcrowded back office in the association headquarters when the most unlikely thing happened: two seemingly capable, enthusiastic, bright young things walked in to offer their help. It was even better when they mentioned their address, as together the addition of Hague and Duncan virtually doubled the existing membership of their particular branch of the association. Before they had left the offices in Webbs Road the two had taken control of their local branch, with Duncan as Chairman and Hague as Secretary.

Working life for William was not proving quite as harmonious as his domestic arrangements. Shell UK was then one of the few big-name companies which ran a graduate recruitment programme and places were in high demand. William had been taken on to deal with special projects in public affairs but very soon found that there simply was not enough for him to do. He reacted to his new job in much the same way as he had to his first day at school. Frankly, he was bored and frustrated with the bureaucracy that accompanied the byzantine hierarchy in which ascending levels of seniority were rigidly denoted by increasingly luxurious office carpeting.

At his own level he was quick to make friends. Much like his arrival at Oxford, his joining Shell had precipitated much gossip among immediate colleagues. A high-profile *Washington Post* article in August 1982 had listed William as a future world leader. Again the expectation was that a political obsessive was about to join their ranks, and again it was an impression which William was quickly able to overcome. The winning formula of a down-to-earth approach and relaxed sense of humour softened the cynics and made him a popular drinking partner in the Shellmex House bar, the Lensbury Club. Unfortunately William found that facing down the occasional critic over a pint was rather more stimulating than the work itself, but although he did not find it a sufficient challenge he was nevertheless circumspect in his criticisms. When a university friend visited him to ask advice on careers, William carefully pointed to all the good points about his new employer. Vivien Godfrey had been treasurer of the Oxford Union during William's term as president. She had been offered jobs at Shell and the management consultants, McKinsey. Although William put in a good account of life at Shell it was not long before he was joining Godfrey on the front steps of the 'Rolls Royce' operation at McKinsey, known simply to insiders as 'The Firm'.

Immediate colleagues who shared the Shell internal communications office with William knew that he was under-utilised and that his real aim was a political career. He was open in his ambitions, but, as he had learned at Oxford, never ostentatious. If other people wanted to discuss political issues with him he would oblige, but William was never the firebrand. It just was not his style to take up time trying to convert people. Not surprisingly, real world politics rushed in to make up for the frustrations that William found with corporate life. On a return trip to the Oxford Union he once again met Leon Brittan, then Chief Secretary to the Treasury. Brittan was particularly impressed with the case

William made in proposing the motion, 'This House would Support the Government's Economic Policies'. It was January 1983 and although the Falklands factor had buoyed the government's fortunes, its economic record was troubled. As Chancellor, Geoffrey Howe had made a vital attack on inflation but unemployment was still rising and national income had dropped to below 1979 levels. William's defence was resolute in its support for the direction of government policy and made a convincing case for sticking to the policy for long-term results. As a result William was called to the Treasury and offered a temporary appointment as speech-writer to Brittan and Howe in the run-up to the 1983 election.

Although it was a rather solitary role for William working alone in a small office churning out drafts, he considered this post a gift, especially as it required a secondment from Shell. The placement proved particularly auspicious for William's future career. Apart from notching up another respected accolade for his political CV, William won himself friends in extremely high places. After the election Geoffrey Howe remained Chancellor and Leon Brittan was promoted to Home Secretary, and they later became the signatories on Hague's application to join the Conservatives' parliamentary candidates list. It would have been hard to have earned a more heavyweight endorsement. The Treasury job was also the genesis of a valued friendship with Leon Brittan, who became a walking partner for Yorkshire excursions and later certainly helped when William applied to stand for Richmond following Brittan's appointment to the European Commission.

Even the high politics of the Treasury were insufficient to meet William's interests fully. After speech writing by day he would return home to Clapham for a relaxing evening of local campaigning. He and Alan would host committee meetings in the front room of their flat to discuss the leafleting and canvassing rotas. Although these were light-hearted affairs, with Hague and Duncan competing to perform the best political impersonation, Alan being particularly good at Margaret Thatcher, locals recognised that their hosts had serious ambitions. However, both wanted to achieve certain things outside politics before standing for Parliament. For the 1983 election they were happy to play a supportive role and helped in the campaigns for the local seats. Rupert Allason was the Conservative candidate for Battersea but despite the impressive victory that the party won nationally in June, the seat remained Labour until it was later nurtured by the more pro-active Prospective Parliamentary Candidate and eventual MP John Bowis.

In the neighbouring seat of Tooting the candidate was one of Hague's colleagues from the Treasury, Robin Harris. William's post had become necessary because full-time Special Advisers have to stand down from their Civil Service jobs when becoming involved with party politics. Under other circumstances Robin Harris, one of the full-time advisers to Geoffrey Howe, would have worked with William, but instead William became one of his campaigners in Tooting. Although the Conservative administration had by this time established its hold on Wandsworth Council, the parliamentary seat of Tooting remained a Labour stronghold at parliamentary level. So although William and Alan enjoyed spreading the Tory message by loud hailer through the streets of Tooting, their efforts did not help Robin Harris become an MP, although he later went on to become Head of the Conservative Research Department.

After the 1983 election the cell of political activity which was 14 Hazelbourne Road continued functioning, although the chairman was soon in absentia. Alan Duncan left Shell UK to join the Marc Rich organisation, an American oil company which later became embroiled in controversy when its managing director relocated to Switzerland, allegedly to avoid US charges of millions of dollars of unpaid taxation. The move saw Duncan leave for Singapore, although he had clearly left his political heart in Clapham – if not his political heart then certainly his wine cellar, which went on to lubricate many a fervoured political debate among the inner circle of the branch. At one meeting Duncan sent back a video dispatch from the Far East, a welcome missive from the leader across the water.

Clapham's proximity to central London and the radical reputation of Wandsworth Council was making it the ideal location for the younger legions of 1980s yuppies fired by the Thatcherite property dream. William found like-minded company among his fellow committee members including Anthony Cole, who later became chairman of the whole association, and Mark Worthington, now a close adviser to Lady Thatcher. Worthington was so impressed by William that years later he relied on his early impressions to advise Lady Thatcher in his favour during the 1997 party leadership campaign: he became convinced that William was 'sound', the accolade that speaks a thousand reassurances among Thatcher's disciples. Apart from a literal commitment to sound money, William's 'soundness' rested on his firm line on law and order, his dislike of political correctness and distrust of vested interests.

Hague's return to Shell after the general election was short-lived. Within weeks he had been headhunted to join McKinsey. First he took a holiday in Portugal with his university friend Gary Jackson. Things did not get off to a flying start because of an air traffic control strike which left the two marooned in Heathrow with only an airport lounge bar array of malt whisky to distract from the boredom of waiting. It rather set the tone of the holiday, during which port tasting was the chief activity. In typical William style this had to be conducted with determined attention to detail, progressively working through from one-year-old to forty-year-old port. He also admitted to having developed a similarly scientific approach to finding a future wife. William's off-and-on relationship with Kim was still continuing in the background but his longer-term plans seemed to rest on a rather complex formula requiring specific age differentials, relative incomes and vital statistics.

William's association with McKinsey has proved a double-edged sword for his reputation in politics. For some the fact that he had a short but brilliant career there is a greater recommendation than even his first-class degree. For others it is a sign of someone whose politics will be characterised by managerialism rather than a hunger to seek out new ideas. The boom in consultancy in the last twenty years has created another social stereotype (to many an anti-social stereotype) of the overpaid, inexperienced twentysomething who climbs up the career ladder by ruthlessly 'downsizing' established companies without a thought for the human cost. It is a caricature that McKinsey is understandably concerned to distance itself from and indeed its long established professional reputation places the firm among a mere handful of similar top specialists in the world. The reputation begins at recruitment level, with exacting standards required of its new entries.

When William joined McKinsey in the mid 1980s the company was reviewing its recruitment methods. It was keen to develop new talent that had not come up through a business route to its first rung of analysts. Brooks Newmark was then working on a project for McKinsey and had suggested name as a possible interviewee, but his reputation had already reached the London headquarters, then in St James Street. Newmark was working in a team with Archie Norman, now in William's shadow cabinet, and Howard Davies, who now heads the Financial Services Authority. Both were involved with William's recruitment, through a series of interviews that involved a number of the firm's associates. Having a first-class degree and having secured the Oxford Union presidency put William into that exclusive band of graduates which McKinsey are keen to develop even if they have not yet shown particular business acumen. William's political reputation was significant in that it denoted a future leader, a characteristic which McKinsey aimed to apply to the business world although 'The Firm' always understood that William had his longer-range sights on Parliament. Now that William Hague is among the best known of McKinsey alumni, quite a few people like to claim responsibility for his appointment, and indeed he would have been interviewed by several associates. Archie Norman was certainly not the only person who saw William for interview but his role has become slightly obscured over time. Nowadays Hague does not like people to reflect on Norman's role in his joining McKinsey. Since Norman has himself played a lead role in Hague's reforms of the Conservative Party machine, Hague is concerned that Norman's rapid rise through the party ranks and recent appointment to the shadow cabinet could be misconstrued as a favour returned. Both men are now uncomfortable about discussing this period as any, even mistaken, hint of favouritism hardly chimes with Hague's commitment to build a fresh, open, meritocratic party.

Shortly after Hague joined McKinsey, Archie Norman left to become finance director of Woolworth Holdings (which later became Kingfisher) from where he called upon the advice of recent colleagues at McKinsey, with Hague as a key member of the team. Hague had already cut his teeth on his first project for the firm, working as a junior analyst on an assignment for Citicorp on a team headed by Michael Mire, now a company partner, and which included Howard Davies, head of the Financial Services Authority, and Adair Turner, until recently head of the CBI. This project would have been typical of the working environment at the firm, revolving around small teams on projects usually lasting several months, often with clients who maintain a long-term relationship with McKinsey. The Firm is known for being extremely discreet about its clients, specialising in dealing with the senior management at top-flight companies and institutions. Unlike Shell, this was a talent-based operation with a sharp learning curve in which bright young things were expected to advise senior, established clients right from the outset. Hague quickly impressed his colleagues and clients with his clear, rational approach to problem-solving and his conscientious attention to detail. This was not a period in which he devoted very much time to politics, or indeed to anything much apart from work. Team members are expected to devote evenings and weekends to the job and William easily met these requirements. It was another environment in which his relaxed manner easily won him friends, but also belied an extraordinarily focused and determined character who thrived on the intellectual stimuli he had so missed at Shell. William's ability to compartmentalise served him very well, for while he was not concentrating on a specific problem of the day he would chat easily in the office. In fact, far from seeming too narrowly focused on work he gave the impression of having varied interests, and some thought him a little eccentric as he often discussed his political ambitions alongside the merits of transcendental meditation. William had taken to practising TM for twenty minutes each morning, convinced that it is the equivalent of several hours of sleep – which given that he has always risen very early was a necessary energy boost. Indeed, when he finally became party leader, colleagues found it hard to adapt to the sight of him meditating in his office with the door open.

Not all of McKinsey's recruits survive the exacting schedule, and of those who stay, perhaps one in around seven makes it to the senior role of partner. Senior colleagues were in little doubt that William would have made it that far and would have looked forward to remuneration far in excess of an MP's salary, even as Opposition leader. Among so talented a group of peers this was perhaps the first environment in which it was absolutely appropriate for him to shine intellectually. At Oxford he had stood out because of his wit and showmanship while keeping his academic prowess in the background; at McKinsey charm was important but delivering the goods even more so. When working on a study for Whitbread on a possible takeover of Scottish and Newcastle, William stunned colleagues by creating an analytical model that spanned two office walls. Paper logic had to be matched by practical ability, however, and his route to promotion came from his popularity with clients. He earned the respect and admiration of far more experienced business people – such as a group of hardened hotel executives when he took on an account for Forte.

The work about which Hague feels most proud is a later project he undertook on his return from business school. McKinsey have some clients for whom they work on a charitable basis, and one such was Oxford University. Hague enjoyed returning to his former stamping ground, this time to advise on fund raising. His advice was bold: based on his study of an American model, his recommendation was that the University should invest far more than it felt it could afford, eventually to bring in far more revenue than it had ever hoped for. The plan worked spectacularly well, over the years bringing in over £340 million for the University. Henry Drucker, the University's Development Director, was highly impressed with William, particularly his capacity for hard work. Although he clearly had a head for business, William's heart was obviously elsewhere. The team leader for McKinsey told Drucker: 'That man will be the next Conservative prime minister.'

Within a year of joining the firm, thoughts turned to further study. Those recruits who have not come via business school are required to attend one early in their McKinsey career. Sitting in the double-height office overlooking St James's, William and Vivien Godfrey, one of five analysts with whom he shared the grand surroundings, swapped thoughts about where he should go. William's fascination with and affinity for the USA might have inclined him towards applying to Harvard, but there was one disadvantage to the American schools: the MBA lasts two years, and it would not have suited William's plans to be out of the country for that long. He intended to fight a seat whenever the next election was called and the chances were that such a long course would prevent him from doing so.

McKinsey Europe regularly sent a contingent of analysts to the continent's main school, the European Institute of Business Administration, INSEAD. The highly respected INSEAD course was concentrated into nine months, while its other attractions rested on its global focus. The majority of overseas students attending American business schools tend to be British, whereas INSEAD attracts a far more international intake. To secure a place there William had to improve his conversational French and German. He is not a keen linguist and no particular fan of French, finding it an unattractive language, but a month's cramming took him to the standard required to follow certain lectures in French. He was Paris bound.

Hague's nine months at INSEAD from September 1985 were the most fun he had had at any point in his education. The coursework was testing but well within his capabilities. He had gone with the intention of making the most of the social life, for once without the need to prove himself in any sort of political arena. In exchange for grey Clapham, William found himself in the relative bucolic paradise of Recloses, just outside Fontainebleau, where INSEAD is based. He and Vivien joined forces to find accommodation and were both determined to establish an international household. They found the perfect setting in a charismatic *auberge* they rented from the farmer's wife Madame Saille, and shared with an Italian, a Swede and a Parisian. The lifestyle suited William well, especially as the village afforded him long walks in the local woodland denied him in London. Both studying and social life were intense, given that these students were achieving the same qualification in half the time of other MBA courses. The pressure of work quickly established a camaraderie between students, most of whom shared the desire to make the most of a student lifestyle before committing themselves to highly demanding careers. It was a community of talented and ambitious people (140 in each intake, or 'promotion', as they are known), among whom William was certainly an equal but, relatively unusually for him, not especially outstanding. Social life revolved around group activities as there were very few women on the course and the intensity of the study militated against romance.

No political significance can be read into William's attendance at INSEAD. This was not a case of an instinctive Eurosceptic facing up to his demons, or indeed of someone inclined towards scepticism having his prejudices either confirmed or disproved. Although the school is called the European Institute, it is not a European Union institution. It exists to further excellence in business techniques, both in a European context and worldwide. Courses include practical business problem solving and relevant academic studies, including economics and studying the European Institutions, but there is no given line on their merits or shortcomings. Some though not all of the academics are very supportive of the European project, but attendance at the school does not denote a particular endorsement of it. William's year at the school coincided with significant developments in European politics as Margaret Thatcher's scepticism hardened, seismic changes in Germany developed, Italy's characteristic political instability rumbled on and Jean Marie Le Pen's malign influence appeared to gain ground in France. William's European Politics lecturer, Professor Jonathan Storey, was keen that a broad range of opinion was represented on his course, although it was rather more about comparative institutions than a forum for political debate. William viewed his academic education as simply that, a practical training for a business career, not an opportunity to hone an ideological conviction.

If not for a career in business, the INSEAD experience might have equipped William for a career in catering. Social life very much revolved around food, both within his household, who would make an effort to eat together in the rustic kitchen every night, and across the whole group, among whom a competitive drive to offer up the best weekend dinner party developed. William's household was at an immediate advantage. Not only did their dining room table seat forty people, but Vivien Godfrey, who had earned her organisational spurs on the Oxford Union ball committee, thought nothing of catering for anything up to seventy. With military precision the farmhouse kitchen was converted into an efficient line-up of choppers, whiskers and peelers. William managed to come off relatively lightly by taking responsibility for providing the wine and the fresh bread from the local boulangerie, and clearly he had learnt something about stock-taking because the supply was always plentiful. The one dish that he managed to prepare perfectly was ratatouille, although the dinner party menu often reflected the different cultural influences at the school. On one occasion they joined with several other British students to prepare a Raj banquet for forty, on another the household contributed to a smoked fish and smorgasbord evening laid on by the Scandinavian contingent. Washing it all down with Schnapps, William ensured that he paid homage to his own cultural inheritance by treating guests to a rendition of 'Ilkley Moor baht'at'.

William's political interest was recognised among his closest friends, in part because his participation in practical course work was marked by his flair for public speaking and the art of persuasion. On one occasion William was practising a negotiation model with

fellow student Chris Latter. Although they arrived at the necessary result the tutor believed they must have colluded in order to
have reached such a textbook conclusion to the set problem.
Clearly a kindred spirit, Latter became William's partner, along
with Canadian Hal Hannaford, in a debating competition.
Although William had temporarily put his political ambitions on
hold, he easily succumbed to the temptation to flex his oratorical
muscle on the initiation of an inter-school debating contest. The
American School in Paris decided to challenge INSEAD and
other nearby schools to a three-round contest. Relying more on
style than content Hague's team was victorious. Their preparation
consisted of rehearsing a few lines during the car journey into
Paris and of arming themselves with appropriate props. The key
to the INSEAD team's winning formula seemed to be reams of
computer print outs, actually irrelevant to their argument, but
creating the impression of empirical back-up to a supreme act of
showmanship.

Like most of his contemporaries Hague played hard and
worked hard at INSEAD. He remembers his time there with
particular enthusiasm, considering it the best part of his education. Academically he did well, regularly appearing on the Dean's
List of the highest grade scorers, and eventually achieving a
distinction along with about a quarter of his group. His European
adventure concluded with a month-long holiday with INSEAD
colleagues in southern Italy, visiting Amalfi, Sicily and the
Aeolian Islands. Here among the constantly bubbling volcanoes
Hague felt he had arrived in Paradise – yet the lure of the
Conservative Party and Yorkshire was sufficiently great to call him
home.

Chapter Five

Westminster Calling

One must not overlook the depressed incomes of the farming community . . . and the appalling and increasing pollution of some of the nation's most beautiful rivers. These are not subjects of today's debate. Nevertheless I hope to ensure that they will not go unnoticed or unaddressed in the House.

William Hague, maiden speech in the House of Commons,

March 1989

It came as no surprise to his McKinsey colleagues when in 1987 William Hague absented himself from work to pursue his true calling. Although his attention to detail and obvious workaholic nature had put him on the fast track towards a certain partnership at the Firm, Wentworth was calling. His home seat seemed to offer the perfect training ground and fitted his career template. He had reached the point in his plan at which it was necessary to chalk up true blue points by fighting a no-hope seat, and there was certainly nowhere better to do that than on home turf, with a home-grown election team.

Although Hague had a distinct local advantage in standing for selection to fight Wentworth, his homeboy credentials did not guarantee success. The Conservative Association had had a habit of preferring outsiders. In the somewhat embattled circumstances of keeping alight the Tory torch amidst an electoral sea of red,

Wentworth Conservatives had taken as a matter of pride the chance to initiate relative innocents into South Yorkshire's small but defiant Tory fold. In William Hague, however, they had more than a local boy made good. Although the turf was familiar, Thatcher's assault on the mining industry had hardened the battle lines. Wentworth saw the sense in recruiting someone who combined a Yorkshireman's disposition with a management consultant's professionalism. Hague's selection changed the mould; thereafter his successors in following general elections, Mike Brennan and Carl Haymer, were also locals who had, like Hague, chaired the constituency's Young Conservative branch.

The general election campaign of 1987 emerged as the most expensively packaged campaign ever, with Labour making full and stylish use of media techniques that the Conservatives had perfected in previous contests. The Alliance of the Social Democratic Party and the Liberal Party, buoyed by positive opinion polls, good local election results and high-profile by-election victories, seemed a credible third force as the two Davids (Owen and Steel) made early impact with a national tour in May. Slick packaging and high-tech resources were thin on the ground in South Yorkshire, although local Conservatives did have their own secret weapon in the shape of the redoubtable Nancy Matthews.

Already in her eighties, Matthews had been a professional agent and stalwart of the party for nearly fifty years. As a young widow she had devoted herself to the cause of Conservatism in Yorkshire, and over the years had provided an invaluable professional linchpin to an area where Conservatives were rather thin on the ground. Matthews had known and encouraged William from his first teenage political awakenings: she was delighted to see him back as candidate, as were other Wentworth association notables including Pat and Ray Swift, William's minders at his first party conferences, with whom he had actively remained in touch.

Professional agents were costly and thus scarce in such strongly Labour areas so Matthews had responsibility for several constituencies, but even her considerable presence could not replace the practical and legal need for election agents to be appointed to each of the seats in her domain. In terms of mixing business with pleasure William could hardly have hit upon a more satisfactory arrangement than having Kim Birch offer to be his election agent. Their long-standing friendship had once again flourished into something more serious when Kim had moved down to London to work in the City for SG Warburg. When William talked of fighting the local seat where she too had been a Young Conservative, Kim volunteered to give up three weeks of her annual leave to run his campaign. In fact William's whole election was a very social affair, for his friend and former flatmate Alan Duncan was another of the Matthews troops. Duncan had been selected to fight one of Wentworth's neighbouring seats, Barnsley West and Penistone. In the progress of their friendly competitiveness Duncan had rather stolen a march on Hague by becoming the first of the two to be selected. He had been chosen for the equally safe Labour seat the previous year, and had in the same week purchased the ideal home for a wannabe MP, at 18 Gayfere Street, virtually overlooking Conservative Central Office and a stone's throw from the House of Commons. William, who would later become a tenant at the Westminster house, had put his first steps on the property ladder by purchasing his own Clapham pad in Marmion Road.

For the Conservatives nationally this would be a far more challenging general election than the previous one and no time for complacency, even though the party started the campaign with a twelve-point lead. Margaret Thatcher's hold over the cabinet had already suffered the blow of Michael Heseltine's resignation over the Westland crisis, and the popular affection in which she had been held was increasingly tested by growing concerns over health and education. Despite his many detractors, Neil Kinnock made a considerably more effective opponent than Michael Foot, with political skills well suited to capturing a resurgent public aspiration for the intangible moral component.

At his adoption meeting on 21 May, Hague tempered his acclamation for the government's dry economics by stressing the Tories' national themes of greater emphasis on social issues, particularly revitalising the inner cities and education system. Inevitably in Wentworth at large Hague was on a weaker footing when it came to defending the government's economic policies, so much of his fire was aimed at the opposition, though not at Peter Hardy, the Labour MP. Hague and Hardy had a considerable mutual respect dating back ten years to when William had made his first schoolboy visit to the Commons for a tour organised by his MP. For the 1987 election they reached an agreement not to criticise each other, but to reserve their negative comments for the mutually distrusted Alliance. This strategy had considerably more advantage to Hague, whose fight for second place was under threat from the Alliance, who had come 1500 votes behind the Conservative candidate in 1983. In terms of giving Hague's party a competitive advantage, Neil Kinnock presented a gift by revealing a damagingly ambivalent position on defence, which Hague happily exposed to shore up his vote.

For Hague this was an election for practice and to get back into the swing of campaigning before fighting a safe seat, but even so he planned his routine with uncompromising thoroughness. Stella and Nigel Hague found their whole house in Wentworth village commandeered for action with the same military planning that young William had reserved for his toy soldiers. The dining room became the committee room, and the kitchen the works canteen with Mrs Hague acting as caterer to a troop of workers who arrived to stay a few nights at regular intervals over the three-week campaign. William had already recruited his girlfriend to be agent. He also tempted Oxford and London friends for a break canvassing in picturesque South Yorkshire. Brooks Newmark and Gary Jackson were among the guests. The campaign vehicle was an inappropriately shabby blue van requisitioned from David Rusby's farm, complete with David as driver. William felt that his Heath Robinson approach to transport contrasted well with the Labour Party's official car that carried Peter Hardy around the constituency. It also looked a little pathetic compared with the Conservatives' national campaign bus. A double-decker bus, festooned with blue election paraphernalia promoting the 'Next Moves Forward' manifesto theme, visited Wentworth on its nationwide tour. Travelling through the whole area it picked up the Nancy Matthews platoon of candidates constituency by constituency. Its national coordinator, Ashley Gray, dealt with hundreds of prospective MPs but remembers only a handful, among whom Hague featured as particularly helpful. Good humour was certainly called for when, having ignored Matthew's route advice, the battle bus was unable to make any moves forward after getting stuck under a low-level road bridge.

Although there were several public meetings and campaign hustings, William's approach was low key, concentrating on a thorough canvass. The result was mixed, with Hague claiming he had increased the vote, by 500 on top of the 1983 poll, but in fact his overall share of vote had fallen slightly. Nationally the Conservative share of vote held up at 42 per-cent, similar to its 1983 result, and it maintained an overall majority of 102 seats. William held a celebratory party in Cortworth Cottage for his campaign team and Alan Duncan. Mrs Hague was somewhat disappointed when faced by ninety glasses to wash up, William having told her that he was off – taking Kim on a well-earned weekend away.

William did not have to wait long before being offered a real opportunity to enter Parliament, which was well within his target of becoming an MP by the age of thirty. He was one of 365 aspirant politicians who applied to represent the North Yorkshire seat of Richmond on the retirement of Leon Brittan. Brittan approached his association in June 1988 to inform them that Margaret Thatcher had asked him to become a European Commissioner. Although the appointment had been rumoured they were nevertheless shocked, as he had been their MP only since 1983. Throughout the post-war years the seat had been staunchly Conservative, but in the mid term of a contentious government that was no guarantee of success in a by-election even though Leon Brittan had achieved a majority of 19,000.

Contrary to the instincts of the central party machine, Richmond's association argued against a quick election. The chairman Sheilah Pitman, a general's daughter with daunting 'handbagging' abilities of her own, wrote to the Prime Minister asking for permission to run the selection according to the local timetable. Pitman, agent Jim Lumb and Brittan were in agreement that the process of finding and establishing a new candidate would take time – partly because of the inevitable competition which meant the selection itself was bound to be a lengthy process, and partly because of the nature of the constituency. Boundary changes since Hague's election have marginally reduced the size of the seat, but it is still around a thousand square miles. The main towns other than Richmond in the north are Thirsk and Northallerton, but the character of the seat is defined by its stunning and varied countryside. The overwhelmingly rural surroundings make farming an important interest group, although only around 12 per cent of the community are farmers. Many of the area's inhabitants are professionals commuting to Teesside, or small business people in the market towns and many villages, and there is also a very high proportion of military personnel based in and around the army camp at Catterick. With a spattering of ancient monuments, ruined castles, valleys made famous by writers and celebrated by television in romantic reflections on the Yorkshire Dales, the Richmond constituency nurtures a proud and independent breed of Conservative.

North Yorkshire has justifiable county pride. It offers a facet of British life totally removed from the pace of metropolitan culture; halfway between Edinburgh and London it does have a self-contained character which locals also believe distinguishes it even from other parts of Yorkshire. There are tangible distinctions from neighbouring seats – of which one, Sedgefield, is Tony Blair's constituency. Whereas Richmond has been associated with prosperous farming, Sedgefield's less privileged profile is, like Hague's childhood home, defined by the historic role of the coal industry. That Hague had family, his mother's sister Marjorie Londin (who famously won £850,000 on the National Lottery in 1997) in Scarborough, would have counted in his favour more than his own South Yorkshire background. South Yorkshire after all is not North Yorkshire.

Though not cut from exactly the same cloth, Hague could claim that his upbringing resonated with the values of the Richmond Conservative Association. The combination of farming and small business background were the ideal breeding for Richmond. His obvious ambition and celebrity were also helpful as Richmond prided itself on choosing high flyers – not for them a merely efficient backbencher but a star player who would draw the nation's attention to the indisputable common sense and uncommon sensibilities of this profoundly English heartland. It was an area that Hague knew and loved, having taken advantage of its spectacular opportunities for indulging his love of walking. It was a habit shared by Leon Brittan and his wife, who had accompanied William on treks through the constituency long before it homed into view as a prospective seat.

Some post-event lily gilding can be assumed in the recollection of then agent Jim Lumb, who believed he was 'walking with destiny' when William visited the Conservative office in Northallerton. Nevertheless Hague certainly made a good impression early in the selection process, not least because of all the candidates he made the first appointment to visit the association and illustrate a commitment to researching its particular concerns.

The key reason why the association had lobbied hard for time to replace Leon Brittan was its sheer size. With fifty-five branches representing the whole constituency, the executive, which would play a direct role in narrowing down the candidates, had more than one hundred members. The formal selection process began in August 1988 with an initial trawl though CVs, leaving a shortlist of fifty to be interviewed by a panel of twenty-two people drawn from different parts of Richmond life. For the first round of interviews the Richmond association noted the efforts of many candidates to endear themselves to a country constituency by wearing tweeds, although most of the male members of the interview panel had considered traditional pinstripe lent appropriate seriousness to their task. The first man to question William Hague, County Councillor Bill Barton, was impressed. He and many of his colleagues felt the interview with Hague was more like an entertaining chat. Barton concluded that they had met a man who 'could bullshit himself out of anything'. During the second round of interviews, when candidates had been reduced to twenty, many had taken a lead from the first round and turned up in pinstripe. This time the association hit back and came attired in corduroy and Barbours. As an intimidatory trick it may have helped to weed out some of the strong competition, which included Steven Norris and Michael Ancram, but did not hold back the four obvious candidates for the final selection. The final shortlist of four consisted of Alan Duncan, whose career path was once again in line with Hague's, Edward Garnier, Mark Robinson and Hague. Richmond is proud that all of its shortlist became MPs soon after, but talented though the final four were, William won by a large majority with Duncan in second place by some margin. Duncan particularly impressed the selectors when, after the result was announced, he immediately offered his help for the by-election campaign. Duncan's enthusiasm for canvassing the remote and frozen peaks of the constituency was tempered by occasional business pressures. By then a very successful oil trader, he was one of the few people with a mobile phone, although the first of such phones were not as portable as today's technology allows. Colleagues remember him cursing the frustrations of an unreliable signal while buying and selling oil on the Yorkshire Dales.

Once Hague's selection was confirmed by an open meeting of the association in mid November the real fight could begin, although the by-election writ was not moved until January, after Leon Brittan had taken up his European role. Despite Hague's undoubted qualities, his youth made him an unusual choice for such a traditional association. Brittan, who had advised him throughout the selection process, felt that William's selection was testament to the degree of concern there was that the seat would be lost. Since the 1987 election the government's popularity had taken a pounding with public doubt over water and electricity privatisation and hostility to the new Community Charge. The long-promised reform of the rating system was controversial in towns, but it also hit hard among tenant farmers in tithe properties throughout Richmondshire. Only weeks after Hague's adoption the extent of unease developing within the Tory party was revealed by Sir Anthony Meyer's backbench challenge to Margaret Thatcher's leadership. Cabinet visitors who came waving the flag for Hague also found that they had to reassure the public about the government's public service reforms, particularly the Health Review launched on the eve of the campaign, which proposed giving GPs greater independence. This was set to be the sort of election that required an energetic, good communicator rather more than a seasoned politician.

Hague's minder, former cabinet minister Michael (now Lord) Jopling, had not met William before the election. His constituency, Westmorland, was in many ways similar to Richmond. Recognising the importance of the election, Jopling volunteered for the minder's role, a wise adviser who should help a by-election candidate through what is always a far more closely inspected process than fighting a seat at a general election. Though he was aware of Hague's precocious reputation, Jopling was surprised and impressed by his talent. The Conservatives held a daily press conference at the Fleece Hotel in Thirsk. Hague was staying at Leon Brittan's house in Spennithorne throughout the campaign, and Jopling would make the journey to Thirsk with Hague each morning, using the time for vital preparation. He quickly considered himself out of a job, concluding that if ever there was a candidate who did not need a minder it was Hague. Jopling believed Hague the most competent by-election candidate the party had had since Peter (now Lord) Walker in the 1960s.

Whatever Hague's strengths, however, it was really good luck which presented him with the circumstances in which he could win. The feud between the two parties of the former Alliance was reaching a crescendo by this election, so much so that the Social and Liberal Democrats and the Social Democrats each stood their own candidates. The SDP's Mike Potter was a strong local candidate and Barbara Pearce for the Liberals had some local connections, but with both standing they had immediately undermined the high possibility that a single party of the centre could have claimed another Tory citadel. Potter, a Richmond farmer, was generally considered the best candidate by the press. Hague fought a thorough grass roots campaign, determined to visit as many communities as possible and hosting a series of pork pie suppers in the area's many pubs. The weather throughout the January 1989 campaign was bleak and snowy, making many of the more outlying areas difficult to reach, and leaving Hague soaked and frozen on a daily basis. Observers from other camps thought Hague a competent, safe pair of hands but not particularly charismatic. Even *The Times*, which early on predicted his success, decried his public image, complaining that he 'reads statements like a speak-your-weight machine'.

With no official opinion polls conducted until the closing days of the campaign, the opposition parties considered themselves at a disadvantage. The SDP thought that proof of their progress would help them to build a momentum, pulling votes away from the Liberals and the Conservatives. As Mike Potter was a farmer they had done well among his many colleagues, and farmland throughout the constituency was peppered with huge hoardings advertising his name. The party had made a great leap forward in by-election techniques by using enormous individual letters to spell out Potter's name on hillsides. It was too much temptation for one over-zealous member of the Hague team who fought back with guerrilla tactics: at night he ranged the hills with a paint brush, changing the 'P' to an 'R'. The reign of the phantom graffiti artist was cut short, though, when he leapt into his getaway car only to find that in his haste he had jumped into the SDP's campaign vehicle. So the posters remained a graphic display of support but, as Hague was pleased to point out, sheep don't have a vote. The Tories' private polls showed, however, that Potter and Pearce were leeching their support, especially in the last week when their predictions of an 8 per cent lead began to look increasingly vulnerable. A Gallup poll on the last day of the campaign, Wednesday 23 February, showed that the SDP were clearly in second place, although sixteen points behind Hague. Between them the SDP and the SLD were beating Hague. It galvanised the SDP team into a flurry of leafleting and last-minute campaigning that proved effective but came too late to change the destiny of the SDP. Three of its strategists for the

Richmond election, Chris Hopson, Andrew Cooper and Daniel Finkelstein, were among group of SDP supporters who later joined the Conservatives in a highly publicised move during the 1992 general election campaign. In February 1989 their candidate came within three thousand votes of beating William Hague. A single Alliance candidate would have meant certain victory for they polled more than 54 per cent of the vote between them on the day. The final tally saw Hague the victor with more than 19,500 votes:

W. Hague (Conservative)	19,543	(37.2%)
M. Potter (SDP)	16,909	(32.2%)
B. Pearce (SLD)	11,589	(22%)
F. Robson (Labour)	2,591	(4.9%)
R. Upshall (Green)	1,473	(2.8%)
four other candidates	456	(0.9%)

William Hague had won an historic victory, the last Tory by-election victory until Hague himself was leader of the party and the Conservatives were in opposition. In an irony similar to when Hague became leader at a dramatic low point in his party's history, he became an MP in an election that also marked a decline in its fortunes. The fall in the share of the vote since the 1987 general election was worse than in any by-election since Mrs Thatcher had come to power, but with the undoubted help of the splintering Alliance, Hague had kept Richmond true blue and had made it to the House of Commons. It was a victory which even his team felt had been saved from the jaws of defeat. Had the election been a week later they believed the SDP's momentum would have taken it to the winning post. In his maiden speech on 20 March 1989 Hague committed himself to championing the causes of the countryside, a theme he was later to pursue with renewed vigour during his first year as party leader in an effort to find a distinctive identity for the defeated and dispirited Conservatives. The speech, made during the Budget debate, was a call to remember the plight of pensioners during an expected rise in inflation, as well as a call to remember the plight of the countryside alongside the more highly publicised inner city problems which had plagued the Thatcher government. Since then the issues that Hague raised have worsened with the beef crisis, collapse in lamb prices and phasing out of subsidies from the reformed Common Agricultural Policy, and the whole of the Yorkshire region has applied for European aid.

Soon after winning the seat William fulfilled his early pledge of moving to the constituency. In exchange for a Victorian terraced house in overcrowded Clapham, Hague purchased a slice of history and, even more valuable, a haven of peace and privacy, on the Brough Park Estate. For a similar price of around £100,000, Hague had bought his two-bedroomed flat in Clapham and now a two-bedroom apartment in North Yorkshire. His salary as an MP was then under £25,000 a year, but a second homes allowance of nearly ten thousand pounds aided the purchase in Brough Park. Hague had looked at only two places when he found his Yorkshire home, right in the centre of the constituency, accessible only by negotiating a way through the lazy sheep who have made a 'chill-out' zone of the narrow road down to the main house.

Once a grand country mansion, the house has been cleverly converted into a number of units, all of which are different. For what is essentially a two-bedroom flat Hague's home gives an impression of serious grandeur. The modest front door, leading off an Italianate courtyard, opens into a magnificent stone staircase progressing up four levels. An iron candelabra hangs down through three of the levels, the walls of which have gradually filled with paintings and political memorabilia. The hallway is testament to Hague's, and now his wife's, fascination with books. Each wall is lined with books, mainly political biographies but also many novels and travel books. The shelves reach so high that Hague recently commissioned a local furniture maker to produce a hand-made set of library steps: they are carved with a Yorkshire rose and a Welsh foxglove to celebrate his and Ffion's mutual love of books. Hanging in pride of place at the bottom of the staircase is a vivid portrait of the couple by Diccon Swan, a wedding gift from Alan Duncan. The living room, which is on the top floor, is similarly imposing. A thirty-two-foot by twenty-eight-foot room with dark beams exposed in the open ceiling belies the size of bedrooms and kitchen, which are quite small. Not so, however, the basement, which Hague quickly converted into a gym, but could have made an indoor tennis court. The couple consider this their home and return every weekend despite the inevitable complications this creates in juggling timetables and travel arrangements, either by car, train, or plane to Teesside airport.

Hague's political career is testament to the adage that luck is as important as talent. Undoubtedly his progression has been hastened by his own conscientious perseverance and flair, but without such fortuitous career breaks his rise would certainly have been slower.

On entering the House Hague determined to keep his head down and make a name as a diligent backbencher. He did not intend to heighten his profile by courting notoriety. In a party striated with factions since the Tariff Reform League, and driven by an internal competitive dynamic of wet versus dry, Hague deliberately steered clear of aligning himself with any particular group. It was a tactic with mixed blessings, keeping him out of trouble and yet arousing suspicions about the true depth or consistency of his convictions. He joined one non-sectarian dining club, a discreet group of a dozen or so MPs drawn together through friendship rather than ideology. The 'Third Term' Dining Group was organised by Tim Yeo and Andrew Mackay with a variety of opinion reflected in its members who included Tim Boswell and David Harris as well as Steven Norris and David Heathcoat-Amory. His colleagues learnt of his instinctive Conservatism and consistent focus on the key areas of Europe, law and order, the family, education and health. It was the foundation of the 'Common Sense' manifesto that Hague has since made the centrepiece of his policy contribution as leader. He often repeated his conviction that those were the five areas on which the Conservatives should fight. In the run-up to the 1997 general election he told his fellow diners that Conservatives would suffer if they failed to reassure people they were serious about the future of the family, the security of sterling, the security of the individual and the delivery of good quality schools and hospitals.

As at Oxford and at McKinsey, William's reputation was a mixed blessing for a new and young MP. His role as hard-working constituency member was necessary to establish a more mature impression among his new colleagues, some of whom would have been amused by his schoolboy speech, others suspicious of his likely ambition. His smooth handling of the by-election had won him important fans in the House. Hague's first promotion came just a year and a half after his election. When Norman Lamont, then Chief Secretary to the Treasury, lost his Parliamentary Private Secretary, Lord Jopling suggested Hague as a replacement. Chatting on the floor of the Commons next to the dispatch box, Jopling told Lamont that Hague was outstanding. Lamont considered it an interesting enough suggestion to meet Hague and then push for his appointment against the advice of the whips' office, where he was considered too young. Lamont got his way and subsequently felt vindicated in his choice as Hague proved a loyal and thoughtful PPS, who did not flinch from reporting back the negative reactions of backbench colleagues. Although Lamont did not consider Hague a philosophical animal, he was impressed by the way he contributed to the speech writing process. Hague's style tended away from embellishment and invective, towards simplifying the message. The two shared a common approach to economic matters and to Europe, although Lamont found it less easy to empathise with Hague's motivating convictions on law and order which saw him vote in favour of the return of capital punishment in February 1994.

PPS to a Chief Secretary is a pretty good job for a new MP, especially when it brings automatic access to the heart of the campaign for the Prime Minister's survival. Hague's appointment to the Treasury – where John Major was Chancellor – came days before the Conservative Party's descent into civil war with the ungracious dismissal of a great leader and his original political inspiration. His role as PPS to Lamont put him right in the middle of John Major's campaign team even before a campaign was under way. The first step was to move to the assistance of a wounded Margaret Thatcher after Heseltine's challenge. The first ballot on 20 November 1990 had left her four votes short of an overall majority. Hague acted as a important sounding board for back-bench opinion and reluctantly had to inform Lamont that he had found colleagues who said they had voted for her in the first round but would not do so in the second. It was evidence that many loyal Thatcherites were pained to hear as it forced them to admit she had been fatally wounded. That was also Hague's conclusion: he believed she should not fight on as a split vote on the right might allow Michael Heseltine to claim the leadership.

After Thatcher's resignation in Cabinet on Thursday 22 November, Hague found himself at the very first meeting of the fledgling Major campaign by dint of his role as Lamont's PPS. Major himself was not there as he had taken leave for a serious dental operation. Hague's particular contribution was to suggest a neutral location for the campaign HQ. When Alan Duncan had bought his house in Gayfere Street several years previously Hague had taken a room there before finding his own flat in Clapham. He knew the house was more than suitable: the location was excellent, the facilities good as Duncan's business had required the installation of extra phone lines, and the layout worked well to accommodate one team dealing with media on the ground floor and another dealing with sensitive voting statistics in the private basement study. William's initial attempt to secure Gayfere Street was thwarted: Duncan was out, on a visit to his tailor. After a few expletives had been hurled down the phone he eventually made contact with his friend and the deal was done: the campaign had a headquarters and Hague was at the heart of operations.

Gayfere Street housed the press team and the number crunchers. Elsewhere in Westminster satellite offices ran out of the Treasury and John Major's office in the Commons. Although Major did not at first want a single campaign manager, in the tense moments after Thatcher's resignation, it soon became obvious that one person had to take control. As Major's closest Treasury colleague Norman Lamont assumed this role, and as Lamont's PPS it followed that Hague remain based in the Treasury liaising between the different arms of the operation. Hague applied his best PPS skills to being Major's gatekeeper, fielding calls, meeting and greeting Members and briefing the campaign whips, Richard Ryder and Francis Maude. Even if Hague had not found himself in the exciting position of working closely with Major he would have been active in the campaign, but his proximity to the future Prime Minister offered a potential for career advancement that would have fired the enthusiasm of a less ambitious man. Although this leadership bid, conducted over a very few days and absolutely concentrated on the MPs, was very different in character from Hague's own, it offered some lessons which would inform the 1997 campaign. Chiefly Hague realised the need for numbers to be closely guarded. Then, as in 1997, the bunker operation revealed their true calculations of support only to the key players. To guard against complacency and to confuse the opposition these figures were certainly more generous than those revealed to the press and even to other team members. It was a tactic that Hague used effectively in 1997.

On Tuesday 27 November 1990 John Major won the Conservative Party leadership. Of all the names that would be discussed as his likely successor, Hague did not become the most prominent until the dying days of his second Parliament.

In person Hague made his first leader's speech to the party conference in October 1997; by proxy he achieved the same thing in 1991. As he was elected late in 1990 Major had to wait almost a year before addressing the conference as leader. He was eager to roam across many briefs. At the time his regular speech writer, Nick True, was away on compassionate leave. Sarah (now Lady) Hogg, head of the policy unit at 10 Downing Street, called in help in the shape of Michael Trend, a leader writer on the *Telegraph*. Trend, an experienced speech writer, was given some guidance on themes and a couple of drafts that had been contributed. One, from William Hague, presented Trend with a problem: how to improve on it. Not only had Hague's draft covered the themes which Major had wanted, it was also written with attention to Major's own style of delivery. With some reworking Trend and a small team of contributors finessed the final speech, but whole paragraphs were lifted from Hague's unsolicited draft. It was Trend's first encounter with Hague, and it made a lasting impression so that when he was later elected MP for Windsor, a firm friendship developed.

Unlike that of some more senior figures in Major's campaign, Hague's loyalty to the new regime was never questioned, even during the troubled years after the 1992 election when his talents were rewarded with a ministerial post at the Department of Social Security and a swift rise to the cabinet. Although he was later to apologise for the ERM debacle of autumn 1992 he did not undermine the policy while in government. In the later years of Major's Government Hague, although a Eurosceptic, was never one of the 'bastards' in John Major's cabinet. Where others had lost faith in the man they had elected to continue Thatcher's work, Hague loyally defended Major when he was challenged by John Redwood in 1995.

Chapter Six

CLIMBING THE LADDER

Of all the jobs I have had in government, the one that has meant the most to me is serving as the Minister for disabled people. The courage and self-confidence of the disabled people I met was an inspiration. I met people who faced up to and overcame the most terrifying physical and mental disabilities. My party will never forget its obligations to disabled people. Their courage and their dignity are an inspiration to every community.

William Hague, speech to the party conference, 1997

Hague loves the Palace of Westminster. He loves the pageantry and the history, its role in defending British freedoms, the hushed corridors and their heritage of plots and deals, and he loves the Commons chamber. As a schoolboy he had looked around in awe when he came to visit, and eighteen years later that enthusiasm had barely diminished. On 7 June 1993 Hague surveyed the green benches with a renewed sense of excitement. He could recite by heart some of the greatest speeches ever delivered there and now he was to make his ministerial debut at the dispatch box. Answering questions about the Maxwell Pensions Unit was hardly likely to give him the opportunity for inspiring oratory, but it was with a sense of occasion that Hague addressed the Commons that day.

John Major had known well the job he chose to make Hague's first step on the ministerial ladder. He too had served as Parliamentary Under Secretary at the DHSS, as it was then known. As one of the largest departments in Whitehall, it had been the proving ground for many senior politicians, including Margaret Thatcher, John Moore and Michael Portillo. At thirty-two Hague was several years younger than Major had been at the equivalent point in his career, but initial doubts about his youth were diminished by shining commendations from Norman Lamont and the whips' office. So on 27 May 1993 Hague became a minister, replacing Ann Widdecombe on her move to the Department of Employment. Widdecombe, whose singular style had emerged in the DSS role, was considered a tough act to follow.

As the most junior member Hague joined a team headed by Social Security Secretary Peter Lilley with Nick Scott as Minister of State, Lord Mackay of Ardbrecknish and Alistair Burt, a second Parliamentary Under Secretary. As the team discussed reallocating responsibilities it very soon became obvious that Hague's skills were well suited to the pensions brief. His colleagues quickly appreciated that he was exceptionally bright and numerate, someone who would relish the challenge of a complicated and technical brief. They also agreed that he was remarkably down-to-earth for a young man of whom great things were already being predicted.

For Hague this was the first in a pattern of appointments which required delicate management of a politically sensitive issue. His task was to prepare the complex Pensions Bill that had been long delayed by the government. The 1991 theft by Robert Maxwell of £350 million of pension scheme funds had threatened to destroy public faith in company pension schemes. Additionally the government estimated that with the number of claimants due to rise by 40 per cent the cost of the State Pension would double within forty years. The pressing need to encourage the uptake of private provision had also been seriously undermined by the scandal of pension mis-selling during the late 1980s. Having been encouraged to opt out of SERPS (the State Earnings Related Pension Scheme), around one and a half million people were given the wrong advice by pensions brokers. There were further complications arising from the European Court of Justice ruling that the retirement age for men and women should be standardised. Raising the retirement age for women would save money for the exchequer, but would be more difficult to sell than lowering the age for men. In short, Hague had inherited a heavyweight brief but one he relished as his first real challenge since leaving McKinsey.

Hague was an immediate hit with his colleagues and civil servants, revealing the strengths that would characterise his ministerial career. He enjoyed the uniquely businesslike approach of the department that had transformed its operation with the introduction of separate agencies to run its different concerns. He responded well to Peter Lilley's preference for delegating tasks, a practice that he replicated in his own sphere. He was well liked by his civil service team although he was considered a hard but fair taskmaster. He was always straightforward about his requirements, setting clear instructions and specific objectives, appreciative of work well done but intolerant of half-hearted effort and particularly of poor time-keeping. In fact Hague immediately distinguished himself from most politicians by sticking closely to a strict timetable, chairing meetings so that they never ran over. This is a habit he sticks to rigidly, so much so that colleagues in his team know that one of the few circumstances in which Hague loses his cool is if he is kept waiting.

Hague's quick grasp of the technical detail and all the nuances of the pensions issue soon convinced colleagues in the House that all the predictions about his golden future were well founded. The ministerial role exposed him to a new set of influential contacts in his party. It brought his first encounter with Lord Cranborne, the man he would later sack in one of the most dramatic disputes ever between Conservative peers and their Commons colleagues. At his introduction to Hague, Cranborne felt nothing but respect for a remarkable debut. As leader of the Lords, Cranborne was keen to fix a meeting to discuss the passage of the Pensions Bill through the Upper House. Cranborne brought together the bill teams from both Houses and booked one of the grand committee rooms in the Lords for a whole afternoon. He expected the meeting might last as long as three hours as they examined the possible political pitfalls that could accompany the bill's passage through both Houses. Hague knew his audience would be supportive but also intrigued to see how he would perform. Many were far more experienced than he in the legislative process, but he was quietly confident. He knew he had grasped the details of his brief. In the event Hague's colleagues were extremely impressed and left with time on their hands. He stripped the bill down to its essentials, running through the key points in fifteen minutes, answered questions and revealed that he had thought through the tactics and the strategy. The meeting was over in only forty-five minutes but it had left a lasting impression on everyone there.

For Hague the pensions brief was largely an intellectual challenge, but it also brought him face to face with the human responsibilities of his role and the issues of this particular political constituency, the 'grey vote'. At a meeting of the Maxwell pensioners he saw the worry and anger etched into the faces of people who had been swindled. It is a meeting he often cites as having a played a formative role in the development of his own 'compassionate conservatism', although that did not mean he would advocate state assistance for Maxwell's victims. Hague believes that handling the pensions brief has given him a certain authority on the issue that he has since used to some political effect. As leader he chose to make the plight of pensioners a priority for his 'common sense' agenda, announcing Conservative intentions to raise pensions by £5.50 per week by scrapping free TV licences and special fuel allowances. It was one of the first of his populist announcements of summer 2000 and was praised by Lady Castle in preference to New Labour's 75p increase.

He had a short-term political imperative to guide the legislation through, but there were also profound long-term issues to be considered. As the bill was largely concerned with implementing the recommendations of the Goode Report into the Maxwell scandal, its passage through the House was relatively uncontroversial. The government was seen to be responding to the 'something must be done' lobby. The weightier responsibility was to consider the long-term implications of pension provision by devising a system that would encourage a cultural shift in favour of the private provision. Sir Michael Partridge, the department's Permanent Secretary, had worked with both Labour and Conservative ministers in more than thirty years at the department. He saw in Hague a serious strategic thinker, someone who was able to detect and deflect political flak while keeping an eye on the long-term political agenda. Hague would have contributed to early thoughts in Peter Lilley's plans for 'Pensions Plus', but he had moved on from the department by the time the scheme was unveiled – to immediate and misleading condemnation from Labour – in the run-up to the 1997 general election. In Sir Michael's experienced judgement a good minister understood that politics is the 'art of the possible', someone who could make their ideas practicable. Of the many junior ministers who passed through his department he considered three outstanding: Margaret Thatcher, John Major and Hague. Of those he thought Hague the best and, alongside the other two, marked him out as a future prime minister.

Few were surprised, then, when Hague was rapidly promoted. The move up one rung of the ministerial ladder came in July 1994, shortly before the Pensions Bill received Royal Assent. His handling of the legislation had received numerous plaudits from the press. The *Financial Times* was typical in commenting that Hague had shown 'exceptional mastery of detail in steering the pensions bill through parliament'. It was exactly someone with that sureness of touch that was required to succeed Nick Scott after his high-profile departure forced by his controversial role in blocking a private member's bill on disabled rights. Hague had earned his promotion, but it was not without some disappointment for his immediate colleague Alistair Burt. Burt had served longer in the department and his 'one nation' credentials were thought by many to make him an obvious person to take on the brief for the disabled. Burt was disappointed to have been overlooked but impressed when Hague dropped into his office to commiserate. He felt that Hague was genuine when he told him that he was quite embarrassed to be taking the job, a job he felt Burt also deserved.

If the pensions role had called for skilful handling, Hague's added new responsibilities for disabled people were a real hot potato. As Minister of State Hague maintained his responsibilities for pensions as the issue moved on to the matter of equalisation of the retirement age, and was charged with the job of saving face for the government over its increasingly unpopular resistance to introducing a disability act. Nick Scott's departure from the department was forced by his own admission that he had misled the House. Although he had initially denied it, he had in fact sanctioned departmental assistance to backbenchers tabling questions that would effectively scupper a private member's bill that had sought to introduce rights for the disabled. The government's opposition to Labour MP Roger Berry's bill was both practical and philosophical. There were certainly significant costs implied in the introduction of a whole range of new rights of access and employment for disabled people, but many Conservatives were also opposed on principle. There was considerable scepticism about the effectiveness of equal opportunities legislation and concerns about adding more regulation to business. Nick Scott had been trying for many years to overcome these barriers to change and was a keen advocate for a government bill. Although his demise was hastened by the intervention of his own daughter Victoria, a lobbyist for RADAR (Royal Association for Disability and Rehabilitation), most of the disability lobby were sad to see him go. They knew that he had actually been working away behind the scenes to change opinions among his colleagues and that unfairly he had had to carry the can for government intransigence.

By the time Hague moved into the role the issue had really built up a head of steam, but that gave him a significant advantage over Nick Scott. *The Sun* newspaper had taken up the cause as a popular campaign. Although Hague appeared to be taking the job at a particularly difficult time, Nick Scott had already done much of the legwork and John Major had become convinced that the government could no longer hold out against public demands for action. Shortly before he left office Scott had announced a green paper, 'Disability on the Agenda', which was put out to consultation for three months. Scott proposed for the first time a statutory requirement that employers should not discriminate against disabled people. Hague had the advantage of an important ally in Major, but he also had to win back the good faith of the press and public and devise measures that were serious enough to meet the approval of disability groups without splitting the government benches.

Hague says that he enjoyed this role more than any other and indeed he took to the cause with great enthusiasm. Unlike right-wing colleagues in the House and in cabinet he had no ideological objections to such legislation. He did not share the philosophical doubts about the wisdom of defining rights by law, although he acknowledged those arguments by stopping short of recommending the creation of a disability commission. To Hague this was both a practical issue and a matter of duty: he believes that government has a responsibility to help people who through no fault of their own are less able than others to make the most of their lives. He went on a fact-finding tour to the USA to study the American legislation, a wide-ranging act which many right-wingers here and in the States consider puts too many burdens on business. But Hague was impressed and is proud to say he based his legislation on the US Act. On an evening off he went out to eat with his colleagues. Seeing the disabled facilities in the restaurant he said, 'The disabled should have the same rights in the UK.' As with his pensions reform, Hague has subsequently pointed to his role as the Minister for the Disabled to illustrate his compassionate credentials. In such a short career it is inevitable that he will seek to capitalise on his achievements, but the extent to which he won the respect and support of the disabled lobby indicates his concern was and is genuine.

His first task was to establish a productive relationship with disabled people's groups. As ever his easy manner and down-to-earth approach was key. Bert Massie is now the first head of the Disability Rights Commission that Labour had called for and have set up in government. When Hague took over from Nick Scott, Massie was the key campaigner at RADAR and the first point of contact with the disabilities lobby. Shortly after he was appointed Hague invited Massie into his office at 79 Whitehall to discuss the consultation paper. Massie was used to dealing with ministers and expected a routine chat. He was surprised and impressed when Hague set a very different tone for their meeting, and subsequent dealings. Within minutes Hague sent his civil servants away and spent an hour and a half talking alone to

Massie, who found him straightforward, honest and sincere. There were important details on which the two disagreed, mainly on the campaign for a commission, but Massie appreciated that Hague had to shape legislation he could get through. Importantly, he knew that Hague was someone the lobby could do business with. Hague was clearly a slick operator, and was not going to make the mistake that his boss Peter Lilley had made earlier that year. At the height of protests against the government's record on disability issues, heightened by plans to introduce incapacity benefit tests, Lilley had aroused controversy by suggesting that some people who turned up to wheelchair protests weren't actually disabled. The Disability Alliance condemned as a slur on the disabled Lilley's suggestion that 'people on our television screens who have been refused benefit will be seen for the first time in a wheelchair'.

But Hague's record as Minister for the Disabled was not completely uncontroversial. Ironically he, like Nick Scott, was also responsible for blocking a private member's bill that was calling for regulations tougher than the government was prepared to consider. Although the government proposed its own Disability Discrimination Bill for the 1994–5 session, the Speaker made the unusual decision to allow time for a similar private bill proposed by Labour MP Harry Barnes. The Barnes Civil Rights Disabled Persons Bill picked up on work of the derailed Berry bill with the aim of introducing a powerful commission to enforce its anti-discriminatory measures. The Speaker considered the bill sufficiently different from government proposals, and the Labour Party was keen to use it to force the government to toughen its proposals. On 24 November 1994 Hague made a statement to the Commons outlining his own plans. The government bill proposed that it would be illegal for any employer with more than twenty staff to discriminate against employees on the basis of a handicap. In the first measures to grant disabled people rights of access to public buildings and transport, public places including shops and pubs and facilities such as buses were to face tougher laws on providing access. In place of a commission it proposed a National Disability Council, an independent body to advise the government on the effectiveness of the new measures and to recommend new ones where necessary. Hague told the House: 'Our objective is clear, to eliminate discrimination against disabled people so that they can take a full part in society. But the changes cannot happen overnight, as disabled people themselves recognise. It is vital that the action we take has a realistic timetable, is practical and takes account of the impact on service providers.'

Although Hague could not have satisfied all the demands of disabled groups without recommending a commission, his proposals were met with a largely positive response. There were a host of different bodies involved in lobbying for the disabled, but RADAR had emerged as the umbrella organisation for the campaign. Privately Hague had told Bert Massie what he thought was politically viable. He was not going to push access to education as lobbyists wanted. The government had included some access rights in its 1993 education legislation and Hague considered it was too soon to revisit that.

There were also disagreements over the measures proposed to cover transport, but Hague was willing to compromise as long as RADAR assisted in bringing the rest of the lobby on board for the bill. It was a complicated negotiation. Hague did not think he would get the backing to include clauses covering the insurance industry and was prepared to jettison them to get the bill through. After much deal-making, insurance did make it into the Act, but Hague remained adamant that a commission was a proposal too far. It was not a view shared by all Conservative MPs, some of whom were privately supportive of the Barnes bill. Despite government efforts to occupy all the committee time,

Barnes did succeed in guiding his bill into committee. Technically the membership of a bill committee is decided by a separate allocations committee, but Barnes was able to influence the outcome by suggesting some MPs for the job. He was assisted by Alan Howarth, then a Conservative, who later defected to Labour on the issue of disability rights. The Barnes bill committee included a number of sympathetic Tories, such as Peter Bottomley, Hugh Dykes and Andrew Hunter, a fairly trenchant right-winger who nonetheless assisted Barnes with tactical abstentions. The make-up of the Tory contingent on the committee ensured that Hague was often in a minority. Although Barnes was encouraged by winning on a number of points of principle in committee, he of course knew that it was Hague's job to see an end to his bill. Following the Nick Scott affair the government could not afford another public relations disaster. Hague's tactics were more subtle than his predecessor's. The progress of the bill to the floor of the House was impeded by Hague's technical amendments. Eventually Hague scrawled a note to Barnes explaining he would get the bill out of committee. By the time it reached the chamber on the last ever Friday afternoon session there were only forty minutes left for debate. Just as the Berry bill had run out of time so had the Barnes bill, its delay in committee ensured by Hague's campaign of amendments.

Harry Barnes was pleased that his bill had some influence on Hague's legislation, but both he and the shadow cabinet spokesman for the disabled, Tom Clarke, thought Hague could have gone further to include their recommendation of a commission. Clarke had been sorry to see the departure of Nick Scott, whom he believed a dedicated campaigner for the disabled. Nevertheless he was impressed by Hague, particularly by his deft use of humour which he used to defuse tenser moments in the progress of the legislation. Clarke respected Hague as very focused and determined, stubborn but not arrogant. However,

William – aged four – in his first school photo.

Aged five, at Scarborough in 1966.

Just William – aged eleven.

'Half of you may not be here in thirty or forty years' time, but I will be and I want to be free': sixteen-year-old William addresses the Conservative Party Conference, 1977. (© *Mirror Syndication International, 1977*)

Holding forth at the Oxford Union.

At INSEAD, 1986.

Below: The Richmond
by-election, February 1989:
to the left of the newly elected
member are Lindi St Clair, 'Miss
Whiplash' (Corrective Party) and
Screaming Lord Sutch (Monster
Raving Loony Party).

5.17 a.m., Friday 2 May 1997: waiting with Michael Portillo and Alan Duncan for John Major to arrive at Conservative Central Office.

The 1997 leadership campaign: 'It's William Hague. Have you got the name? Vote for William Hague to follow the same kind of government I did.'

19 December 1997.

Photo-opportunities in 1997: *that* baseball cap, and getting in the mood with Ffion at the Notting Hill Carnival.

The burdens of office.

Labour believed that the disabilities lobby had successfully created a climate of opinion in which Hague could have gone further and pushed his colleagues into accepting the commission. In opposition the Conservatives have not opposed the introduction of a commission by Labour but in government Hague had an uphill struggle in cabinet even without that proposal. Opposition was not limited to one section of the party. The cabinet was split down the middle with Major and Lilley backing Hague, but Ken Clarke, Heseltine and Howard adamantly opposed. For Clarke the cost of the measures was simply too much for the Treasury to cope with. As President of the Board of Trade, Heseltine was opposed because the bill did not match Conservative rhetoric about reducing red tape for businesses. Howard doubted the ability of legislation effectively to counter discrimination.

Hague saw no conflict between the bill and his Conservatism. In America he had bought the argument that this legislation enabled people to help themselves, to move from dependency to independence. On balance he also believed it was good for business by opening it up to new contributors and new markets. The political clamour for such a bill helped Hague to overcome the serious obstacles, but quietly many Conservatives agreed with the unnamed minister who told newspapers that Hague had taken through 'the most socialist piece of Tory legislation that session'.

Hague had proved himself a wily operator, a skilled negotiator and tactician. In one other important arena the brief also gave him the opportunity to shine. His political skills were evident in his dealings in the House and behind the scenes, but the other crucial testing ground was the media. John Major's government certainly needed fresh faces to put the best case for Conservatism. Introducing a bill that for the first time gave legal rights to the disabled was a positive story for Hague to convey, but it was not all plain sailing. He had taken on the job just as the Conservatives' reputation in the field had reached rock bottom, and he faced a well organised and media-friendly lobby that automatically appealed to the sympathies of the public. Although he was offering something new in the Disability Discrimination Act, Hague also had to explain his department's parallel initiative to clamp down on invalidity benefit fraud. The measure to introduce tougher qualifications for a new incapacity benefit was met with strong resistance from Labour, who argued that it went much further than eliminating fraud and would exclude worthy claimants. It was a high-profile initiative that threw Hague into the media spotlight to defend a controversial change, and his dexterous performance in delivering and defending the measure added another gold star to his CV. It was not long before the whispered admiring comments of Westminster colleagues reached the diary columns of the press. In April 1995 the London *Evening Standard* described Hague as 'the brilliant thirty-four-year-old social security minister. Mr Hague is being spoken of as potentially the youngest Tory cabinet minister since Churchill.'

Despite his art of self-deprecation Hague knew he was in line for an early promotion to the cabinet. The circumstances which hastened that move were as much a surprise to Hague as to the rest of the Westminster village although it certainly was no secret that John Major's leadership was coming under increasing review by his parliamentary colleagues. In June 1995 things took a turn for the worse as Major's handling of the European issue raised the spectre of a likely challenge to his leadership in the autumn under the old rules of the party.

Having been heckled by members of his own party at a back-bench meeting, Major moved to seize the initiative. On 22 June the Prime Minister shattered the calm of an unusually perfect English summer afternoon by issuing his 'Put up or shut up' challenge. Hague was speaking in committee when the Social Security whip Andrew Mitchell handed him a note explaining Major was about to resign. Calmly he continued as the Labour members of the committee grew increasingly restless, sensing the excitement of a huge Westminster drama about to unfold.

The brilliantly diverting tactic gave Major's leadership only a short-lived boost but paved the way for a promotion that would bring his unexpected successor to prominence. With the entertainment of a political pantomime over, John Major emerged the fool, John Redwood the villain, Michael Portillo the coward and William Hague the only real winner with a principality all of his own and a flaxen-haired princess as his reward.

Chapter Seven

WALES

I found him a charming man. Very easy to talk to and get on with . . . The most interesting thing for me is that he was interested in Wales. I've met the last three Secretaries of State and he came over to me as the most positive. I was prepared to think of him as a whippersnapper but he didn't come over like that at all.

Peter Andrews, owner of Llanerch Vineyard, Vale of Glamorgan,
March 1996

I found him full of humour and he had done a lot of research into the subject. I vote LibDem and I found him quite impressive. He's a little chap who's not very big in stature but he was very personable.

Jo Exell, Information Officer, Glamorgan Wildlife Trust,
February 1996

As Hague gulped down the fresh salty air and surveyed the view, he had plenty of reason to feel content. He loves walking; the steady pace of his feet on the crunchy coastal path, the refreshing sting of the sea breeze on his face, the feeling of boundless energy powered by the rhythm of the exercise. He had seen imperious cliffs, pale yellow beaches edged with shimmering rock pools, rare sea birds swooping over ruined castles. This must surely be the perfect way to combine business with pleasure. At thirty-four he was the youngest cabinet minister since Harold Wilson, the fellow Yorkshireman whose policies he had despised but whose political journey he had sought to emulate. Hague's progress thus far had taken him south from Rotherham to Westminster and now west to Wales. The distance between his home county and his new base seemed irrelevant. Hague felt an immediate kinship with the Welsh; the run-down coal fields of the south reminded him of his childhood in industrial Yorkshire, the dramatic scenery of North Wales and Snowdonia of his Richmond constituency and its surrounding countryside. It was a pleasure to leave London and immerse himself in the country and the culture which were to leave their mark on him in a very personal way.

It was summer 1995. Hague's first move as Secretary of State for Wales had immediately signalled how his style would differ from his predecessor. John Redwood had never regained his stride since being caught on camera miming awkwardly to the Welsh national anthem. Redwood's aloof manner, efficiency drives and unwillingness to pander to nationalist sentiment branded him an unsympathetic Englishman representing a government that the vast majority of the Welsh wanted out. In substance Redwood and Hague had much in common. Both were on the right, both were Eurosceptic and both were ardent defenders of the Union, but Hague would mark significant changes in tone. Where Redwood believed that signing official letters in Welsh was the thin end of conceding the case for devolution, Hague had no such objection. Where Redwood celebrated budget savings by returning the money to the Treasury, Hague preferred to spend it back in Wales. Hague was happy to sign letters in Welsh, just as he was more than happy to be on this walk along the Pembrokeshire coastal path. He had chosen to spend his summer break getting to know Wales. Redwood had been seen as distant and unaccountable, but Hague would not make the same mistake. His ascent of Snowdon, his countryside break in farmhouse bed-and-breakfasts and his trek through the Pembrokeshire National Park had two aims. He wanted to get to know the people of Wales and their concerns, and he wanted to be seen to be doing it. The press had been invited along to report on his progress. He could have held a meeting about funding the coastal path in his Cardiff office, but instead Hague made the important gesture of going to walk the walk himself.

It had been no great surprise when Hague was made the beneficiary of a recently vacated seat at the cabinet table, following Redwood's departure in the wake of his leadership challenge. His former boss Peter Lilley had told colleagues that as a minister Hague had been 'just excellent'. Hague himself had expected promotion, although not necessarily this post. When the call from John Major came Hague thought he was bound for the Treasury, as the new Chief Secretary. The rumours sounded likely and the corollary, that the concerned and reasonable William Waldegrave go to Wales, made a lot of sense. Ken Clarke, it seems, did not agree. Hague was too Eurosceptic for his team. Hague was not concerned. Chief Secretary was considered the weightier job but Secretary of State for Wales put him in charge of a nation. His responsibilities covered the whole domestic agenda from education and health to the environment and industry. Privately Hague had decided that his job was about the three Es: economy, education and the environment. Politically his task was to repair the image of the Tories in Wales whilst also making the case against Labour's proposals for a Welsh Assembly. In real terms this was an uphill struggle. The Conservatives had hit an all-time low in Wales by the time Hague came to office. Of thirty-eight parliamentary seats in the principality the party held only six, and had failed to take control of any of the twenty-two new unitary authorities at local elections in May 1995, emerging with only forty-one councillors in the whole of Wales.

The difference in approach between Hague and his predecessor quickly made a good impression within the Welsh Office. As in his previous job, Hague was well liked by his civil service team. His private office, headed by Kate Jennings, who has now moved on to the private sector, had had another recent recruit.

Fast-track entrant Ffion Jenkins had been appointed Assistant Private Secretary under John Redwood. She had narrowly missed an appointment to serve in John Major's private office at Number 10, which had she taken would have taken her life – and Hague's – down a different course. Her frustrations at Redwood's lack of enthusiasm for her native language were relieved when Hague indicated a far more open attitude to private coaching. Along with press officer Richard Lehnert (now working for BBC Wales) and journalist Julie Kirkbride, (now Conservative MP for Bromsgrove) Jenkins accompanied Hague on his grand tour. Although he was on official duty the unbroken August sunshine ensured that the trip did not feel like work. In a series of perfect days one stood out, a trip to the Blaenau Ffestiniog Railway and a group dinner at the White Horse in Capel Garmon overlooking Snowdonia National Park. Later that evening Hague rehearsed his lines for an imminent baptism by fire, an appearance the next day singing the national anthem. Sitting on the churchyard wall he was taken through his initiation test by his earnest assistant, Ffion Jenkins.

It was to be another year before the relationship passed from professional to personal, but Hague knew from the start that she and he would be good friends. To the wider public Hague's eagerness to learn about Wales was a plus, but his political hue and Yorkshire accent were bound to impede his progress. When Hague's fact-finding tour took him to the National Eisteddfod in

Abergele his trip was marred by protesters from the Welsh Language Society campaigning for a devolved government with responsibility for Welsh education. Jenkins had tried to put potential protesters off the scent by planting news of ministerial appointments elsewhere in Wales. On a similar occasion with John Redwood the two had been locked into a school by nationalist protesters and had had to escape over a dry stone wall. Such protests were the more graphic end of a general scepticism captured in more light-hearted style by the *Western Mail* cartoonist Mumph. With a flat cap, a blazer and a liberal smattering of 'ee bah gums', the new Secretary of State for Wales was portrayed as a Yorkshire schoolboy.

So how would this relative political novice attempt to build a grown-up reputation in Wales? To add substance to the astute PR exercise of touring the country and signalling his willingness to learn Welsh, Hague looked to reversing some of the more unpopular of Redwood's decisions. He wanted to prove that his grand tour had taught him something about the unique requirements of Wales, that he had been genuinely impressed by what he had seen. Fittingly his first move was to mark the environment as one of his priorities. This was consistent with his own beliefs, reflecting the heritage of his brand of traditional Conservatism and pride in Britain.

An early visit to the Countryside Council for Wales in the northern cathedral town of Bangor convinced him to reverse John Redwood's budget cuts to the quango. Redwood had considered the organisation wasteful and cut its funding by £3 million as well as moving to reduce its powers. Hague overturned the decisions and delivered an early white paper on rural affairs. The paper, 'A Working Countryside for Wales', was launched to mixed reviews in the Llanerch Vineyard, Vale of Glamorgan, in March 1996. Although there was little new money available for the initiative it was a mark of Hague's genuine concern to acknowledge the particular needs of a largely rural economy and its under-resourced village communities.

Hague's second U-turn on Welsh Office policy concerned a far more sensitive issue that was to become the focus of a national outcry. Before his departure John Redwood had ruled against a public inquiry into allegations of child abuse in North Wales children's homes. There had already been a lengthy inquiry resulting in some arrests but the local authority involved had cited legal reasons for not making its findings public. It had not been an easy decision for Redwood as it was quite possible that a second inquiry might achieve little more whilst once again forcing victims through a harrowing process and diverting millions of pounds of funds away from core services. In early 1996 it began to become obvious that the government would have to rethink that decision. The campaign was taken up to effect by the Opposition. The shadow welsh secretary, Ron Davies, raised the unedifying prospect that the results of the existing report were being suppressed to prevent victims making costly compensation claims against Flintshire County Council. Officials in the Welsh Office knew that Hague felt minded to act but would have to devise a strategy for reopening the issue. Against the background of a growing campaign for a media inquiry, any delay by the government would open them to accusations of complacency, but Hague was in no position to rush a decision. He was the most junior member of the cabinet having to convince colleagues that the government should overturn its previous decision, and he had to consider a way of doing this that would not automatically imply that the government had made a grave error of judgement in their first decision.

Where he was able to Hague indicated that he favoured a review of the original decision. In meetings with the Opposition and in dealings with Flintshire County Council between April and June, Hague would not rule out a public inquiry. By the time that he was able to announce a new judicial inquiry, his lobbying had helped galvanise a coordinated campaign by the Conservative Government. In June, John Major announced a national investigation into sexual abuse in children's homes to be led by Sir William Utting, Chairman of the National Institute for Social Work. A few days later Hague unveiled plans for a judicial inquiry into the specific case of the Clwyd allegations to be carried out by High Court judge Sir Ronald Waterhouse. At the same time the Home Secretary Michael Howard tightened laws covering the care of children, and Health Secretary Stephen Dorrell launched a review of childcare. The Waterhouse Inquiry finally issued its harrowing report in February 2000.

Whenever possible Hague would indulge his enthusiasm for walking in the Welsh countryside. In typical Hague style these were never relaxing meanders. Instead he would undertake serious outings around Snowdonia. Colleagues at work were rather intimidated by his casual references to having completed the Three Peaks Walk on a day off from the principality. By most people's standards a twelve-hour walk (which Hague now completes in under eight) through Pen-y-Ghent in the Yorkshire Dales would be testing exercise. For Hague it was a pleasant way to keep fit for a lifestyle that was physically demanding. Many weekdays started in his office at the Welsh Office, Gwydyr House in Whitehall, and ended back at the House for a late vote, having travelled down to and back from Cardiff. Occasionally he would stay overnight in Cardiff at the official ministerial flat: this was a functional affair with basic accommodation, floral wallpaper and kitchenette, but as with all apartments the main selling point was location, location, location. The flat was just across the hall from his office. At weekends he would make the round trip from Cardiff to Richmond and then back to London for Monday mornings.

Consequently his bachelor lifestyle was quite ascetic. His homes in London and Yorkshire were neat and bare. He had little time for entertaining and was generally catered for by official events and constituency functions. There were plenty of Yorkshire matrons happy to indulge their talented young MP with chicken dinners and chocolate cake teas. In the Welsh Office he was even offered help buying clothes. His diary secretary Ruth Thomas went shopping with him, not because he was especially sartorially challenged, but because he is colour blind.

When asked about his own aims for office Hague always named as his top priority assisting the Welsh economy and bringing jobs to the principality. He was unapologetic about the 'Yes it hurt, yes it worked' rhetoric of the Major government, but also assiduous in playing his part in attracting new business to the valleys. Redwood had cut the budget of the Welsh Development Agency. Hague increased it, although never to the levels it had reached under Redwood's predecessor David Hunt. Whereas there was always a suspicion that Redwood's free market convictions would make it difficult for him to embrace the full panoply of state mechanisms for attracting private investment, there was no such concern about Hague. Similarly Hague was more than willing to take full advantage of EU membership for negotiating a better deal for Wales. Brussels was Hague's first overseas visit as Secretary of State. His trip was to sort out a row about European funds for Wales held up in a dispute between the Commission and Welsh Office. Later he visited the Wales European Centre in Brussels to encourage its role in promoting the interests of Wales in Europe. It was something that Redwood had never done, but Welsh Conservative enthusiasts for Europe recognised that the difference between the two men was largely presentational. Their representative on Europe's Committee of the Regions, Lord Kenyon, suggested that as far as Europe was concerned Redwood and Hague had similar views but a different approach: 'Hague is no great Europhile, but certainly when he says no he says it with a smile.'

If Hague had wanted his time at Wales judged according to his success in attracting investment he had certainly set the right criterion. His record as Secretary of State was notable for unprecedented levels of inward investment. In the year to April 1996 the Welsh Development Agency secured 120 projects creating and safeguarding 12,000 jobs, a total investment of £970 million. In the House of Commons, Ron Davies accused Hague of offering Wales Korean 'cast-offs'. He said that manufacturers Ronson had transferred production from Korea to Wales because wages were 20 per cent lower there. Certainly labour costs and flexibility were an attraction to overseas investors but Hague played an active role in securing investment for Wales against stiff competition from other parts of the United Kingdom. The real jewel in his crown was the LG (Lucky Goldstar Group) project, which brought over six thousand jobs to Newport in Europe's biggest ever inward investment project. Although such deals are months in the making with all the relevant machinery of government geared toward securing the contract, the individual contribution of a minister can make all the difference. Key members of the Welsh Office staff noted Hague's determination to win the electronics deal which involved motivating all his departments to deliver the necessary infrastructure requirements as well as establishing his all-important personal relationship with the South Korean negotiators. It took ten months of intense negotiations to secure the package. Hague informed none of his cabinet colleagues about his progress, lest he display his cards before the game was won. When at the eleventh hour the deal was nearly lost because an early leak of its successful conclusion appeared on BBC news, it was Hague who repaired the damage. To the company this was a dishonourable breach of confidence. The crisis was overcome only with Hague's direct intervention and diplomatic reassurances, although once he was sure of the deal he leaked the news himself.

Hague was taking a weekend flight to Korea to sign contracts. The day before he had delighted John Major with the news and had informed William Waldegrave that the deal was done and the Treasury would have to fulfil its obligations to inward investment. Television news crews based in Singapore were already gearing up to fly to Korea to cover the triumphant news conference. Waldegrave was bounced into rubber stamping what turned out to be the largest ever selective assistance grant to an incoming company. Hague had one more duty, to drink for Britain, and he and the British Ambassador left the final dinner with LG bosses upright, but only just. In customary style the celebrations were marked with alcoholic toasts, but the cocktails of choice were strangely prosaic. The first few rounds were Atom Bombs, glasses of beer with shots of whisky dropped into them. When the tipples progressed to Hydrogen Bombs, whisky with shots of beer, Hague was grateful for his now well-documented capacity to hold his drink. The hangover was bearable, as delivering the LG deal to Wales brought Hague glowing write-ups in the Welsh press and the first serious suggestions that he could succeed John Major as his party's next leader.

Wales's good fortune in attracting the multi-billion pound deal was won at the expense of her key national rival, Scotland. The industrial deal had brought Hague into direct competition with Scottish Secretary Michael (now Lord) Forsyth. It was an irony because the two worked very much in tandem on the Conservative campaign against Labour's devolution proposals. Hague had made his ministerial debut at the party conference in 1995 concentrating not so much on Wales but on his youth. Along with Seb Coe, then MP for Falmouth, Hague cast a 'Spotlight on the Young'. Two years before the Tories were resoundingly defeated Hague told his predominantly elderly audience that 'for the first time since the 1930s we are seeing a young generation which is not the natural ally of the political left. His next double act at conference featured Michael Forsyth. The constitution debate at the 1996 conference brought Hague, a relatively low-profile member of the cabinet, his starring moment. 'It is deep in the instincts of our party that where the flag of the Union is in greatest danger we must fight as hard as we can. . . They can fly the white flag of surrender but we will fight for the Union Jack.' It was stirring stuff delivered in an engagingly relaxed manner, Hague and Forsyth in shirt sleeves. Of the two it was Hague that shone, a successful profile-raising exercise only months before the 1997 General Election.

From the start Hague made it clear that he was implacably opposed to plans for a Welsh Assembly but he was to go much further than his predecessor and others on the right, in acknowledging Welsh aspirations to self-government. Ron Davies handed Hague an early PR coup by leading a boycott by Labour MPs of his first session of Welsh Questions in the Commons in July 1995. The tactic backfired, giving Hague a free ride in the House and a sympathetic hearing in the Welsh press. There was little love lost between Hague and his Labour shadow. Davies had protested about Hague's tour of Wales, suggesting he was taking a holiday at the taxpayers' expense. When Davies later remarked that Prince Charles was unfit to be King, Hague relished his retort. He branded Davies a lager lout and decried the 'rash, crude, intemperate remarks by a man who's not fit to be in government in a party not fit to govern.'

Although Hague had never been less than blunt about his objections to an Assembly – 'a waste of time, a waste of space and a waste of money. It would weaken not strengthen the position of Wales in the United Kingdom' (Welsh Questions, 17 June 1996) – his tactics were to offer some concessions towards devolution. His first move was to back a reform of the Welsh Grand

Committee. This committee had been set up by David Hunt, when Secretary of State, as a mechanism for making the Welsh Secretary and his ministerial team more accountable to MPs in Wales. Hague suggested the Grand Committee meet more often in Wales, calling at different locations around the principality. Following a precedent established in Scotland, the Committee would also have the right to question cabinet members on matters affecting Wales, but it would have no power to scrutinise legislation. A dispute between Hague and Davies held up the meetings of the Committee and succeeded in making it little more than an academic concession. Although Hague saw a certain value in encouraging Welsh members to meet in Wales, his plan was essentially a tactic to divert attention from the arguments for an Assembly. At least one of the then Conservative MPs in Wales, Walter Sweeney, criticised the tactic as a sop to the nationalists.

Similarly, Hague's move to increase the powers of Welsh local authorities did not meet universal approval within his own party. In a move that again echoed arrangements in Scotland, Hague told the Commons in February 1996 that he would devolve powers over European funding programmes and regeneration schemes from the Welsh Office to local authorities. He described it as one of the biggest transfers of functions towards local government set out by a recent Secretary of State. The move was welcomed by shadow minister Rhodri Morgan, only reinforcing the doubts of those Conservatives who questioned the political sense in bolstering the power of Labour local authorities. Hague saw a definite political advantage. Devolving powers to local authorities would give them a vested interest in opposing an Assembly likely to claim back those responsibilities.

Hague's strong defence of the Union and obvious successes in Wales were winning him a good press and vindicating Major's decision to promote him. In cabinet Hague had his natural allies in the fellow Eurosceptics, but Major never considered him anything but loyal. Major was angry and dismayed when Hague later made his speech criticising the 'constantly shifting fudge' of his leadership. As far as Major was concerned, if there had been a fudge then Hague had been a part of it. In April 1996 Major's decision to hold a referendum on future Euro entry presented Hague with a dilemma. Although he agreed with Michael Portillo that such a referendum was not desirable, he decided not to oppose it. Major knew that Portillo considered such a referendum an abrogation of government responsibility, but he was not aware that Hague doubted its wisdom. Hague was able to convince himself that since the government was not going to rule out Euro entry, a referendum was at least a way of delaying it.

He took an equally pragmatic line on another issue that never became policy but which nevertheless came to be seen as a litmus test for defining different shades of opinion on the right. In the search for an answer to Tony Blair's dynamic soundbite, 'tough on crime, tough on the causes of crime', the Conservatives flirted with the idea of recommending identity cards. Some on the right were appalled at the implications for individual liberty: the move threatened to make people accountable to the state rather than maintain the British tradition that the state should be accountable to the people. As ministers in the Department of Social Security, Hague and Peter Lilley had investigated the option of ID cards to counteract fraud, but found no convincing arguments that they would achieve this. Hague lined up with colleagues who opposed the proposals, but his objection was not on libertarian grounds: he simply did not think they would work in cutting crime.

In Wales later that year Hague suggested a remedy he favoured for indiscipline in schools. He found himself quickly having to deflect a potential political embarrassment brought on by his admission to a Welsh newspaper that he was in favour of the use of the birch – exactly the sort of policy that gave the over-enthusiastic Young Conservatives a bad name. It had been a policy of Hague's as a YC, but in a Secretary of State it was more contentious. Hague had to sidestep the matter by stressing that it was his personal view and that he was not advocating a change of government policy.

There was one issue on which Hague was pleased to declare his hand. Along with Michael Howard, Peter Lilley and Stephen Dorrell, Hague led an open campaign to defeat John Major's plans to reform divorce legislation. This was not a full-scale revolt as whips anticipated significant unease and granted a free vote. Lord Mackay's Family Law Bill was significantly compromised with its proposed cooling off period of twelve months extended to eighteen months as a result of the protest. The issue had spilt the Tory party for months with considerable criticism from the Conservative press. Family and marriage had always been a linchpin of Hague's Conservatism. His objections to Mackay's bill were born of conviction.

Progress towards establishing a marriage and family of his own was initially slow, but Hague had increasingly come to enjoy the company of his private secretary, Ffion Jenkins – a fellow Oxford graduate, clearly bright, efficient and charming. He was impressed by and attracted to her passionate love for Wales and its culture. It was, as Hague says, 'friendship at first sight'. Hague had always reasoned that regional differences should be valued, but until he met Ffion he had not appreciated the particular role of the Welsh tongue in defining a sense of nationhood for her country: it was her and her family's first language.

In some respects the relationship was an attraction of opposites. Coming from a hard-working, matter-of-fact background, Hague had little interest in the arts or literature. Jenkins, however, hailed from the relative exotica of the Cardiff literati, her father Emyr a former director of the National Eisteddfod. She could broaden his horizons as far as music and culture were concerned but would not presume to challenge his political beliefs. As a civil servant Ffion had to rise above party politics, but as she was far more motivated by the cause of Wales than by a particular philosophy this did not present her with a problem.

The working relationship turned to friendship and then to romance, and it was soon clear that politics would not be a cause of arguments. Unlike the Blairs, who share political conviction and motivation, politics is not a subject of conversation for the Hagues. This suited William well: he knows what he believes and prefers not to debate it off duty.

Ffion too had come to enjoy the company of her boss, but as a conscientious career civil servant she was in no rush to complicate matters. She admired Hague's intellect, ability and his ambition. Eventually, after they had worked very closely together for fifteen months, Hague spotted an opportunity to take things further at an official function the two were attending, the Prudential Arts Awards at the Tate Gallery. That evening Ffion faced stiff competition: at dinner William was sitting next to Deborah Ball, and he quickly discovered an enthusiasm for ballet. In fact he was less interested in the ballet than in the dancer, who definitely met his number one physical requirement in a woman – slim ankles. Even more precisely than a 'legs man', Hague is an 'ankles man'. In Hague's eyes Ffion had the advantage both of slim ankles and blonde hair so, emboldened by the bonhomie of the evening, Hague suggested they go on for a drink at the end of their official duties.

It was hard for Jenkins to switch off. Hague suggested she stop calling him Secretary of State. 'OK, Secretary of State,' she replied.

The ice was broken. It was October 1996 and the romance was to move on in leaps and bounds although both were remarkably discreet. They were keen to keep the relationship a secret until they were sure it was serious enough to survive public scrutiny. No one else in the Welsh Office knew about the relationship until it was well advanced, not even the three other women who shared an office with Ffion.

For less self-disciplined people the illusion of normality would have been difficult to maintain. The Hagues are equally composed and self-contained. Ffion particularly guards her privacy fiercely, sometimes too fiercely, as she deters positive coverage as much as more prurient press interest. Hague has always had the ability to elude close inspection. He remains an unusually private person, who friends and colleagues find frustratingly hard to read. He often uses humour to deflect criticism and control a conversation, but sometimes at crucial moments the jokes run out and he is left unable to make small talk. As leader his containment has been a mixed blessing, helping him to maintain an even temper but inclining him against developing relationships beyond the clique of his private office. Few people in the party feel they have established a rapport with Hague. Criticism early in his leadership that he foolishly avoided seeking advice from more experienced figures has persisted. Others just think he is socially awkward.

His and Ffion's discretion and consequent lack of displays of public affection have been interpreted as signs that this was not a serious romance and that the relationship was more about mutual advancement than love. Not surprisingly the couple dispute this, and the testimony of Hague's friends and family suggest the two had fallen very much in love. Once the couple married they later visited Hague's parents for Christmas. His family were left in no doubt about their closeness. One of his relatives said, 'The Hague family are not particularly demonstrative but William and Ffion couldn't keep their hands off each other. We didn't know where to look.'

The furtive nature of the affair was enhanced by the excitement of early meetings. Dates were either spent at Hague's Dolphin Square flat or at Jenkins's flat in Putney. Neither were particularly bothered that Hague's relative celebrity kept them holed up. After all, as Hague told friends, in the early stages of a relationship 'there are better things to do than go out!' The situation involved careful planning. Hague would often take a ministerial car back to his own home, and then make his own way over to Putney. Of course they would travel to work separately, Hague sometimes returning to his own flat in the early hours of the morning.

On the personal front the relationship seemed to work effortlessly. Hague found himself fascinated by this very cultured, arts-loving literature fan. She was drawn to his sense of humour and remarkable knowledge of history and the world.

That Christmas Hague travelled to Montana for a ski-ing trip with his university friend Gary Jackson. Even if he had wanted to keep his relationship with Ffion a secret, his demeanour suggested that something was up. Jackson had never seen him so distracted and excited. It was the first time Hague had seemed in love. He caused a great fuss in having to find an international calling card so that he could phone Ffion from the slopes. His friends were delighted that at long last Hague had entered the real world. He was even prepared to try new restaurants: on previous trips with Jackson he had insisted on sticking to tried and tested options.

Of his previous girlfriends three had been serious enough to meet his parents, but he had never felt he wanted to make a life with any of them. His friendship with childhood sweetheart Kim Birch had long survived their romance. She had been particularly popular among Wentworth Conservatives who thought her devotion to William would make her an excellent constituency wife. They probably underestimated her as Birch has made a successful career for herself in a Sheffield law firm although she has never married. Kim and William's relationship was off and on for a while but they drifted apart for the last time when she returned to Yorkshire after a spell working in London. The two have remained good friends, so much so that when William first fell for Ffion he asked Birch for advice.

'There is a girl in my office I'm quite keen on, but as we work together I'm not sure what to do,' he confided in her.

'If you like her, go for it,' was Birch's suggestion.

When William first became an MP he went out with Barbara Kyriakou, now Commons secretary to Archie Norman. Hague met her while he was working on John Major's leadership campaign, when she was secretary to Sir Graham Bright, Major's PPS. Commons rumours have it that the relationship never progressed further than a friendship, although it lasted a couple of years. Kyriakou, also a slim blonde, was a hit with Hague's family, particularly Nigel Hague who was very keen for his son to marry. Despite his father's encouragement William did not feel that Barbara was the one for him. Her ballgown was still hanging in his spare bedroom when he became engaged to Ffion. According to friends of William it was John Major who unknowingly precipitated the end of the relationship. They say Major happened to ask Kyriakou how things were proceeding with Hague. When she replied 'too slowly' he suggested she force the pace. The tactic backfired and Kyriakou was heard to say that she would never listen to John Major again. Major does not recall the story but it has become the stuff of legend among close friends of Hague.

Hague's next girlfriend was Jane Hardman, a city PR executive. Hardman's relationship with Hague prompted gossip-column speculation as she was a rather glamorous associate for the highly tipped young minister. Hague's parents were of the impression that the Conservative Party hierarchy rather approved of this match. To Nigel Hague's incitement to marriage were added the approving comments of John Major and Jeffrey Archer. Hague told his mother that they had said, 'Go for it, she's a stunner!' But Hague treated their suggestions with the same lack of seriousness as his father's regular mentions of marriage: he ignored them. The circumstances of Hague's split with Hardman remain unclear. Friends of Hague understood that Hardman enjoyed going out and attending functions with him but was reluctant for things to turn more serious. Rumours in the House suggested that the two had broken up because of Hague's control-freak timekeeping, that he had been unforgiving when kept waiting at the start of an evening. Hague flatly denies the newspaper rumours that surfaced during his leadership election that he proposed to Hardman, or indeed to anyone other than Ffion. Hardman has never commented.

Hague had always told his family he would marry when he wanted to and not before, and he would not allow his career to dictate whom he should marry. His mother knew immediately her son mentioned Ffion that the relationship was far more serious than any previous. The early days were delightfully effort-less. They knew each other well from fifteen months working in each other pockets, and as each knew intimately the details of the other's working days there was a built-in incentive not to discuss work in their private time together. It established a pattern that suits them both.

Temperamentally William and Ffion are very similar. Like Hague, Jenkins is very self-motivated and self-assured. They both have their own careers but prefer to leave discussion of them in their respective offices. Since Jenkins left the civil service she has worked for Arts and Business, an agency finding commercial funding for the arts, and now for Leonard Hull as a head hunter. Her current job has allowed the couple more time together, since she has fewer evening events and can sometimes work from home. Hague's prominence has also given her access to other opportunities, such as her role on the British Council. Adjusting to the demands of her husband's job has been hard. She attends more than a hundred functions with him in a year, and although she professes to have had no interest in a political career, she certainly works a room better than most politicians. Naturally graceful and attentive, Ffion has proved a very valuable asset to Hague's progress through the reception circuit. It has taken time for Hague to grow into the demands of high office. More seasoned colleagues noted his early, rather clumsy dealings with foreign dignitaries. Lord Cranborne described his handling of a meeting with Henry Kissinger as 'an embarrassment'. Hague was certainly aware that what he lacked in charisma Ffion would add in polish. When she was at Arts and Business he accompanied her to one event, such are the demands of his schedule. Even if she has had to make more concessions towards supporting his work than can be helpful for her own career progression, the couple are jointly agreed that they will not be rushed into having children. In essence they are a model professional 'power couple', married with good incomes and no children and enjoying the lifestyle. They take as many holidays as schedules allow, particularly enjoying cross-country ski-ing, and they are in no hurry to disturb this just yet.

When Hague proposed to Ffion over dinner at the Black Bull, a Richmond hostelry famed for its cooking, it was not a great surprise. Although the two had only been going out for five months they had now known each other for a year and half. It was 21 February 1997, Ffion's 29th birthday, and the day after she had left the Welsh Office, having decided a short while previously to look for another job.

She said yes immediately. Hague telephoned his mother the next day but warned her not to go public with the news. For one thing he had not yet asked Ffion's father for permission, a rather old-fashioned habit but appropriate when winning the respect of the tight-knit, traditional Welsh family that Hague was marrying into. For another, Hague wanted to keep the news private until he was able to announce the details to the press, which he did in early March to the *Yorkshire Post* and the *Western Mail*.

With an election in the offing William and Ffion decided to postpone planning their wedding until the campaign was over.

Hague's period at the Welsh Office had paid him personal and political dividends, yet the benefits to his party's fortunes were less obvious. His record was marked by an increase in public spending by the Welsh Office, in line with the general increase in the run-up to the election, but Hague did cut administrative costs more than his predecessor. He expected that the remaining six Conservative seats in Wales would be lost in what was always likely to be a severe defeat for his party. With the prospect of a leadership election looming, he was happy to accept Major's invitation to a special role as one of four cabinet ministers with particular responsibility for presentation of policy. It offered him the chance to impress his peers and seemed to some party insiders more of a priority to him than his own brief: as a minister with broad-ranging responsibilities he took surprisingly little interest in the development of the Conservative manifesto for Wales, frustrating party staff trying to finalise the document.

His own election campaign was efficient and low key, and he did not put a foot wrong although he was right in anticipating a Welsh wipe-out for the Conservatives. In Wales as elsewhere Conservative fortunes had been dwindling for years. It was perhaps too much to expect that he could reverse the trend single-handed in less than two years. His political contribution is best reflected in the very close results for the 1997 referendum on Welsh devolution. As leader of his party Hague continued a high-profile campaign against the proposed assembly. Labour managed only a very narrow victory, suggesting that Hague's consistently practical objections had made some impact.

Fortunately the devolution campaign was over and done with by the time of the wedding late in 1997, since it is likely that William and Ffion held different views on that subject.

With the option of a service in the House of Commons chapel, Ffion was content to have the wedding in London. By now Conservative leader, Hague was busy planning the reorganisation of the party, so she set to organising the nuptials. The added advantage of a marriage in the Palace of Westminster was the built-in privacy: the whole event, service and reception, could be catered for within the secure area.

The Speaker, Betty Boothroyd, played her part in ensuring the couple avoid the paparazzi. Seb Coe visited her to ask if it would be possible for the newlyweds to depart via the river. At first she was not too happy with the idea. The Speaker's Steps were coated with years of slippery grime from the Thames. She predicted a disaster of really embarrassing proportions if either party were to slip while trying to climb the steps to reach a boat. After a couple of drinks Boothroyd decided to take Coe out to inspect the steps, and rather enjoying the prospect of reviving a much neglected feature of Westminster she relented: as long as Hague paid, she was prepared to have the steps cleaned and a special platform built to enable a river departure.

Alan Duncan was to play the similar role of fending off embarrassments at Hague's stag do. The event was very Haguian, a little too much so for some of his friends. Those who had known Hague before his most recent and most serious fitness fad were ill prepared for the physical feat that awaited them. School and university friends like David Rusby, Guy Hands, Brooks Newmark and Gary Jackson would have been happy with wine, women and song. Others who had accompanied Hague on his more physical pursuits – Seb Coe and Nick Gleave (a constituency aide who now has an election planning role in Central Office) who had worked out with him, and Nick Levy (best man) with whom he had trekked through Northern Thailand – were less surprised at the activity weekend. In a male bonding session more redolent of an outward bound course than a boys' weekend, Hague led an expedition climbing Ben Nevis. Not everyone made it to the top. Even one of the guests mused that this was more 'men behaving sadly' than 'men behaving badly'. Hands attempted to divert to Fort William to arrange some less salubrious entertainment but was restrained by Duncan. The evening was spent at the Inverlochy Castle Hotel where good food and wine was the priority, but by Hague's standards this was a fairly sober affair. His old friends sensed that the responsibilities of leadership were cramping his style. At a previous stag event where Hague had been the guest of his school friend Keith Washington he had initiated the festivities and was later held responsible for the breaking of the honeymoon suite bed in a wedding day prank.

In London, Hague held another even more decorous event at the West End's least hip location, the Carlton Club. The true blue reception for MPs was made slightly bluer by the arrival of some strippers courtesy of a cable TV channel. Two days before the wedding Hague was still relishing his duties at the dispatch box, telling the House, following the difficulties of Paymaster General Geoffrey Robinson: 'The Prime Minster will forgive me for suggesting that just as his honeymoon is coming to an end mine is about to begin.' On his wedding day, 19 December 1997, he returned to the Carlton for the ushers' lunch. The previous evening he and Ffion had entertained family and friends at the St Ermin's Hotel in Victoria – a high Gothic building which provides a romantic backdrop for television and film sets. Guests included old family friends who went back years. Pat and Ray Swift, who had accompanied Hague to the party conference in

1977, thought he seemed even more proud than he had done at his national political debut.

The wedding in the Palace of Westminster was an Anglo-Welsh affair at which the Welsh definitely outsang the English. The Hagues successfully evaded the press and made their dramatic departure down the Thames after a wedding supper in the Members' dining room. The honeymoon had also been planned with absolute privacy in mind. Hague had chosen to revisit India, the site of an earlier adventure holiday with Nick Levy during his early twenties. The Indian High Commissioner Dr Singh Vi, who had become a close friend, arranged for escorts to take the couple through Delhi airport and suggested a grand fortress hotel on the way to Jaipur. It was a luxurious, exotic break with camel treks and elephants and tigers for company. After an idyllic two weeks it was time for Hague to return to the Westminster jungle.

Chapter Eight

THE FRESH FUTURE

No change is not an option. We need to renew our organisation, rebuild our membership and rejuvenate our party if we are once again to become the dominant political force in the land, representing the whole country in local and national government.

William Hague, Leader of the Conservative Party,
23 July 1997

A few minutes before four o'clock on 23 July 1997 an expectant hush fell over the press conference room at 32 Smith Square. In the same room a month before, William Hague had been inaugurated leader, confirmed in the role by a Party convention that he had vowed to abolish. For the first time since then, Hague was to address representatives from all sections of his party – voluntary, professional, councillors, MPs, peers and MEPs. The windowless meeting room was packed to the brim as anxious, excited advisers paced around the edges, aware that as players in the new regime they were contributing to a radical overhaul of one of the world's oldest political parties.

The meeting was the closest thing to a 'special conference' that it had been possible to arrange hastily in the month since Hague had become leader. Aware of the grass roots clamour to democratise his party, Hague had promised a special conference at which members could confirm his appointment. His new Chairman, Lord Parkinson, had had to temper the enthusiasm of those he privately called Hague's 'boy scouts' by reminding them of the logistical problems and, more pressingly, financial strictures which made a full-scale conference ahead of the annual October meeting a practical impossibility. So 23 July became the first stage of that process, outlining Hague's principles for reform and promising to put them before party members in a ballot before the October conference.

Having prematurely achieved his life's ambition to lead the Conservative Party, Hague now had everything to prove. His rise through academia, business and politics had been swift and trouble-free. Inevitably the leadership, his biggest challenge, held the greatest potential for failure.

From the start he faced the constant jibe that he was merely a caretaker, holding the fort for a bigger figure to return to the House. In the early months his low public profile was heightened only negatively by a series of public relations disasters which served to reinforce the impression that while in Blair youth equalled dynamism, in Hague it equalled inexperience. Some Conservatives argued that the new leader needed to give the opposition a sense of policy direction quickly if it was to find a coherent position from which to counter the government. This was not the view of Hague or his advisers: he feared tying his party to premature policy commitments, and believed that Conservatives could not compete with Mr Blair's honeymoon for media coverage. In human terms as well the party was exhausted after the long haul of the general election and a divisive leadership campaign, and simply no match for the machine that New Labour had thrown behind its 'First 100 Days' campaign. However, Hague had already identified a common cause for his party. The reforms were more than a politically convenient project; they were a vital necessity.

Throughout the Thatcher years the popularity of the government had given rise to something of a myth about the brilliant party machine at Conservative Central Office and in the country. Not only was it creaking, inefficient and poorly resourced by the time of the 1997 election, it was rendered even less effective by the decentralised structure of the party as a whole. In fact the Conservative Party as a single entity did not exist. In an appropriately organic fashion it had grown up over the years with a separate body, the National Union, representing the party members, the parliamentary party comprising both MPs and peers, and a professionally staffed Central Office working ultimately to the leader. Each section had guarded its power base with vehemence. During the good times the system seemed to work, but during the troubled Major years its weaknesses were exposed at the party's expense. Local constituency associations cherished their independence – so much so that many had grown suspicious of a Central Office that they considered unaccountable. Why should they work hard to contribute funds to Central Office if the chairman made all the decisions as to how the money should be spent and the party frequently ended up in debt? Many activists blamed MPs for the fate of the party. Disunity at Westminster stoked resentment at the grass roots. In the face of Labour's democratising reforms, many Tory members wondered why their unreliable MPs had sole domain over the choice of the party leader, and why it was so difficult to remove them once their contribution had ceased to be effective. MPs, on the other hand, felt that the National Union had allowed the party in the country to grow old and wither. In the midst of this mutual suspicion, the leader John Major had no ultimate sanction against disreputable MPs.

The case of Neil Hamilton, the Tory MP deeply implicated in the 'Cash for Questions' affair, pointed to the crisis in the system. In defence of its independence the Tatton Conservative

Association backed its MP, whose crass vulgarity was enough to deserve reprimand of itself, whilst party leaders were technically powerless to intervene. The party appeared corrupt, complacent, and inept, hardly a good advertisement for winning an election or motivating its own supporters.

In the month since Hague's victory it had become clear that he would need to summon up all of his highly celebrated management skills if he was to unite his party, divided as it was by more than ideological schism. For years the public had watched the factional warfare conducted in the glare of the media spotlight. Less known was the power-brokering and consequent personal antagonisms that were bubbling beneath the surface. The reform process and later streamlining of the professional operation were set to intensify these divisions in a negotiation that pitted the bullish Sir Archie Hamilton, chairman of the 1922 Committee, against the cunning Robin Hodgson, leader of the voluntary party's National Union, and the ruthless new vice-chairman of the party Archie Norman against the resistant campaigning chief Sir Tony Garrett.

During the leadership campaign William Hague made party reform the unique selling point of his bid to become Conservative leader. Other candidates took up the cause, but none with quite the enthusiasm or urgency of Hague's campaign. It was a platform that had offered him a distinctive mantle for the competition, but his advocacy of it was more than expedient. Although in the early days of the campaign Hague had not known exactly what remedy was needed, he did become convinced that comprehensive reform was vital. Apart from the practical need for change, New Labour's modernisers had shown that a commitment to democratic reform was popular with the general public. Both Hodgson and Norman discussed their proposals with Hague, with many of these early ideas shaping the later progress of the project.

It was not the first time that defeat had forced the party to look at its structure and effectiveness: the most comprehensive reforms of modern times had followed the defeat of 1945, when party leaders revamped the Conservative Research Department and tightened up the rules governing the amount of money which candidates could contribute to their own campaigns. The then party chairman, Lord Woolton, also developed a way of attracting new members by establishing the new Young Conservative network and a policy consultation programme through the Conservative Political Centre. Attention was turned to Central Office in the 1990s, when Sir Norman Fowler made the first steps in establishing a governing board for the party.

As Hague was the least known of the leadership contenders, his stance on party reform risked reinforcing the common view that his politics were little more than managerial. To Conservatives looking for the 'vision thing' Hague's emphasis on internal reform seemed to confirm their worst fears that conviction politics were becoming swamped by the culture of management consultancy. There was also the risk that with the youngest candidate and an obviously youthful team, the Haguites seemed too eager to replicate the moves which New Labour's key players had taken to rejuvenate their own cause, without taking account of the cultural differences between the two parties. For all its administrative weaknesses the Conservative Party had always been less centralised than Labour, a feature that often frustrated the leadership but which was popular with the members. More experienced members of staff worried that the lust for change risked throwing the baby out with the bath water: there was certainly a sense of the prefects taking over the school in the manner of the keen young things poised to take the party's leadership and its incumbent patronage. As he developed his views during the leadership campaign Hague contemplated not appointing a party chairman. Attracted to an idea developed for him by John Maples, he considered replicating the Labour model that separated party management from political strategy. Hague wondered about replacing the post of chairman with a more anonymous role of party manager, or general secretary. His fantasy model saw the management team in one building, and the political operation housed elsewhere in a modern media centre.

As a first draft it was rather too ambitious, both culturally and financially. Hague was attracted by the idea that in opposition the leader was in a stronger position to promote the big changes which he realised he would have to undertake and take the Central Office traditionalists with him as he did so. Although he seriously considered scrapping the role of chairman, he thought again after appreciating that such a step could convey the appearance of arrogance.

The rethink was underlined by strategic reality, as during the leadership campaign two of the party's power bases had already come to blows. Robin Hodgson, head of the National Union, had campaigned to break the MPs' monopoly over voting in the leadership election. In the shell-shocked aftermath of the general election it was Sir Archie Hamilton, chairman of the 1922 Committee, who won the short-term battle to keep that particular leadership contest the sole preserve of MPs. Hodgson, who had been campaigning for months to give the National Union greater prominence, hoped to force the pace of change by employing the Electoral Reform Society to poll constituency chairmen at each stage of the leadership ballot. The published poll certainly achieved Hodgson's aim of giving the party members' grievances a higher profile, but it also made MPs even more aware that when choosing a party leader their views weren't necessarily shared by the members. If anything, the poll hardened the resolve of MPs to cede as little as possible in any future debate on the introduction of an electoral college for the leadership elections.

Hague was well aware of this tension, as he was the poor state of the party's professional machine in Central Office and throughout the country, and in those circumstances the suggestion of Lord Parkinson as Chairman made a great deal of sense. At the time it was becoming clear that Hague's line on Europe would exclude the best known of the big guns of Major's cabinet, and Parkinson offered the weight of experience and association with the grandest of Conservative grandees. Although Parkinson's return seemed at once to undermine Hague's message about a fresh start, it was a necessary manoeuvre. Hague believed Parkinson brought the stature and diplomacy necessary to take all sections of a cautious, and in some parts unwilling, party along with the reform process.

Lord Parkinson (who had no vote in the leadership election) was the only appointee whose post was offered before the final ballot. Indeed, until the revelation of the Clarke-Redwood pact he was not keen to take up the offer. Hague had offered him the job on the Tuesday of the second ballot, 17 June, but Lady Parkinson had been less than enthusiastic about the prospect of her husband's return to so high-profile a political role. Another by-product of Wednesday's incredible alliance was the response to Lady Parkinson, whose reaction to events was to urge her husband to back William wholeheartedly. Throughout the day on Thursday, Hague had tried to contact Parkinson for an answer, but had been unable to reach him at Royal Ascot. He had his answer in person at the celebration party in the campaign head offices. Lord and Lady Parkinson went straight from the traditional finery of Ascot to toast the new leader and confirm their role in the next phase of Conservative history.

The first tasks were to appoint the personnel to carry out the reforms and to develop the key themes that were outlined to the party on 23 July. Parkinson's appointment was not uncontroversial – Archie Norman, for one, eager to see his former professional colleague modernise the Tories, pondered the wisdom of bringing back a figure from the *ancién regime* – but as surprise dissipated it was soon understood by most as a pragmatic, consolidating move. Amid the gloomy post-election pall and anticipated job losses, Central Office staff appreciated the return of Parkinson, whose avuncular charm softened the blows of adjusting to opposition. More controversial was the extent to which less tried and tested members of Hague's leadership campaign team were given permanent roles at Central Office.

Despite, or perhaps because of, his background in management consultancy, Hague is not a 'hands on' manager. He did not search out particular talent to build a team with complementary skills but rather took what was offer. In some cases he inherited some very good people, but throughout his leadership people have asked what his very mixed team says about him. The revived position of Chief of Staff and its deputy were offered to former MPs Charles Hendry and Sebastian (now Lord) Coe. With effectively a blank sheet of paper, Hague's team was not sure how best to structure their operation. The inspiration for bringing back a coordinating Chief of Staff came from New Labour, as did much of the enthusiasm for their 'project', but it was not sensible to invite comparisons with the heavyweight personnel in the Prime Minister's private office. Hendry had been PPS to Hague during his time at the Department for Social Security, and on his advice and that of Deputy Chairman Michael Trend, Hague later (September 1997) moved his base of operations from the Commons to Central Office so that he could oversee the reforms directly.

With an abundance of chiefs in the new structure Hendry's role soon seemed redundant, and by the end of the year he had been moved sideways into Business Liaison, making room for former Olympic athlete Sebastian Coe to reinterpret the role of Chief of Staff. Although Hague had not known Coe for long, their close friendship was cemented through the leadership contest. Others were less impressed. Coe had made little impact as the short-lived MP for Falmouth (he took the seat in 1992 and lost it in 1997) and had left a poor impression on Central Office staff during the general election campaign by suggesting he wanted to broker a deal with his opponent from the Referendum Party, which came as a surprise to those who had never associated Coe with Euroscepticism. Nevertheless Hague was – and is – a defiant supporter of the man who has become his closest aide and acts as his very loyal gatekeeper, and will not countenance any questions about his role, even from other senior party officials. In private Lord Parkinson complained continually that he found Hague's office (which George Osborne had also joined from Hague's campaign as Political Secretary) less accessible than he would have liked. As Chairman he was also aware that some more established professional staff were suspicious of Hague's team, particularly of the protective role played by Coe. Hague has always dismissed such criticisms, pointedly saying that Coe is 'his mate'. As a champion athlete Coe would obviously impress the fellow fitness fanatic in Hague, but their bond is rooted in something more fundamental than their highly publicised interest in judo. Like Hague, Coe, who grew up in Sheffield, is a Tory hewn from the challenging political landscape of South Yorkshire.

Hague's next key appointment was Archie Norman, the newly elected MP for Tunbridge Wells. It was hardly traditional practice for a new backbencher to be appointed straight to Central Office as a vice-chairman, but it was a sign that Hague would break with convention to get a job done. As a former McKinsey colleague, Norman's joining Hague's team added to the impression that the new leader was creating a clique in his own image, but it was a hit worth taking to bring proven business acumen to the heart of the reforms.

Norman was immediately put in charge of the reform process. His arrival was something of a surprise to Michael Trend, the party's deputy chairman whose position had forced him to appear neutral throughout the leadership campaign but who was none the less an enthusiastic Hague backer. As Parkinson's deputy, Trend was entitled to feel Norman's appointment ate into his own role, but he reached an accommodation. Along with Parkinson, Trend was to play an important role in acclimatising Norman to the small 'c' conservatism of the institution he was set to reform, since Norman's uncompromising business approach would not always sit easily with some of the quaint customs of a voluntary organisation or its professional wing.

Parkinson too was initially wary of Norman and the role he would play. He had thought the reforms would be his domain, but in practice he was to act as the facilitator for Norman's initiatives by chairing the working party which Hague set up in June. Although Parkinson admired Norman's reputation as the man who turned round the failing supermarket chain Asda, he feared Norman had too little appreciation of the culture of a political party. Norman, on the other hand, was hardly likely to be impressed with the less than straightforward way in which politics sometimes operated. He was furious to find himself the subject of Westminster gossip. One Sunday he opened his newspaper to read with disbelief a blow-by-blow account of a supposed reprimand he had received from Parkinson. According to the article he had been put in his place by the chairman when at an early meeting Parkinson had told him about his background in the party. 'I've been with this party many years, I was a branch chairman, chairman of my local Conservative Political Centre and I progressed to being an association chairman. I was a young MP and then promoted into the cabinet. I became party chairman. After a break I returned to the cabinet and now I've been brought back as chairman again, but all this experience does not qualify me to run a supermarket.' Always the entertaining raconteur, Parkinson may have been dining out on the story, but the newspaper had missed a vital detail: Parkinson had never actually had this conversation with Norman. Later that evening Parkinson telephoned Norman at home to apologise.

When the story became the stuff of Westminster gossip it left Norman even more determined to inject some disciplined professionalism into a system that apparently leaked like a sieve. He considered it essential that he bring his supermarket experience to bear on finding a modern structure for the party, and called in assistance from the PR company Lowe Bell. (Sir Tim Bell had famously transformed Margaret Thatcher from a blousy matron into The Iron Lady and had been advising the party on and off ever since.) Norman was offered Nick Herbert, who worked as his right-hand man, starting by writing a study of New Labour's reforms, while Norman spent the summer fine-tuning his own set of proposals, a template that he believed constituted the ideal solution. When the review was later under way it was Hague who often had to suggest the most practical interpretations of Norman's ideal options.

From the start Hague was keen to give a lead on the principles of the reforms, so that his team could work on the details. The Fresh Future speech was thus his framework for reform and his first big test as leader. In the race to influence the new leader, the National Union was off the starting blocks first. Shortly after Hague's victory Hodgson, who had been touring constituencies with proposals for several months and had already briefed all the candidates during the leadership race, showed Hague a slide show on the National Union's preferred reforms. In fact the National Union had been so eager to seize the initiative that it had called a meeting (not their first) to discuss reform for the day after the general election, a move the rest of the party considered a deliberate tactic to exclude them. Hodgson's key demands were to give a greater role to constituency chairmen, establish a national membership list, reinvigorate the Conservative Political

Centre (the policy discussion group for party members) and, crucially, give members some say in future leadership elections. Other unofficial members' associations, chiefly the Charter Group and the Campaign for Conservative Party Democracy (both of which lobby for a greater role for members), have long argued with some potency that the National Union had itself become a clique whose preferred reforms stopped far short of really empowering the whole membership. None the less, Hodgson's priorities chimed with Hague, who was open to any suggestions which would professionalise the party machine and encourage activity at the grass roots. A national membership list would allow the party to recruit centrally, to target specific mailings and to test the opinion of its activists far more effectively than the decentralised, constituency-based system allowed. Conservative Party membership had dwindled miserably, and there were important lessons to learn from New Labour's aggressive approach to recruitment.

Work began on drafting the Fresh Future straight after Hague was elected, and the speech that he delivered on 23 July was largely his own work. An initial draft was prepared by George Osborne and then polished by a team including Alan Duncan, David Lidington and Michael Simmonds.

Duncan, who had moved seamlessly from Hague's campaign to assume a media management role for the new leader, admired the way in which Labour had transformed itself, especially through skilful use of the media, and hoped to fashion himself as a Tory Peter Mandelson. To that end he soon became frustrated by the lack of attention being paid to improving the system within Central Office. Duncan and Parkinson were to disagree strongly about the pace of the reforms, with the Chairman preferring to wait until the management reforms had been completed before looking at the professional operation. Lidington was Hague's newly appointed PPS; Simmonds was special adviser to the previous chairman Brian Mawhinney and later to become membership director.

When the team met for an all-day speech writing session, Hague led the conversation. He was clear about the six principles he wanted to shape the reforms: unity, democracy, decentralisation, involvement, integrity and openness.

The accusations of sleaze that had tarnished the last government were a particular concern. At the last minute Hague decided to strengthen the commitment to openness by promising to publish the names of major donors to the Tories. To have overlooked that point would have mired the party in past mistakes, but it did later cause problems with existing donors who had already made their contributions in good faith that they would remain anonymous. Publication had to be delayed until the next financial year.

When Hague stood to deliver what was a template for his leadership, he knew he had to convince both those in the room and the wider audience that this project was as much about policy regeneration as it was about structural reforms. The point was to redesign the party so that it once again would become the best delivery mechanism for Conservative ideas. His assessment of the party's weaknesses was unsentimental: the membership was old and unmotivated, councillors were thin on the ground, and there were too few women and ethnic minorities involved. The principles that he had outlined were intended to revive the party by making it 'fresh, open, clear, clean, outgoing and listening'. Of course the one thing it could never be was 'new'. Although Hague's formula that 'we must be true to our past but in touch with the future' sounded very like the mantras of Labour Party modernisers, Labour had first call on the word 'new', which was studiously avoided in reference to Hague's reforms.

It was the responsibility of the working party to hammer out the details of the reforms. The specific commitments that Hague promised in the speech were to establish a new governing body for the party's organisation, which would bring together all interest groups, and to produce a 'green paper' for debate at the party conference. He was also to honour his earlier pledge to put his election up to vote by the party members, by promising a secret ballot on his leadership and the six principles of reform. The ballot results were to be announced at the conference. With no alternative leader on offer this was a sop to the party members, but it was at least a gesture towards democratisation and, significantly, towards the principle of One Member One Vote, which had done so much to turn round the public view of the Labour Party.

With an initial deadline of the October conference the working party had its work cut out, and it is typical of Hague's management style that he made his appointments and stood back. The group reported to him weekly under Lord Parkinson's chairmanship, although Norman would also talk to Hague over the telephone at weekends. The atmosphere in the Custard Room, a yellow conference room on the first floor of the Smith Square HQ, grew more fractious as weekly meetings lasted longer and longer. On one occasion Parkinson drew the meeting to an early close, and Norman was furious to discover that the curtailment was due to Parkinson's appointment at a rugby match.

Not surprisingly, the ballot of party members announced at the October conference overwhelmingly backed both the new leader and the principles which he had issued for the reforms. Eighty per cent of those members polled backed Hague and his plans. This was of course an important public relations exercise for the Tories, but it would be unfair to dismiss it as superficial, since it constituted a significant event in Tory party history. Never before had the members been consulted in such a way, as this was the first time the central operation had ever had a list of its national membership.

The Conservative Party had had two conferences a year.

Traditionally the October conference was the key political event of the year and the opportunity for set piece 'debates' to showcase policy and its loyal adherents. The spring conference, or Central Council, was a meeting of the National Union and more concerned with issues to do with the running of the party. This October 1997 conference, the first for Hague as leader, brought an uncharacteristic display of grass roots dissatisfaction. After knocking heads together for several months Parkinson was persuaded that it would be appropriate for all the antagonists to face the conference and debate the proposals suggested in the 'green paper', the 'Blueprint for Change', and members duly heard from Hodgson, Norman and Hamilton.

It was the first time Sir Archie Hamilton had ever addressed the conference and stood in front of the party members. When he tried to defend the need for MPs to maintain the lion's share of the vote in leadership elections the mood of the meeting turned sour. Hamilton was booed, yet he remained unrepentant. The hostility was further whipped up by Lord Archer, who had decided to contribute to the debate in the guise of members' friend, and used his own brand of popular invective to turn up the heat on Hamilton. Archer had his own agenda – to win the hearts of party members so that they would back him as Conservative candidate for the race to become London's mayor. As a direct assault on the MPs' exclusive power base it proved the most significant moment in the evolution of the reforms, ushering in the certain prospect of OMOV.

Armed with the backing of the party members, the process moved on to a consultation on the proposals in the 'Blueprint for Change'. The main areas of contention were the proposed powers and structure of the management board, the composition of the electoral college for the election of the leader, and how to encourage broader representation at all levels of the party. It was to be a particularly fraught period for Sir Archie Hamilton: as chairman of the 1922 Committee his role was to bring MPs on board for a move that would see the end of their monopoly over the selection of the leader. Hague had already put his weight behind the case for a more inclusive system, and after the party conference the only question was to debate not whether the reforms should take shape, but how. Once the party started to debate the composition of an electoral college it became increasingly difficult to reach any consensus on how such a system should be administered. Although the Labour Party had dramatically heightened its democratic credibility by introducing OMOV, the members' votes only made up one third of the total ballot. Hague was keen to gain the public relations advantage of taking the Conservatives' democratising reforms even further. As Hamilton and Hodgson debated how to divide up the system between the party members, MPs, MEPs, councillors and peers, the whole focus of the argument shifted. It became clear to MPs that the way to retain most control was actually to throw their support behind OMOV. Offering all party members, whether an MP or a grass roots supporter, a vote would clearly be the most inclusive system and outflank Labour. MPs, however, would still maintain the crucial role of initiating a leadership election and then narrowing down the candidates to be presented to the membership in a final vote. By resisting earlier calls from the National Union for a say in Hague's election, the 1922 Committee now found itself unable to resist the move towards OMOV.

The next problem for the executive was to achieve consensus on a system to include in the party's planned 'White Paper', due for distribution to members in advance of their spring conference, and this was to bring Hamilton into conflict with Hague.

Under the existing rule a leadership contest could be triggered if ten per cent of the parliamentary party called for a contest within a month of the opening of Parliament. After lengthy negotiations the 1922 executive sent out a complicated questionnaire to all MPs, listing various alternative procedures. The results were inconclusive – to Hague's considerable irritation. The process had been going on for months and it seemed the 1922 Committee was unable to make progress. Very little disturbs Hague's disarming composure, but poor time-keeping and general 'faffing around' is guaranteed to do so, and on this occasion he took the unprecedented step of calling his own meeting of the 1922. He paged Hamilton and demanded an immediate showdown with him, to be followed by a gathering of the whole of the parliamentary party. After a heated exchange Hague and Hamilton agreed a set of rules to recommend to the MPs. In a system that was being sold as offering more power to party members, the recommendations actually bolstered the security of any sitting leader. The percentage of Tory MPs required to trigger a challenge was raised from ten to fifteen. Unlike the previous system this would progress to an election only if the leader then failed to win a simple majority in a vote of no confidence. In a third stage, MPs would be responsible for narrowing down the candidates to be put before the party members. MPs have been able to hold on to much of their control of the process as they maintain responsibility for narrowing the field of competitors down to a final shortlist of two: by the time party members get to have a say in the choice of a new leader, their decision will be between those two candidates. Nevertheless, MPs do face the possibility that their favoured candidate might not win.

For Hague, heading a party that had been undermined by constant speculation about challenges to the leader, it was right and sensible to ballast his own position. Selling the reform as a democratising move was also a brilliant way of invoking the rights of the members to outflank intransigent MPs while actually strengthening the role of leader.

The case for OMOV was also intensified by the pressing need

to find a new way of selecting candidates for the European elections of 1999 and the London mayoral race of 2000. The European elections were to be the first in which voters would place their cross against a party rather than an individual candidate, in line with the list system used by continental members of the EU. The more votes a party received, the more of their listed candidates would be elected, those closest to the top of the list thus being more likely to make it into the European Parliament. Labour Party officials were responsible for ordering their lists, and Hague's advisers recommended regional hustings after which candidates would appear on the lists, ranked in descending order of popularity according to the votes of the party members. This seemed dangerously democratic even for many in the party, particularly the MEPs and the National Union. Both groups were considered more sympathetic to the European project than the rank and file members, and their reluctance to submit themselves to judgement by popular vote certainly suggested that was an accurate assessment. It proved a successful move both tactically, in out-democratising New Labour's far more élitist system, and politically: Hague rightly predicted that party members would favour Eurosceptical candidates, adding popular backing to his own policy agenda.

However, employing a similar system for selecting the mayoral candidates has severely dented his credentials as a strong leader. Hague may have argued that the choice of Jeffrey Archer was up to the party members, but the impression left is that he abrogated a leader's responsibility. Even if that were not the case, the Archer affair at the very least begs questions about the effectiveness of Hague's reforms. He established the Ethics and Integrity Committee as the key move to rid the party of its 'sleazy' image, but its formal, legalistic structure proved too inflexible a system for investigating the doubts about Archer. The party still seems to have insufficient informal means of investigating rumours and suspicions and can only act once concerns have already become embarrassments. Although Archer was eventually banned from the party for five years, the sanction only came after the much predicted scandals had emerged.

Hague had committed himself to creating a party that had more women and ethnic representatives, but whereas he and Archie Norman were prepared to consider a target system, the voluntary party and MPs vehemently opposed anything which hinted at positive discrimination. When Hague came up against the power of the party's existing women's organisation, the Conservative Women's National Committee, he was forced to back down. Under the old system women members were represented on the National Union Executive Committee. They had established their own organisation which Hague and his team believed was not representative of the range of women they wanted to draw to the party. It was considered anachronistic and unlikely to foster wider representation of women throughout the party: the women's organisation was more similar in tone to the Women's Institute than a contemporary rallying point for the younger, professional women that the party needed. Norman was to raise their ire by suggesting that the women's organisation should no longer have an automatic right to places on the executive of the proposed new party convention, feeling that this tokenism gave disproportionate influence to a particular type of Conservative woman. The consultation paper suggested creating a new Women's Network, aiming to recruit women of all ages and backgrounds. The executive of the Women's Committee was furious at the prospect of a rival body. By creating its own constitution to fit with the newly proposed structure of the party it effectively shored up its own position and handbagged the new leader, although at the significant cost of conceding its automatic right to executive places. Hague did not want to provoke rebellion at the grass roots – of which the Women's Committee was very much an important part. In the longer term the manoeuvring of the Women's Committee has contributed to a diminution of the role of the Women's Network, which has lost its women-only focus to become a vehicle for attracting young professionals to the party through drinks receptions.

The Italian waiters in the goldfish bowl of the Atrium restaurant at 4 Millbank were at work early, clearing away tables to make way for the morning's big event. For Westminster's marble media palace it was yet another press conference; for William Hague it was the unveiling of his prescription for the Conservative Party. Central to the Reform White Paper that Hague launched there in mid February 1998 was the new streamlined structure bringing together the previously disparate sections of the party. The organisation was to be united in the National Convention, a representative body of about 800 people drawn from all sections of the party. From there members are elected on to the ultimate governing body, the board.

Hague returned to the Atrium, where he had launched his own bid for the leadership, to unveil the 'Fresh Future' document. In the four months since the party conference the whole of the party had been involved in an active consultation process, and the press conference set was cool, blue and immaculate, giving the event an appearance of confident professionalism. Behind the scenes, however, a last-minute panic had threatened delay.

On the morning the White Paper was due to go the printers, Lord Parkinson arrived at Central Office to find Sir Archie Hamilton sitting in reception. The previous night the 1922 executive had met to sign off the last draft. Chaos had broken out when colleagues discovered an infuriating clause that had been overlooked by Hamilton. They had ceded quite enough on the votes for the leadership and had no intention of relinquishing any more power to the National Union. There had been a protracted argument about the rights of members versus the rights of MPs in reselection battles. The National Union, with considerable support from Archie Norman, considered it too hard for local associations to remove MPs who were past their best. The procedure required association members to register their protest in a public show of hands. In negotiations the 1922 Committee had effectively fought their corner, but on viewing the final draft of the document it appeared that Sir Archie had allowed greater concessions than his executive would stomach. Indeed, Sir Peter Emery, a vice-chairman of the 1922, took them personally, as the proposed reforms were rumoured to be aimed at those like himself who had been in the House for many years. Certainly Norman was keen to find a way of clearing the path for the selection of younger, more dynamic candidates

In the Central Office foyer Hamilton told Parkinson that he would not be able to sign the White Paper. Archie Norman refused to consider a redraft. Parkinson the conciliator had to step in. Robin Hodgson was called to the Chairman's office for a show-down with the 1922 executive, well aware that having secured OMOV it was now his turn to back down. He knew well the depth of feeling on this point. At a recent party function, John Townend, a member of the 1922 executive, had told Lady Hodgson that her husband was the most hated man in the Conservative Party. A redraft was ordered but by that point Hamilton was so anxious that he refused to leave the building until the final script had been typed up. Parkinson then insisted that Hamilton and Hodgson sit by Michael Simmonds as he made the changes on the desk-top publishing system. The 'Fresh Future' White Paper made it off the presses with the necessary signatures of Hodgson, Parkinson and Hamilton, and the document was ready to be distributed among members for their final approval in a ballot before their spring conference. At a more recent meeting of the National Convention changes were made, making it easier to deselect sitting members.

At the spring conference at Harrogate in March 1998 Hague confirmed the White Paper in a speech that tied the reform of the party to the aim of reclaiming the One-Nation mantle from New Labour. He argued that invigorating the grass roots would broaden the base and appeal of the party so that it would once again represent the needs and aspirations of the whole nation: 'I will achieve unity by making sure the Conservative Party is a broad and tolerant party in the mainstream. I have no interest in leading a bunch of Blue Trotskyites trotting into the wilderness.' Specifically he pointed to the makeover of the CPC into the Conservative Policy Forum, though three years on it is hard to see how the newly formatted policy discussion group has increased the participation of members in the policy making process.

As the result of one significant gesture, however, party members can claim some limited ownership of the election manifesto, which like New Labour's prior to 1997 has been put to a ballot of members. Proposals for a draft manifesto were distributed to all members in the run-up to the 2000 party conference, asking for a yes or no vote in response.

On recruitment Hague also boldly repeated his campaign pledge to double the party's membership within two years, half of the new recruits to be younger than himself. Before the introduction of the national membership list, when local associations held individual lists, the central party had no accurate way of counting or contacting its members. After the last election estimates stood at around 350,000. In the run-up to the turn of the century Hague even spoke of recruiting thousands of new members, 'a million for the millennium'. More recently membership has started to increase, but Hague's target is a considerable way off. Figures released by the party in late 1999 still put membership in the region of 350,000.

The Fresh Future changed the structure of the party in the country, simplifying the hierarchy of the voluntary party under the National Convention. These changes were to mark the next and bloody stage of the process that would see a whole layer of the professional machine culled to mirror the new structure of the voluntary party. Even if efficiency was a motive, ultimately the moves were financially unavoidable.

Finding that the party was £4 million overspent and that six months after the 1997 party conference it still had not paid its hotel bills, Lord Parkinson realised that drastic action was needed, and acknowledged that, for all their differences, this was a task for Archie Norman – who, still Chairman of Asda, had now considered his reform task finished. It was agreed that he would come back to the party organisation as its first Chief Executive.

Once again the Custard Room was to play host to bitter exchanges. This time round Norman was pitted in an uncompromising battle with the Campaigns Director, Sir Tony Garrett. Garrett was one of the party's longest standing agents and professional staff, with a wealth of election experience and a thorough soaking in the culture of the party.

He and Norman approached the review from completely opposing positions. Garrett was determined to defend the role of his deputies who staffed the party's regional HQs. Norman wanted to shorten the chain of command, close all the regional offices and redirect efforts to smaller county-based operations. This was the most acrimonious of the changes, with Garrett opposed from the start and a whole layer of party professionals fighting for their jobs. Garrett soon found himself fighting a losing battle but he never wavered, believing the new regime was pulling the guts out of the party. In the end regional offices did close, with the loss of around forty staff including Garrett himself. Garrett, an obstructionist in Central Office, was never going to win over Norman, but it was unfortunate that the two could not reach an accommodation to prevent a painful episode and the loss of an experienced campaigner.

Though Norman's tough approach was respected, this did not make him liked. In Central Office, where he chose not to have an office, he was considered remote and unpersonable. On one occasion Parkinson completed his evening tour of the building to find great laughter in the press office. He greeted with a wry smile the news that the subject of fun was Norman. At that day's Prime Minister's Questions, Norman had stood up to ask a question, but inexperienced in the art of the Commons had fluffed his lines and was upbraided by the Speaker before he had even had a chance to question the Prime Minister. Parkinson requested that the tape be played again for the entertainment of the troops.

Although Parkinson sometimes baulked at Norman's manner, he recognised that the party could afford nothing less than a radical approach. As usual after a general election, the operation had been scaled down quickly, but the parlous state of Conservative finances demanded an even more drastic approach. Parkinson recommended businessman Michael Ashcroft as deputy to Sir Graham Kirkham, Hague's first treasurer. As the scale of the problem became apparent Kirkham moved aside within six months to let the more motivated Ashcroft take over. Ashcroft had been a seven-figure donor to party funds for a number of years, and after May 1997 was the only one remaining. The extent of Ashcroft's overseas business interests raised doubts about his suitability to act as treasurer for a party now turning its back on foreign donations, but with bankruptcy a real possibility Hague had little choice but to support the man whose donations the party still thought fit to accept. As treasurer Ashcroft told

Norman that the party's expenditure was £14 million a year, its income £8 million. With the added costs of the general election, the Conservatives were looking at debts of ten million pounds.

Conservative treasurer (more appropriately called fundraiser) was not a job for which applicants were queuing up, and indeed it was made even more challenging by the party reforms. On the one hand Hague's pledge to publish the names of donors (pre-empting an expected legal obligation to do so) and to end overseas donations immediately made fundraising more difficult (Between one third and one quarter of Conservative donations had come from overseas). On the other hand, the constitution of the new party board was a disincentive for any prospective treas-urers. Ashcroft, with a considerable personal fortune, is probably the only member of the governing body who can afford the impli-cations of sitting on the board of an unincorporated association. At his first board meeting as Treasurer, Ashcroft watched the colour drain from his colleagues' faces as they fully realised that each could be held personally liable for the party's debts. Of the fourteen members of the board, each representing a different section of the party, the majority (eight) come from the voluntary side of the party, elected by the National Convention. This is an arrangement which suits the treasurer as it means that the expen-diture of the professional machine is held to account by its members, more likely to be looking at the long-term health of the party rather than the short-term requirements of their political careers.

Norman's reforms of the party machine created immediate savings of about £3 million, but for the first year such changes incurred their own costs. There were the one-off costs of redun-dancies and buying in new technological back-up to replace the old regional offices. As the board meets monthly, Ashcroft and Norman agreed that all expenditure over £250 should be cleared by the Chief Executive. Although the moves seemed stringent, the state of the party finances worsened as the knock-on effects of the general election expenditure (in all £28 million) made their impact on two sets of accounts following 1997.

Ironically the party which doesn't believe in state funding was thrown a lifeline from the public purse. In February 1998 Lord Parkinson represented the party at the Neill Committee inquiry into party funding. It seemed like yet another indignity for the Conservatives to admit that they were on the verge of bankruptcy, but by arguing the constitutional case for a strong opposition Parkinson negotiated an increase in allocation of Short money, funds from the public purse which go towards running the offices of the official opposition. The funds amounted to £3 million a year to spend on parliamentary activity and, since 1999, have been a crucial boost to meeting the opposition's day-to-day running costs.

As a proportion of income, donations from the party treasurer have risen since 1997, but there has been considerable success in broadening the base of contributors.

The swish of designer evening frocks and the clink of champagne flutes announced a moneyed audience for Hague's tribute to his treasurer and the party's new supporters. The Team 1000 Spring Ball in May 2000 at London's Vinopolis was an opportunity for the well-heeled and well-groomed members of a club of those who contribute £1,000 or more a year to party funds to eat dinner with the shadow cabinet and watch Hague in action. Over fusion cuisine and *petits fours* Hague addressed his unusually glamorous audience. A week earlier he had made a similar speech to party members 250 miles away in Wensleydale, where the local branch hold a fundraising cheese auction each year. His routine was adapted from his Commons response to the 1999 Budget, when he teased Gordon Brown: 'The Chancellor said that the Budget is good for families. It is good for families who do not have a mortgage, who are not married, who do not run a car, who do not smoke and who do not save for a pension. . . There may even be a family like that somewhere in the country. It sounds suspiciously like the Chancellor to me.'

In the grand arched dining room of the Vinopolis the party was auctioning exclusive holidays and tickets for the best boxes at the races. Two very different audiences – but the same jokes travelled well from the grass roots to the green shoots. The serious business of the evening was to acknowledge that Team 1000 had expanded under Ashcroft from 120 members to 800. Of higher contributors, those giving more than £5,000 a year had risen fourfold to 120 and the number of those giving more than £10,000 was up from 10 to 52. As a result of the reforms to the structure of fundraising, which have established six separate boards throughout the country, the party has broken even in the year before a general election. Ashcroft and current Chief Executive David Prior have costed an election campaign and launched a separate fighting fund to earn £15 million for that purpose. In real terms the party is in a worse financial position approaching the next election than it was at the same stage before May 1997, but it has finally established the necessary mechanisms for longer-term improvement. Hague's policy on the Euro is attracting back big donors, but the long-term resilience of party funds will depend on building and keeping a wide base of small donors whose interest will be won by attractive policies as much as new fundraising techniques.

Throughout his leadership campaign and first year as leader, Hague's reforming rhetoric was bold and extravagant. In identifying a positive project that would motivate his party at its lowest ebb, the reforms were a sensible strategy. On a technical level there are still arguments about detail – hardcore democratisers say the reforms are superficial and an elected chairman and treasurer should follow – but useful, practical improvements have been made. Unfortunately the worthwhile time and effort devoted to such changes does not easily transfer into public acclaim and attention was allowed to drift from clarifying a popular message.

Foolishly perhaps, Hague sounded too evangelistic about his reforms, as though they would in themselves transform the party into an open, inclusive, multicultural, sleaze-free modern organisation.

They do at least lay the foundations for that. The success will depend on convincing people that the party's policies, more than its internal workings, meet those aspirations.

Chapter Nine

FROM BASEBALL CAPS TO FLATBED LORRIES

John Humphrys: *There's a poll out again this morning says 14 per cent think you'd make the best Prime Minister, 60 per cent say that Blair would make the best Prime Minister. You've got a problem yourself, haven't you? He's got the confidence of the country and you haven't.*

William Hague: *You can forgive me for not proceeding on the basis of opinion polls. We should never be put off by opinion polls. I was shown opinion polls which said no way could we win the European elections, that we were twenty-eight points behind in those European elections, that a breakaway faction from our party was going to do almost as well as the official party. All of that turned out to be complete nonsense. We've won the elections outright. We've had the biggest swing to the opposition in any election since the First World War, so I can be forgiven after that for not taking too much notice of opinion polls and for getting on, steadily, with rebuilding my party and winning support, which is what we are doing.*

On the Record, BBC television, 16 January 2000

Archie Norman's return to Chief Executive also turned the spotlight on other less than successful areas of the party operation.

From the start of Hague's bid for the leadership his team had prided themselves on having learnt from the media-savvy approach of New Labour, but in practice they had failed miserably to live up to the impression created by their own early successes.

Hague's initial outings as a candidate for the leadership were marked by their slick presentation. The press operation was far more sophisticated than those of his rivals, and Alan Duncan, although occasionally over-enthusiastic, had injected an authoritative tone to briefings. Once Hague was ensconced as leader, however, the weaknesses of the team became apparent.

Duncan had raised the game by talking up the need to deploy the same sort of techniques as New Labour, but the Conservatives had neither the money nor the status to recruit heavyweight press and media professionals. Although Duncan had considerable flair and energy, his judgement did not always serve Hague well, and his expertise was not in television image-making. Having taken on most of the burden of managing media relations since the start of Hague's leadership campaign, Duncan was keen to recruit help. Scornful though many Conservatives are about the value of image-making, Hague's poll reactions showed that he really suffered for not being as televisual as Mr Blair.

Hague has had a lot of luck in his career but in one area he could have done with some more. Among his peers in the House of Commons, his dispatch box skills have always marked him out as an exceptional performer. Unfortunately the debating aptitude which would have made him a giant in a nineteenth-century context is less relevant to a mass audience in the age of the soundbite and the image-conscious television appearance.

Hague's performances at Prime Minister's Questions very

quickly helped to establish him as party leader, with early successes against Tony Blair the only cheer for his dispirited Commons colleagues. A combination of quick thinking, wit and aggression gave Hague's exchanges authority right from the start. A few weeks after he became leader, the Labour government faced problems over the financial arrangements of the Trade minister, Lord Simon, and Conservative MPs relished the prospect of turning the sleaze accusations that had dogged their party back at New Labour. In a bad-tempered exchange Blair told Hague to 'go away and grow up'.

Hague replied, 'When the Prime Minister gets patronising, you know he has lost the argument.'

On the continuing saga of BSE, Hague was able to deflect criticisms of the Conservative government's record with his spirited criticisms of Labour ministers in October 1999: 'We have the Prime Minister saying that meat fed on human sewage is safe, but British T-bones are lethal. We have British lorries being broken into and barricades on fire and no effective action being taken. Is it not clear when we look at ministers that it is not just the dead cows that have had their spines taken out?'

The most demanding performance for an opposition leader is the budget reply, a spontaneous response which has to be decided in the chamber as the Chancellor unveils his plans. This is exactly the sort of challenge that Hague loves, and his replies have been admired throughout the press. In March 2000, for example, he proclaimed after Gordon Brown's budget speech that 'The Chancellor is like a mugger who grabs someone's money and then wants that person to thank him for providing the bus fare to get him home. At the same time he has done that, hospital waiting lists have risen, police numbers have fallen, class sizes have increased, asylum controls have collapsed and the transport system is at a standstill.'

The weekly confrontations with Tony Blair earned him status

and admiration in the forum of the Commons chamber, and the *Spectator* magazine's prestigious Parliamentarian of the Year award in 1998, but with less and less attention paid to these set-piece encounters such successes had relatively little effect on his public image.

From the start there was some concern to correct the impression that Hague was 'nerdy', a 'political anorak'. The many articles written about him during the leadership campaign had focused attention on his unusual single-mindedness and composure, admirable characteristics but unlikely to endear him to a general audience. The depiction of him as a *Hansard*-reading teenage conformist and tweed jacketed Young Conservative was accurate and deadly. His chief of staff Charles Hendry and Seb Coe thought it would be useful for Hague to spend his first summer as leader travelling around the country, meeting people and being seen to do the things that 'normal' people do. That would be followed by a trip to Eastbourne for the first annual away-day for all Tory MPs. The emphasis of this pre-conference retreat would be on team bonding – an opportunity to seat old adversaries and new friends together at dinner. It was a management consultant's dream of motivational training with lectures on the party's image and aims. The Eastbourne weekend was greeted with disdain by a few traditionalists, but has since become an annual fixture, most noted by the press for the opportunity it offers to photograph Tories in casual clothes. So far John Redwood has scored the most highly in the dressing down stakes, for his ensemble of sweatshirt and combat trousers.

Alan Duncan agreed that there could be some media advantages in a strategy of getting Hague out and about, but there the judgement seemed to run out, as these efforts served only to reinforce Hague's 'geekiness'. Having him don a baseball cap for a photo shoot on a water slide at an amusement park, and the damage done to Hague's image by the ensuing photos in the press was compounded when the cameras were invited along to cover his first trip to the Notting Hill carnival in 1997, where he and Ffion were photographed self-consciously sipping rum punch to display the Tory leader's multi-cultural credentials. Neither Hague nor his team had the flair to pull off the art of rehearsed spontaneity. Far from appearing natural, Hague's seemed forced and unconvincing.

But far more damaging was his genuinely natural response to the death of the Princess of Wales.

Fashioning a tribute to the Princess played to all the media skills of the Prime Minister, and to none of Hague's. The tragic death of Diana in Paris revealed that he had neither the appropriate professional back-up nor the instinct for the popular mood of the time. Breaking on the Sunday morning, the news caught Hague at home at Brough Park. Duncan had been taking press calls since the very early hours of the morning, and at around 6.30 a.m woke Hague with news of the fatal accident and called his constituency press officer, Graham Robb, warning him to be prepared for a flood of media requests. By 8.30 there was already a long list of interviews to be done. The arrangements were coordinated with Downing Street because the Prime Minister was in his Sedgefield constituency, only twenty minutes away from Hague by car. It was decided that the television crews would interview Tony Blair outside his church and then drive on to Hague's home. Everything was done in a great hurry, and little thought was given to how the pictures would come across. Hague was to walk towards the cameras across the grounds surrounding his flat, but the image of a formally dressed man walking through a field looked very awkward. Before the crews arrived Alan Duncan had called Robb again to tell him that he and Hague should listen very carefully to what the Prime Minister had said and should pause after each of his interviews. In the heat of the moment his advice was overlooked and Hague stumbled into his most unexpected blunder.

Unlike Blair, Hague had never met the Princess, and unlike Blair he has a Yorkshireman's unease at public displays of emotion. Hague believed his restrained tribute was entirely suitable, but he had simply and severely misjudged the mood of the nation. His old friend Guy Hands, watching at home, despaired. Like millions of others, he thought Hague seemed ill at ease, stiff and uncaring. The press and many of his own party members were similarly unimpressed. It was a revealing insight into a man who in his late thirties had only known stability and success in his own life. Unlike many people watching, Hague had not suffered the trauma of bereavement, illness or divorce that might have made his response more empathetic. To make matters worse, the initial misjudgement was then compounded in a series of mistakes that underlined the inexperience of his whole team. The following week, *en route* to the BBC's Television Centre for *Breakfast with Frost*, Hague found out from the Sunday papers that the Conservatives – following a line spun by Alan Duncan – were accusing Tony Blair of making political capital from Diana's death.

Privately Hague thought that many people believed that to be the case, but having had his fingers burned, he recognised it was inappropriate to make the point in public. Reluctantly he then had to do just that in a defence of his aide's briefing. In a later effort to make up some lost ground Hague, on the advice of George Osborne, associated himself with calls to rename Heathrow Airport after the Princess of Wales. Again it backfired, and again it just made Hague seem out of step with public opinion.

The period of national mourning that followed the Princess's death meant that normal political activity was more or less suspended until the party conference period. For Hague his first party conference as leader was both daunting and exciting, and

he hoped that the occasion would give him the opportunity to
play to his strengths: public speaking and the cut and thrust of
real politics. But even before he arrived in Blackpool, attempts to
focus attention on his private life were attracting more attention
than his core skills.

This was not only Hague's first introduction to the massed
ranks of the party faithful; it was also Ffion's. To Tory image-
makers this was a great blessing, Hague's standing could be
enhanced by the presence of an accomplished and beautiful
fiancée, and in much of the conference coverage Hague was not
so much enhanced as eclipsed by stories of his bride to be. Once
again the urge to show Hague in '3D', more than just a politician,
had led to briefings about Ffion's transparent evening dress and
the couple's sleeping arrangements. Short of briefing 'Yes, Hague
has sex!', the intended message of Central Office spinners was
clear, although both the dress and the insight into the bedroom
arrangements covered more than they revealed.

William and Ffion's hotel suite in the Victorian pile of
Blackpool's Imperial Hotel was surrounded by the party's high
command. If the proximity of so many old fogeys was not sufficient to dull the libido, Hague's standard conference regime was
probably just as effective. He will not drink for the whole week
and keeps his energy up for the marathon effort of conference
with a pasta-dominated, carbo-loading diet. The ultimate passion
killer, though, would have been the comments of Lady Thatcher,
reported as disapproving of William and Ffion flaunting their
unmarried status. With more than a touch of mischievousness
Hague invited the Thatchers to take drinks with him and Ffion
in the infamous suite. It passed with no mention of their private
arrangements and Hague was reassured that Baroness Thatcher's
visit to the inner sanctum had more than confirmed her approval
on all fronts.

Although Hague questioned some of Alan Duncan's judge-ments in his quest to generate positive coverage, Duncan's task was never going to be easy. After the general election Central Office had been left with a depleted press operation. Charles Lewington, John Major's Director of Communications, left to set up his own business, and the head of the press office Frances Halewood left in the autumn of 1997, reputedly dismayed at the Tories' response to Diana's death. The party made one appointment to assist Hague in the lobby: Gregor Mackay, a former special adviser and election press officer, was recruited from PR company Hill and Knowlton before the first party conference. Mackay's roguish charm and quick wit made him a hit in the boys' club of the Westminster lobby, but without a Director of Communications his task as Hague's press secretary was set to expand beyond one person's capability.

Duncan was increasingly frustrated at the lack of attention being paid to modernising the operation of Central Office. Although he appreciated that Hague's priorities were party reforms in the country, he felt that important political progress was being hampered by the lack of a sharp machine, and this brought him into constant tension with Lord Parkinson, who felt that the reforms of Central Office could not be implemented before the review of the party in the country had been completed.

It was not until Archie Norman was appointed Chief Executive that full attention was turned to the vital operation in 32 Smith Square. Much fun was had at the expense of Norman's ideas to revolutionise the culture of a building that had been a breeding ground for cliques and counter-cliques, and Hague himself had even considered the advantages of moving to open plan offices, along the lines of New Labour's headquarters at Millbank Tower. But this was simply not an affordable option for his cash-strapped operation. Instead, Norman imported some of his Asda expertise in a compromise arrangement, and literally tore down many of the partitions that had divided Central Office since an irresponsibly expensive refit under Kenneth Baker's chairmanship.

Key to the changes was the merger of the old research department and the press office. The two were brought together in a so-called 'war room' designed to put the party on a permanent campaign footing. The Director of Research, Danny Finkelstein, moved over to become Hague's personal policy chief, while Roderick Nye, Finkelstein's former SDP colleague and director of the Social Market Foundation, was brought in by Norman to head the new research operation. It was a structure that Duncan had been campaigning for, as he felt it would build a media focus into all of the research department's work. Under this arrangement Andrew Cooper was made Director of Political Operations with a brief to build opinion research into the strategy.

Inspired by Labour's Rapid Rebuttal Unit at Millbank Tower, Duncan introduced a computer programme named 'Context' which was designed to coordinate the efforts of all members of the team. These were much needed changes. Newcomers to the shadow cabinet in the reshuffle of May 1998 were struck by how little had been done in the preceding year. Ann Widdecombe, the new shadow health secretary, was astonished at the shambles of a press room that sometimes took so long to allocate television appearances that the programmes started without Conservative guests.

No party can exist on spin alone, but the Conservatives had been trying to improve their profile without any effective media relations strategy. Faced with the most PR-conscious government in history, the Tories had to polish up their act, but internal changes would not in themselves turn around the fortunes of a failing party. Hague himself took much of the brunt of the media onslaught, but his colleagues never detected that it depressed him: the shadow cabinet found him amazingly resilient in the face of consistently low personal ratings and jibes about his appearance. Occasionally Seb Coe would see in private the effect it had on his mood, although Hague would say that his chief worry was that he was letting down his colleagues.

The most graphic personal criticism arrived on the first day of the 1998 Conservative Party Conference. Hague had gathered his team for an early morning meeting in his suite at Bournemouth's Highcliffe Hotel. The news was supposed to have been dominated by his victory in the ballot of party members on Euro policy, but *The Sun* chose instead to deliver with characteristic bluntness a verdict on his leadership: Hague as a dead parrot, the Conservative Party extinct. It was a biting critique of what was indeed a disastrous period in the opinion polls. According to Gallup, support for the party had actually fallen since the decision to announce a ballot on Europe. At the beginning of September 28 per cent of voters had pledged to back the Tories in the next general election. By the end of the month the figure had fallen to 23 per cent, and on those figures the Tories were facing an even greater reduction of seats at a general election.

The swing against the Conservatives under Hague's leadership went against the normal expectations for a party in opposition: 68 per cent of Gallup's poll were satisfied with Tony Blair as Prime Minister, only 28 per cent were satisfied with the Leader of the Opposition, and *The Sun* had encapsulated the position with their dead parrot.

Hague's advisers were embarrassed at having to discuss the newspapers with him that morning. Those who had pushed for the party ballot felt guilty. The high-profile concentration on the European issue had reminded the public of perceived Tory splits over Europe, and that had affected the poll ratings. At the start of their meeting Hague picked up *The Sun*.

'Well, that tells us bloody nothing,' he said, tossing the paper aside and continuing on apparently unconcerned. His determination not to be put off raised the spirits of his team.

With the new war room in place, Hague and Norman were

concerned to speed up progress on improving their media operation, but it was proving impossible to find a big enough figure
to come on board as a Communications Director. In this, as with
many of their other innovations at Central Office, there was a
strong sense that New Labour had led the way by recruiting a
press man, Alastair Campbell, to represent Tony Blair. That was
creating an expectation which the Tories could not live up to.
Norman had put Gregor Mackay in charge of recruiting himself
a deputy and was becoming increasingly frustrated at his inability
to find a suitable person.

Hague's team believed the most effective way to address
Hague's personal ratings was to improve his television appearances. Where he was able to give considered interviews Hague
had always been a strong television performer, but the demands
of soundbites and photo-opportunities did not play to his
strengths. Long-time public relations consultant Sir Tim Bell
contributed regular tips, but Bell had his own business to run and
Hague needed full-time support. Andrew Cooper and Michael
Simmonds suggested Norman recruit Ceri Evans to advise
Hague on the best way to capitalise on the demands of television:
Evans had known Hague as Welsh Secretary through his special
adviser Barnaby Towns, and had later worked at Central Office
during the 1997 election campaign as a media adviser. With a
background at the BBC, he had then moved to Channel Four to
assist with channel identity. Evans was to divide his time between
his work for William and his role at Channel Four. Quietly
spoken and low key, Evans fitted in well with the band of thirtysomething advisers, Finkelstein, Cooper and Nye, who all
shared a keen desire to rid the party of its fogeyish associations.

A big cultural shift was marked when a television studio was
built where there had once been a bookshop in the foyer of
Central Office. Hague has always poured scorn on Tony Blair's
concern with image and spin, and has stressed his own 'what you

see is what you get' personality as a direct contrast, but there is more than a little disingenuousness in Hague's criticisms of Labour's image-consciousness, as he had himself used public relations advisers to sharpen the image of his leadership campaign. Anthony Gordon-Lennox, who advised him then, has since set up a PR company, Tasc, which Hague has hired to assist with the next general election. The much derided focus groups are simply part of modern politics and despite their public scepticism the Tories certainly use them, and would have done so more if budgets had allowed. However, Hague himself is very much his own person and has had comparatively little image counselling and no voice training. By the time Evans arrived Hague had already had some advice on his clothes and had developed an expensive taste in hand-made Jermyn Street shirts and suits. Style and etiquette specialist the late John Morgan was a supporter of the party and had offered his help after the pictures of Hague in a baseball cap had appeared. Such casual garb would have been anathema to Morgan, an immaculate ambassador for the formal suit. Unlike his own bespoke three pieces, he recommended Hague stick to well cut dark suits and gold ties to give his appearance a cleaner line. Evans agreed, and added that the occasional coloured shirt and red tie would work particularly well for set-piece television appearances.

The most obvious and controversial change to Hague's look has been his hair, since to set off the sharper suits a more definite hairstyle was called for. Hague, although naturally neat, is not vain: the time he spends on physical training is aimed at enhancing his fitness and stamina, rather than building a more attractive physique. When Seb Coe became his private secretary, he suggested Hague should review his exercise regime if he wanted to achieve peak fitness for the long haul ahead of him. The choice of martial arts was Hague's, fitting in both with his practice of transcendental meditation and his competitive streak.

Through his connections Coe was able to suggest judo and recruit British Olympic silver medallist Ray Stevens to be their coach. The now regular practice (at least twice a week) has sharpened Hague's powers of concentration and given him a more sculpted appearance. To match the latter the hair has also been fashioned combat-ready.

Knowing that Hague would consider any discussion about his hair rather frivolous, the decision to change its style was taken out of his hands. Evans and Coe briefly discussed it and decided it was worth experimenting with a shorter cut. When the House of Commons hairdresser arrived for her regular appointment with Hague, Evans took her aside.

'You know how William usually has his hair?' he said: 'Well, don't do it like that. This time we are going much shorter.' Evans told Hague he needed to chat something through with him while he was having his hair done so that he would not notice that rather more hair was falling to the ground than usual. At the end Hague put his hand up to his head to find very little left. On seeing the cut for the first time he was slightly surprised but merely remarked, 'Fine, let's get back to work.'

When news later leaked of concerted attempts to give Hague an image boost it immediately undermined the move to reveal the 'real Hague', although the arrival in March 1999 of a much needed Communications Director signalled the intention to turn round the perception of Hague as bookish and out of touch.

The appointment of Amanda Platell, former managing editor of the *Sunday Express*, followed the sacking of Gregor Mackay from Central Office. When Hague took the decision to entrust the press briefing on his new strategy 'Kitchen Table Conservatism' to Ceri Evans and not to Mackay, it seemed the official press secretary was out of favour. In fact the briefing to *The Times*, which stressed Hague's determination that all members of the shadow cabinet should stick rigidly to the policy, was a spontaneous idea.

Central Office colleagues of Mackay recognised that he had not succeeded in raising Hague's profile, but that his job demanded more than one person could offer. There was some surprise at the cold way in which Hague dropped him, giving no clear reason. Hague told Mackay that 'you no longer have my trust', and Mackay was shocked and dismayed by a dismissal that seemed to come out of the blue. Apart from the uphill struggle that Mackay had been having, Hague had held him responsible for negative briefings about some members of the shadow cabinet. The briefings were never sourced, although Gary Streeter later admitted to revealing information about the commitment of his fellow shadow cabinet members to Hague's new strategy and was forced to make a grovelling apology in shadow cabinet.

What consistently frustrated Hague's team was their failure to capitalise on the wit and effectiveness of his Commons performances, but their progress in presenting him as a strong, attractive leader was impeded by a string of policy problems, including the sacking of Lord Cranborne and the furore over Peter Lilley's attempts to reposition the party on key issues.

Amanda Platell had no easy task when she inherited the communications mantle. A private note from Alan Duncan warned her that 'the party has established almost no influential contact with senior journalists, has no appreciation of which media vehicles are weak or powerful, and is relying on an arbitrary system to devise 'lines to take'. Briefings are often crafted on a wing and a payer with no reference to the shadow teams who are most familiar with the brief.' Platell was to bring with her the necessary contacts to build better relations with the press, even if some soon doubted her political acumen. Politics did not need to be her forte, as Norman had also recruited former *Times* political journalist Nick Wood to handle the lobby briefings.

At last it seemed as though the party was gearing up its act, although early leaks of the new media strategy showed that the ship was not as tight as it should have been. Competing for the country's affections against the televisual Prime Minister and his photogenic family was never going to be easy for William: the Hagues were reluctant to turn their marriage into a photo-opportunity, especially as early experiments had failed, but Platell was determined that the media portray a fuller picture of her subject. Ceri Evans had developed the characters of Chris and Debbie, an ordinary couple with 'kitchen table' concerns to front the Conservatives' election broadcasts for the local election campaign in May 1998, and Hague liked the advertisements; Chris and Debbie and their kitchen table were a long way from the demonised Islington dinner party set that Hague believed people would increasingly associate with an élitist prime minister. Platell thought Hague and Ffion could also come to be seen as a couple who embodied the aspirations and concerns of real people, generally and in the run-up to the European elections. How better to illustrate the couple's mutual support and love than have Ffion pictured in a necklace with a Sterling pound sign pendant?

Evans was far from convinced that this was an image that would convey normality, but was prepared to support the idea as long as Ffion was comfortable with it, and Platell and Evans went to the Dolphin Square flat to discuss the idea. Initially Ffion was uncomfortable about it but her musings were interrupted by a telephone call. It was William. The couple chatted about nothing in particular and when Ffion returned to the conversation with Platell her mood had softened. It was worth a try.

As a PR stunt the pound sign pendant blew up in their faces. When it was revealed by the jeweller, disgruntled at not having been paid, that Platell had bought the necklace it confirmed the view of advisers who agreed with Hague that the best way to sell him was not to try too hard. In reality Hague's ratings were only likely to improve once he had something distinctive and consistent to say politically, but there was an understandable wish to correct the negative perceptions of a man considered by his colleagues and friends funny, charming and good company.

'Project Hague' was devised at a weekend meeting in Yorkshire. William and Ffion entertained Platell, Evans, Coe and Alan Duncan – who had himself caused Platell the first panic of her new job. In May he had warned her that he had given an interview to the *New Statesman* magazine, saying that the Conservatives were still struggling to find a purpose. Platell and Ancram, who had replaced Parkinson as party chairman, had not agreed with Duncan's assessment that the article was thought-provoking and instead considered it insubordinate. As a result Duncan's severe reprimand from Hague was spun as a news story. Privately Hague agreed to meet his old friend, who had been working on the health brief for several months, to discuss his concerns over a long walk in the Dales: Duncan's advice was to start thinking the unthinkable, but the main subject of the weekend was to sell the unsellable. The aim was to highlight all the things about Hague that were not appreciated by a wider audience: his enjoyment of the countryside, his keen sportsmanship and his love for his family and friends. All these were true, but when the plan appeared on the front page of the *Telegraph* it looked contrived and unconvincing. At last Hague had a senior woman in his team, but the PR advantage of that was temporarily lost as the Project Hague leak gave the impression of an emasculated leader whose image was being decided by two strong women, his wife and his communications chief.

Once Project Hague was exposed its purpose was completely undermined, although Platell's desire to broaden the media interest in Hague has continued. His summer 2000 revelations about teenage drinking exploits, expertly spun by *GQ* magazine, spoke more of his aide's concern to sell him to a wider audience than of his actual alcohol intake. Although his obvious taste for beer makes the claim of an occasional fourteen-pint binge quite believable, the opposite impression has been created because everyone knows that Hague's team would like him to appeal to the 'laddish' readers of that magazine.

In terms of the 'froth' of politics, Project Hague was a great story for the media and an embarrassing one for Hague. More seriously damaging to Hague's image as a leader were the continuing associations with the weaknesses of the former Conservative government, particularly sleaze. When Hague told his party conference in 1999 that Lord Archer, the newly selected candidate for London mayor, was a man of 'probity and integrity', few people outside the hall were convinced – and plenty closer to Hague were similarly unpersuaded. Although there were warnings to Hague right from the start of his leadership, he allowed the problem to take its own course.

In the first two years his priorities were the party reforms and Europe, and in championing a democratic system for selecting the mayoral candidate as part of the party reforms Hague could claim that the decision was not his to take. Technically that was true once the system was in place, but even before he had established it Hague was aware of the potential problems with Archer. During the leadership bid he had turned down the chance to have Archer involved. At the start of the campaign Archer had backed Peter Lilley. When Lilley had dropped out he immediately backed Hague and offered to bring his own backers on board. Of Archer, Hague had replied, 'That man has had to resign from every post he's had in the party: what possible role could I find for him?'

By default he found for him the role of potential mayor of London. Hague's apparent inaction to prevent another embarrassment was backed by his chairman Lord Parkinson, who felt his leader was taking the only course available to him, since it seemed that there was no new evidence to further implicate the millionaire novelist in the problems which had long dogged his political career. Together Hague and Parkinson agreed that the party's Ethics and Integrity committee could not reopen a libel case that Archer had already won, or allegations of share misdealing which the DTI was no longer investigating. In addition, Archer was a tremendously popular figure among the grass roots and had devoted himself to the party, attracting many powerful friends along the way. Was Hague to reject the advice of two former Prime Ministers, John Major and Margaret Thatcher, who had endorsed Archer's candidacy, as well as senior members of his own shadow cabinet who backed the man? There were others who thought that he should have done so, as much for policy reasons as anything else. Regardless of any scandal that might emerge, Archer was hardly a serious, heavyweight candidate who could articulate a new Conservatism for a complex city.

In retrospect Hague admits that he should have handled the Archer affair differently. Privately he admits it was an error of will as much as of judgement. As a new leader among old friends he had not quite grasped the extent of his power. Hague simply found it easier to let matters take their own course, than to rise to the occasion and ask Archer not to stand. By the time he was sufficiently free of his other projects to turn any attention to the problem, Archer had been campaigning for two years and was the obvious favourite to win the party's nomination at the primary meeting in September 1999.

Advisers noticed that as the need for a resolution became more pressing, so Hague seemed less willing to talk about the issue. Early reports of New Labour's attempts to prevent Ken Livingstone from standing as their candidate reinforced Hague's preference to leave it to the party to decide. Hague rejected suggestions that Archer be knifed from inside, and worried that if such stories were to come out the Tories would leave themselves open to criticisms of New Labour-style 'control freakery'. His dilemma was that although many people had suspicions about

Archer but no one could offer any concrete reasons why he should not be selected as the party's candidate.

The journalist and broadcaster Michael Crick had written a fairly damning biography of Archer, and for most people in the media that account was enough to raise sufficient doubts about the man's suitability for office. Crick wrote to Hague, whom he had known at Oxford, offering to brief him with more up-to-date information – with the result that several weeks later Crick was reprimanded by a senior BBC colleague to whom Lord Archer had complained. Deliberately Crick had not included any written allegations in his letter as he had feared a leak back to the litigious peer. His fears were well founded because news of his letter did reach Archer's office: hence the complaint to the BBC. Although Seb Coe is an old family friend of Lord Archer's and had arranged for himself and William to practise judo in Archer's gym, he has denied responsibility for the leak. Archer's office has suggested that they heard about it from someone else in the private office. Coe maintains that Crick would have been invited to see Hague although Crick never received such an invitation from anyone in Central Office. Rather than invoke the Ethics and Integrity committee, as Hague had been asked to do by the former Richmond MP Sir Timothy Kitson in a letter requesting an investigation into Archer, he entrusted his new chairman Michael Ancram with the task of checking Archer's suitability.

Not everyone had been convinced of the case for making Ancram chairman. Hague had considered giving the job to Ann Widdecombe, but was talked out of it by Seb Coe and Gregor Mackay. When he told colleagues he had decided on Ancram, a senior policy adviser said, 'You do know Michael is a complete chump, don't you?'

'He is very solid,' replied Hague.

As far as his dealings with Lord Archer were concerned, the former description seemed more appropriate. Ancram asked

Archer whether there was anything else to come out that could embarrass the party. Lord Archer told him there was not, but he had woven so complicated a net that even he was surprised by the nature of the revelations that led to his resignation in November. A former friend had revealed to the *News of the World* information that suggested Archer's libel case against the *Star* newspaper could be reopened. Archer had misled the party, and Hague's patience ran out too late.

Archer hoped he might be able to see out the crisis, but Hague insisted he stand down immediately. Only then was he referred to the Ethics committee, excluded from the party and had his membership revoked for five years. Those who had been awaiting firm leadership breathed a sigh of relief, only to be amazed when the process to replace Archer dissolved into a similar chaos. Steven Norris, runner-up to Archer in the September hustings, had been led to believe that he would be automatically appointed to succeed Archer as the official candidate. It was clear to Ancram that Norris was not impressed when he telephoned to tell him that the party had decided to hold another hustings.

'Don't be like that,' Ancram told Norris.

'Don't be like that!' replied Norris. 'Don't be like that! How else am I supposed to be when the people out there will look at the party and think it can't run a fucking whelk stall on an Essex pier.' Norris was furious. He wanted to stand but refused to throw his hat back into the ring until he knew whether William wanted him to be the candidate. He felt that by being too hands-off, William had already allowed the process to descend into chaos. Now he had to assume direct responsibility, and Norris needed a sign that he would have William's backing if he were to win.

A few days later Shaun Woodward, shadow minister for London, was sacked for opposing Hague's campaign to retain Section 28, the legislation banning the promotion of homosexu-

ality in schools. Norris supported Woodward's line. He telephoned Seb Coe telling him he had found the perfect excuse to
stand aside. 'If you have had to sack Woodward, you'd have to
sack me. I agree with him. How can I be candidate for the Mayor
of London and oppose your policy?'

Shortly afterwards Coe returned the call. It was the sign
Norris had been looking for. 'It's fine for you to stand,' Coe told
him. 'The leader thinks diversity of opinion is a marvellous thing.'

In the run-up to Christmas 1999 the damage to the party's
image caused by the Archer affair and the subsequent administrative dithering was reinforced by the return to the front pages
of Neil Hamilton, embarking on an ultimately unsuccessful libel
case in the High Court against Mohammed Fayed.

Fortunately for Hague, another problem had been averted when
his Treasurer settled a dispute with *The Times* out of court. Since his
appointment Michael Ashcroft had acquired a new title: 'controversial'. Newspaper articles about the millionaire businessman, whose
overseas businesses and ownership of a Belize passport provoked
the enquiries of journalists and political opponents, frequently
referred to Hague's 'controversial treasurer'. Ashcroft has since
acquired another title – Lord – but in the unusual circumstances of
requiring his return to live full time in Britain.

There is understandable interest in a man whose own fortune
has been the largest single source of revenue for the
Conservatives under his own period as treasurer. In twist on the
Yorkshire assumption that Hague had not himself made, the press
concluded that 'where's there's brass there's muck'. Given the
party's nagging associations with sleaze and Hague's avowal to
deal with it, Ashcroft was automatically a target for investigation.
The Tories were accused of breaking the spirit of the Neill
Committee recommendations on foreign funding by accepting
donations from Ashcroft that had come through overseas
accounts, and the revelations undermined Hague's high-minded

pledge to render the party's funding whiter than white.

Ashcroft's donations did meet Hague's new rules, as he is eligible to vote in Britain, but these were pending tougher legislation from the government: the necessary pragmatism driven by the need for funds was understandable, if not quite up to Hague's rhetoric about his reformed regime. More persistent were the suggestions that Ashcroft was not an appropriate treasurer. He had held the position for a year by the time that many of these accusations were made, and his record had bought him the support of his immediate colleagues on the party board, but there were murmurs of disapproval among some MPs who wondered why he had once been refused a peerage.

Hague addressed a meeting of the 1922 Committee to inform it, as John Major had so often in the past, that he would not allow any of his staff to be hounded out by the press. Many MPs sensed a vendetta against Ashcroft, so Hague's determination to resist media pressure was well received. He knew that without Ashcroft he simply could not turn around the fortunes of the party, literally and thus politically. In the face of unproven allegations against Ashcroft, Hague was unflinching in his support, especially when the accusations culminated in a law suit against *The Times,* which had alleged Ashcroft's businesses were under investigation in the States. Nevertheless, Hague wanted the issue dealt with as quickly as possible and Ashcroft was aware of the political sensitivities of such a case coming to court in the run-up to an election. *The Times* also faced the possibility of a potentially expensive law suit. The parties reached an out-of-court settlement in December 1999, the deal having been done directly with Rupert Murdoch at the brokerage of a mutual friend Jeff Randall, editor of *Sunday Business.* This was not the cleanest outcome for either side as neither had proved their case in public, but for Hague it was certainly a blessing.

It was the only blessing in a bad month that saw Hague

having to face the frustrations of his shadow cabinet as 'events' overtook their control. What seemed like an inept sacking of frontbencher Shaun Woodward hastened his defection to Labour. Much though Central Office and other Tories attempted to rubbish Woodward's claims that the Conservatives had lurched dangerously to the right, his departure did not reflect well on the party or on Hague.

A poll in mid January showed Hague's status remained as low as ever. Only 14 per cent of people polled by Gallup said they thought Hague would 'make the best prime minister'. But mid January also brought news that would mark a more positive phase in Hague's relationship with the public.

Since his first speeches as Leader of the Opposition, Hague had made clear his expectations of the public's affair with New Labour. He told the party conference in 1997 that the new government would provoke 'fascination, admiration, disillusion and finally contempt', and Hague always believed that his own standing and the fortunes of his party would never begin to improve until the shine had started to come off Tony Blair. His progress through the four stages of Labour had been slow, as the state of the economy had almost of itself allowed Blair to become 'Teflon Tony', but by mid January 2000 the mood of the nation had palpably changed.

The issue at the heart of this change was health. Stripping away the distractions of spin and personalities New Labour had been found wanting on one of its key pledges, to improve the National Health Service. The terrible winter flu crisis that had hit the country in December was highlighting bed shortages which dismayed both Middle England and the Labour heartlands, presenting Hague with his first real opportunity to attack Labour on delivery and for Blair to be found wanting.

It was not that the Tories had agreed an alternative vision, but the flu epidemic marked the return to normal politics and a real opportunity for Hague to make a mark.

In terms of establishing a brand, the first 'Project Hague' had proved a non-starter. It might have been based on Hague's real interests, but with nothing more substantial to offer than an image-making exercise it was bound to fall flat. Throughout 2000 Hague has embarked on his own project, championing what he believes are popular concerns about crime, asylum and the family, and sharpening policy on health, education and the economy. The image that he has wanted to convey is of a tough Conservative, prepared to represent the views of the 'mainstream majority' against the insidious incursions of political correctness and self-satisfied metropolitanism.

The essence of that message has been most graphically illustrated in Hague's 'Keep the Pound' rallies, an invention of Nick Wood and Sir Tim Bell. While Hague brands Blair the ultimate example of the 'liberal élite', he was seen out in the country, campaigning for the Pound from the back of a flatbed lorry. It is not the most sophisticated brand of Conservatism but it proved distinctive, and memos leaked from Number 10 demonstrated that it was worrying the once invincible Prime Minister.

Chapter Ten

FROM COMPASSION TO
COMMON SENSE

I believe in freedom. I believe in enterprise. I believe in education. I believe in self-reliance. I believe in obligation to others. I believe in the nation. So let us hold our heads high and say to New Labour and the whole world: these are the things we believe in, these are the values from which we will never retreat.

William Hague to the Conservative Party Conference,
October 1997

The qualitative factors underlying the poll position of the leader are more serious than the polls themselves. The perception of William Hague is beginning to settle into a non-specific general negative. It is precisely this bad: when people are asked in focus group discussions to think about the Conservative Party, the increasingly standard reflex first response is, 'They've got to get rid of Hague'.

Conservative Party Internal memo, late 1998

I t was early 1999, eighteen months into his leadership, that Hague was forced to confront the obvious. His advisers' concern had been building for months. The party was making no headway in the polls (one had just put the Tories seven points below the 32 per cent of the vote achieved at the general election) and its leader was almost as unpopular with Conservative voters as he was with the rest of the country. However despite the public perception of a party in pieces it had been an eventful year and a half, with some considerable achievements. Hague had carried out a thorough review of the party machinery, against the odds he had neutralised the Tories' problems over Europe, and he had set out on a high-profile campaign 'Listening to Britain'. Throughout 1998 he had also embarked on a series of speeches attempting to define a contemporary role for his party, but even those nearest to him remained to be convinced that he had a coherent set of views or a discernible political strategy.

There were still weaknesses in the Central Office machine, particularly in its media operation, but these doubts were about something more fundamental. Privately Hague himself admitted that he had not yet found a way of articulating a straightforward message to capture the public imagination. The problem was that his own views, although fiercely held, could sometimes seem to contradict each other. For a party that had always eschewed unbending philosophical purity this was nothing new, but set in the much celebrated post-ideological landscape where Labour had convinced many Conservative voters that it met their aspirations, it was making it particularly difficult to give Hague or his party a distinctive identity.

Those who had worked alongside him in the shadow cabinet and in his private staff recognised his unquestionable qualities: his unflappable composure, his concise businesslike manner, his oratorical flair and his razor-sharp mind. He held firm in a crisis, as he had only a few weeks previously when forced to sack his leader in the Lords, Lord Cranborne, even if most believed his actions had heightened the resultant political storm. He had attempted to analyse the dilemma facing a party whose clothes appeared to have been stolen. However, the steps towards finding a solution had been tentative.

As a young leader of an old party Hague's management style had been cautious. He had talked big about changing the party, but had appointed many old faces to his shadow cabinet. Supporters had said this was typical of his Ronald Reagan-inspired inclusiveness – that he would include in his team people from all sections of the party and some who had not supported him. He had avoided confrontation by floating off complex policy issues, such as reform of the upper chamber, for consideration by commissions. The radical meritocrat who as a student had argued for a democratically elected second chamber was nowhere to be seen in shadow cabinet when discussions started about shaping a response to New Labour's proposed reforms to the House of Lords. Here was Hague as party leader adopting a characteristically pragmatic approach, well aware that he had to bring the peers along with anything he might propose. To some modernisers the Government's two-stage reforms offered the Conservatives an opportunity to outflank Labour with democratic proposals. It seemed an ideal chance for Hague to prove he was really serious about modernising his party, yet he chose not to send that signal. What seemed like a failure of party management that blew up into Cranborne's sacking had been allowed to develop out of a lack of clear direction over policy.

The tension between moderniser and traditionalist, between libertarian and authoritarian, is an inevitable fault-line in any Conservative, but Hague was aware that his gut instincts and his intellect sometimes led him in opposite directions. He wanted to champion the family, but he also wanted the party to reach out to other types of household; he wanted to celebrate national pride but also to embrace globalisation. These were not automatically inconsistent ideas but at times they could seem so, particularly to sections of the media requiring complex arguments to be expressed in a soundbite. In early 1999 Hague came to realise what his policy advisers were struggling with – that on most issues it just was not very clear what he really stood for.

In one area, however, Hague had eventually risen to the demands of a leader's role. On Europe he had developed the line 'In Europe but not run by Europe', which neatly encapsulated the dual aims of preserving sovereignty while also engaging positively with the European Union. Wholly Hague's invention, this line had been developed while in John Major's cabinet and had been used throughout the 1997 general election campaign. It was a rallying call behind which all sections of his party could unite, even if Euro-enthusiasts believed that Hague's personal instincts were far more in tune with the spirit of the second half of the equation. On the substance of policy he had also succeeded in moving the party to the right.

With Michael Howard as shadow foreign secretary and Peter Lilley as shadow chancellor there was every expectation that under Hague the Conservative line on Europe would move beyond Major's 'wait and see'.

In government Lilley had been considered one of Major's three 'cabinet bastards' and although the dubious accolade was not aimed at Michael Howard, he had aspired to such a sceptical branding. The day after Major's off-the-record outburst to Michael Brunson of ITN, Howard told Lilley that he would stand by his 'fellow bastards' even though Major had never considered the loyal and discreet Howard qualified for the triumvirate. Although Hague's loyal support for Major excluded him from similar branding, the so-called bastards knew he was similarly illegitimate: Hague had been a junior minister when Major signed the Maastricht treaty.

Privately Hague is ambivalent about Major's decision, suggesting that he would not have signed the treaty if he had been Prime Minister, although he had supported Major through this period. He is adamant that Maastricht represents the furthest that Britain should go towards integrating with the EU. Like Howard, Hague would express his scepticism in cabinet and in meetings with John Major, but in public he was scrupulous about maintaining the cabinet line.

So at the start of his leadership race, with several competitors from the right, the pressure had been on Hague to prove to a wider audience that the Eurosceptic cause was safe in his hands. His solution was to promise that his party would not take Britain into the Single Currency at the next election, or during the lifetime of the following parliament (the 'two parliaments' line). To each side of the Euro argument this was little more than another fudge, too negative for the pro lobby, insufficiently principled for the 'never' camp. Had they asked, their fears would have been reinforced by John Major. If his policy could be characterised as 'wait and see', he considered Hague's line was really 'wait and see a little longer'. Though Hague would not have welcomed such an endorsement, 'wait and see a little longer' was to prove an effective solution for the majority of his parliamentary colleagues through the leadership campaign.

Once leader, the challenge for Hague was to make the 'two parliaments' line stick. The problems were to come not from the 'nevers' whom John Redwood counselled but from the ardent pros who saw chinks in Hague's sceptical armour. Accepted into the shadow cabinet as shadow trade secretary, Redwood told those supporters of his who favoured a once-and-for-all rejection of the Euro that they would achieve nothing by agitating for such a commitment. Hague's line had won over the vast majority of the parliamentary party, besides which those close to him suspected that his heart told him 'never' even if his head dictated that in public he take a less controversial line.

The pro-Europeans were less willing to fall into line. Their man might have lost the leadership battle, but Ken Clarke was free along with other high-profile figureheads to advance their cause on the back benches and in the media. Although he had given the biggest jobs in the shadow cabinet to sceptics, Hague met his stated commitment to inclusiveness by including some positive Europeans in his team: Stephen Dorrell, David Curry, Sir George Young and Sir Norman Fowler were in varying degrees more enthusiastic about the Euro than Hague and his chief lieutenants.

Although Hague had vowed to end the 'constantly shifting fudge' of the Major years, the weeks leading up to his first party conference as leader were weakened by a fudge of his own.

Less than two weeks into his leadership, Hague's first policy pronouncement signalled his intention to pursue an increasingly sceptical course by calling for a referendum on transfer of powers included in the Treaty of Amsterdam. Yet only three months later Hague agreed a watered down version of his own key phrase on the Euro. In his first conference speech as leader of his party Hague stopped short of saying he would oppose the Euro for the lifetime of this parliament and the next. Instead both he and Michael Howard used a less precise construction: they would oppose the Euro 'for the foreseeable future'. On his most identifiable policy, this was hardly a promising start.

Instead of a Majorite it seemed for a while that the party had chosen Major-lite. In much the same way as John Major constantly felt his hands tied over Europe, Hague had adopted a more conciliatory line to avoid damaging splits at the party conference, his hand having been forced by the non-attendance of the three key Euro-enthusiasts, Dorrell, Curry and Young, at a crucial shadow cabinet meeting. During his campaign Hague had made it clear that he expected everyone who joined his shadow cabinet to agree his line on the Euro, and consequently the policy had never been debated or formally adopted. It was the leader's policy and had not been confirmed by a collective vote. Hague believed that the Euro-enthusiasts would not have joined his team if they had had serious objections to the policy, but not debating it had allowed them to assume that the policy had already been watered down. What discussion there had been in shadow cabinet made it clear to the leadership that the 'two parliaments' line was not universally popular. When Hague's team came together in the Pugin splendour of the shadow cabinet room to agree the line for the conference, three of the chairs around the long oak table were empty. Whether a deliberate snub or not, Hague was worried that these Euro-friendly absentees would later claim they had been deliberately excluded from discussions on the line, and to avoid a shadow cabinet row during conference Hague agreed the softer line, to which Howard and Lilley agreed for the sake of unity in Blackpool.

The fragility of the compromise was evident to Hague as tension remained palpable throughout the seaside outing. Over the weekend preceding conference Hague and his speechwriter George Osborne, had hoped to build themselves a creative cocoon in Yorkshire, but their progress was constantly interrupted by anxious calls about the Euro-fix. Then behind the scenes at Blackpool the shadow cabinet threatened to split open.

On rumours that Hague had sounded a distinctly sceptical note in a television interview Stephen Dorrell paced his hotel bedroom in barely suppressed rage. It took half an hour for one of Hague's aides to calm him down and persuade him not to resign.

Elsewhere Hague's official press team was finding that journalists were taking their briefings directly from the two Euro camps: the prime suspects were the sceptic David Heathcoat-

Amory and pro-Euro David Curry, and over the last thirty-six hours of the conference Hague's inner team seriously debated sacking them both. It was a high-risk proposal, but even so Hague gave the option lengthy consideration before rejecting the plan his team had nicknamed 'Operation Poppadom' (so called because they go down well with curry), preferring to maintain a public display of unanimity. Once the candy floss of conference was over, however, sceptics including Heathcoat-Amory, Iain Duncan Smith and John Redwood insisted the line had to be agreed once and for all – but it was Sir Norman Fowler, Hague's shadow environment secretary, who forced the pace.

As Fowler had supported Ken Clarke's leadership bid he was definitely not considered a sceptic fellow-traveller, and many (including himself) had been surprised that Hague had given him so high-profile a role. He was, however, the only member of the team who had already been in a Conservative shadow cabinet, and in moving to bolster the new leader his experience was evident. Fowler's argument was non-ideological and non-partisan: rather he played the role of 'honest broker', pointing out that the party conference line on the Euro would prove untenable. It had constituted a move away from Hague's clearly stated policy, to which the shadow cabinet had tacitly agreed, and as such seriously undermined their credibility. Eurosceptics were pleased and impressed with Fowler's intervention, which effectively secured a return to the old line.

On 24 October the shadow cabinet formally adopted Hague's policy of opposing entry to the Euro for that parliament and the next. David Curry and Stephen Dorrell implied they would resign, but left the room that day still members of the shadow cabinet. Five days later the party's spokesman on Northern Ireland, Euro-enthusiast Ian Taylor, did resign. Shortly afterwards David Curry also found his position untenable and stood down from the shadow cabinet. Some months later Stephen Dorrell returned to the back benches to contemplate his own Conservative vision, of which the world has heard little.

Somewhat ironically the help of Norman Fowler gave Hague the confidence to pursue his sceptical line on Europe, but it would be another year before he would make his boldest gesture in confirming the Conservatives as the party of the pound. In speeches over the following year he articulated a rational case for keeping Britain out of the Euro, and a month after the party conference took this argument to one of the Conservatives' most testing audiences.

In becoming persuaders for the Euro, the Confederation of British Industry had turned away from its natural position as political ally of the Conservative Party, and Hague chose the CBI conference to make his first full statement on the European Union. Notably he sought to differentiate between being anti-European and being against entering the Single Currency. It was a distinction that the party had allowed to become blurred by adopting too shrill a tone and falling back on patriotic sentiment to argue an economic case.

'We should all be pro-European,' Hague told his audience: 'Pro about a Europe that is flexible, not rigid, that is about diversity, not uniformity.' Against its expectations, Hague impressed his audience with a cool, authoritative dissection of the economic arguments against the principle of committing Britain to Euro entry. He reiterated the party's recently agreed line, opposing entry at the next election, and confirmed that he would be putting the policy to a ballot of his members nearer the time.

To make the constitutional and historic case against British entry and further integration, Hague returned to his own continental base, the INSEAD Business School. In May 1998, only thirteen years since he had been a student there, Hague addressed a group of future business leaders and potential politicians, laying out his vision for a wider, less regulated, more competitive union of independent nation states. He discussed the nation in terms of shared human cultural values and historic bonds, summoning up a far more tangible version of community than Blair's ill-defined communitarianism. The lecture analysed the last fifty years of European history to argue that the federalist agenda is outdated and that the development of global markets required Europe to think again. It was a broad-ranging and thoughtful discussion of the issues, which impressed its immediate listeners and wider commentators. But however thoughtful, it was a not the view of the whole party, and Hague was to suffer the effects of noises off throughout the following summer.

If the run-up to Hague's first conference had been blighted by covert threats of disunity, these became overt in the months before October 1998, and it seemed that under Hague's leadership the party would continue to dance on the fault-line of Euro-discord.

The month after Hague's INSEAD speech Michael Heseltine delivered an impassioned defence of the Euro at the twentieth anniversary of the Tory Reform Group. Earlier that year Heseltine and five other former Conservative cabinet ministers had publicly rejected Hague's policy in a letter to the *Independent*. A usual-suspects line-up of Tory grandees had emerged, including Heseltine, Lord Brittan, Lord Howe and Sir Edward Heath, whose every contribution to the debate was interpreted by the press as a direct stab to the heart of Hague's leadership. When Peter Temple-Morris, a man whose Conservatism had been for years not so much semi-detached as on a different planet, finally found the resolve to join the Labour benches in June, it was painted as another embarrassment for Hague.

How would Hague consolidate his position on the Euro? In July 1998 he and his recently appointed deputy Peter Lilley launched their campaign to Listen to Britain. It was a staged exercise in humility designed to demonstrate an inclusive approach by travelling the country listening to the views of ordinary people and particular interest groups.

At the outset Hague had stressed that regardless of what they heard, the policy on the Euro was set. It might have sounded out of step with an announced mission to listen, but Hague's gut instinct (and informed opinion) was that his European line was the majority view. Indeed, at the first of his town hall meetings in Shrewsbury, a 'Middle England' seat the party had lost to New Labour in 1997, the vast majority of the unsolicited questions were about Europe. His self-selecting audience was almost certainly predominantly Tory, but of those there the prevailing European view was totally in tune with Hague's. He was faced with the irritating problem that a high-profile group of grandees could dominate the media with views that didn't represent the mainstream opinion of the party. It irked him.

It was bothering his closest advisers as well. At a late summer lunch in the Atrium restaurant a plan was hatched.

It can't be the food, and it certainly isn't the service, but there is something remarkably politically potent about the Atrium. As the only café bar serving Westminster, it is the obvious meeting place for all the inhabitants of the political village, so even an ordinary snack is enhanced by the proximity of others power-lunching.

On that particular day the restaurant was relatively quiet: it was late August and most of Westminster was still on holiday. Andrew Cooper, Michael Simmonds and Stephen Gilbert had abandoned Smith Square for a think-in over lunch. Along with Hague's policy director Daniel Finkelstein, the group had in the past been labelled, with varying degrees of accuracy, as Portillistas. They were among the coterie of Eurosceptic advisers who had so raised the ire of then chancellor Ken Clarke that he had famously warned Central Office spinners to 'get your scooters off my lawn'. On this occasion their sceptic leanings were united in one cause, and it was certainly the same as Hague's. Cooper's opinion poll work reassured him that Hague's Euro policy was popular. Simmonds and Gilbert had worked together on the party reforms and knew how to organise a lightning campaign. Together they decided that the time was ripe for Hague to take his Euro policy to the party: he had already promised to consult party members on all aspects of a future manifesto, but the policy on the Euro was not set to change and so it was appropriate to put it to a ballot soon. They knew that Hague was naturally cautious and that it would be hard to persuade him of the merits of an early ballot, but by the time coffee was served their plan had been finalised. Ideally Hague would return from holiday to seize the initiative by calling a snap ballot over Europe. The results would be announced on the eve of the Conservative Party Conference, focusing media attention on Hague's policy and, assuming the right result, undermining the opposition for the duration of the conference.

After lunch the lobbying began back at Central Office, although the leader and chairman were still away. Archie Norman supported the idea of a bold initiative and immediately named it 'Operation Sunrise'. Lord Parkinson's deputy Michael Ancram was non-committal, living up to his Central Office caricature of a man who avoided sitting on the fence by taking cover under the nearest desk. His advice to Hague was detailed in a memo he entitled his 'balancing memo': 'I believe the benefits are clear but the risks are real and should not be underestimated. This concept almost certainly needs a further and major brainstorming session before a clear pattern of advantage and disadvantage will emerge.' The crucial link to Hague would be Seb Coe, and it was important to try to bring him round to the idea so that it would receive a positive spin when put to Hague. Francis Maude, the shadow chancellor, was very keen. He telephoned Hague, on holiday in Utah, with news of the plan. As expected Hague was characteristically measured and avoided rushing to judgement. Coe had not been enthusiastic and both Hague's political secretary George Osborne and PPS David Lidington were firmly opposed. However, by the time Lord Parkinson returned from his break some days after Hague had flown home, he found the leader convinced.

Hague had called Parkinson to a meeting at his Dolphin Square flat. Parkinson was alarmed at the idea: he had grave reservations, not least about the cost of organising and publicising a ballot at that point, and he also feared that the result might not be as clear cut as the leadership hoped. Anything short of the 80 per cent who had voted in favour of Hague's reform programme the previous year might not look sufficiently decisive.

When the proposal was put to the morning political meeting held in Hague's Smith Square office, Parkinson found he was not in a minority of one. Hague had called the meeting to clear the plan and had distributed a written proposal at the start of proceedings. While some of those present were familiar with the idea, for others it was their first encounter with it. Hague went round the table asking for reactions. Most were favourable although Osborne and Lidington spoke out in criticism, and the chief whip James Arbuthnot, a man whose tremulous demeanour leads some backbenchers to question his role in the party hierarchy, was also critical. He worried that it constituted an act of aggression against the party's left. Once Hague had made clear his own attraction to the plan, Arbuthnot swiftly reconsidered. By the end of the meeting Arbuthnot was in favour and Operation Sunrise was on.

Hague announced the ballot and its rules on 7 September. Ballot papers would go out to party members on 21 September to be returned by 1 October, and the result would be announced on 5 October, the eve of Conservative Party Conference. The question was simply a 'yes' or 'no' to supporting the shadow cabinet policy of opposing entry to the Euro at the next election.

Hague explained that the purpose was not to kick people out of the party if they voted against him, but to settle the matter according to a majority vote.

It was a controversial strategy, which when judged too quickly seemed like an own goal, and unsurprisingly it provoked withering criticism from Hague's opponents. Ken Clarke, Sir Edward Heath and Chris Patten dismissed the tactic and its intended effects. Michael Portillo and John Major were supportive. Press reaction was mixed with much comment suggesting the ballot was a superficial gesture that could not resolve the nation's most persistent political debate. The Euro-friendly fringe meetings would still go on at the conference and fronted by the party's most charismatic grandees would attract much attention.

Those criticisms proved accurate for the duration of the conference week, but also missed the point. The ballot, if decisive, would draw a line in the sand confirming official party policy. The views of others would be just that – the views of others.

Hague received the backing he required and had expected: 60 per cent of voting papers were returned, of which 84 per cent voted to back the policy. To short-termists it seemed a hollow victory when only a day later *The Sun* newspaper depicted Hague as a dead parrot, but over the longer term Hague had been vindicated. Confirming the policy at that stage in his leadership has allowed the Conservatives to campaign on a clear and distinctive platform for the European elections in 1999 and towards the next general election. Of course those principled advocates for a Single Currency can and do argue their case, but there is no confusing their views with official party policy confirmed by the party members. Throughout a period in which the Conservatives have struggled to rediscover their sense of purpose, Hague's Euro policy gave his party a platform which clearly differentiated it from New Labour and has ensured that voters have a choice on the key constitutional issue at the next election. To that extent it is qualitatively different from 'wait and see', especially as Hague has said that any practical argument for joining the Single Currency would have to be so strong as to overcome his objection in principle to doing so.

Although it seemed as though the Conservatives were a spent force, identifying and articulating legitimate concerns about the Euro certainly affected the national debate and has successfully frustrated the Government's freedom of movement on the issue. Initial enthusiasm for the Single Currency has been tempered as the Prime Minister recognised that Hague's line is more popular than his.

The European elections of May 1999 were some proof of that and brought Hague's leadership a much needed boost. The Conservatives were the winners with 36 per cent of the vote, beating Labour's 28 per cent and becoming the largest UK party in the European Parliament with thirty-six seats. The national turn-out of 23 per cent, however, indicated that this election had only motivated voters who were already exercised by Europe. In short, Hague had successfully shored up his core vote, a necessary endorsement but insufficiently enthusiastic to indicate the beginning of a substantial Conservative recovery. For Hague personally, though, the election results brought him survival at the end of a tumultuous few weeks.

In one area, European policy, Hague had eventually brought clarity and leadership, but it had not translated across a wider agenda and the weeks leading up to the June 1999 elections had been the most troubled of his leadership. Early doubts about his baseball-capped image had been replaced with more fundamental concerns.

From the moment he became leader in 1997 Hague and his team had been groping for a formula which would enable them to acknowledge the reasons for their defeat and move on. If too apologetic it would seem that the party was doing down its real achievements; if too confident it would seem to have learnt nothing. Based on the experience of regenerated right-wing parties abroad, and indeed of New Labour, Hague's advisers, particularly Danny Finkelstein and Andrew Cooper, were convinced that an extended period of public atonement was essential if the message of a changed party was ever to get through. This did not mean, as some interpreted it, that the party needed to decry any of its significant achievements – rather that it had to accept that it had lost and why.

Many of the senior members of the shadow cabinet, who were rightly proud of what they had achieved in government, were never convinced by the strategy. It seemed an illogical irony that the Conservatives should distance themselves from their own successes while New Labour had risen to success by convincing people that it had accepted the logic of those same achievements. However, the risk to the Conservatives of patting themselves on the back was that, whilst an appropriate fillip for the party faithful, it only reminded the public of all the associated negatives of the party in power. Finkelstein told the shadow cabinet: 'No matter how many times you replay the tape of the last election, we still end up losing. We need to accept that and move on.' Hague understood and commended the logic, but even he had found himself pulled both ways.

It was a confusion felt throughout the party. During the last period in opposition in the 1970s Margaret Thatcher and Keith Joseph had fostered a climate of creative thinking. Although the 1997 election had left the Conservative ranks devastated, the new intake had included forty newcomers, and the fresh blood brought hunger for political regeneration. But many of the newcomers had themselves been steeped in the culture of their failing party for years: previous Central Office insiders and ministerial advisers seemed to find it as hard as their more experienced Commons colleagues to adjust to the shock of being out of power and facing a pragmatic Labour government.

The problem that weakened the Conservatives' attack on Labour before the general election had ensured their defeat. It seemed the Conservatives were never really sure whether to attack the newness or the oldness of Labour. Without being able to set the agenda, the Conservatives were inevitably forced to oppose in a piecemeal fashion.

Within weeks of his becoming leader the first policy change that Hague announced was to back the proposals for a London mayor. In government the Conservatives had opposed the idea, but in opposition Hague was forced to accept it. Faced by the prospect that Londoners would vote in favour of a mayor, Hague had no practical alternative but to concede that the Conservatives had not understood the aspirations of Londoners. Yet in government it had been Hague himself who had mounted some of the party's strongest opposition to Labour's other devolution proposals. He dealt with Londoners' desire for self-government in one way, he dealt with nationalist aspirations in another. At the autumn referenda for a Scottish Parliament and a Welsh Assembly, the Conservatives pressed for a 'no' vote. Where he was able to employ a pragmatic response he had done so; where it would constitute too great a U-turn he had stuck by Conservative principles. Such day-to-day decisions were forced by Labour's agenda; Hague's responsibility was to identify a wider, positive agenda for the Conservatives and to re-engage with public opinion.

Although he received little credit for it, Hague, inspired by the Thatcher and Joseph precedent, did set about such a considered evaluation of his party's philosophy. This was a serious effort by his immediate team, although more seasoned members of the party believed Hague relied too heavily on close advisers and missed the opportunity to reach out to academics and specialists outside the party. His first two years have been crudely characterised as an exploration of 'compassionate' or 'caring' Conservatism, while the attention-grabbing, news-driven statements of the period leading up to and following the local elections of 2000 suggest a grittier Conservatism from the gut rather than the head. It is not surprising, if not wholly welcome, that the Conservative impulses Hague learnt during his formative years should have reasserted themselves as the prime influence in his policy pronouncements, especially as the 'common sense' approach certainly has the strategic advantage of contrasting him more definitely with Tony Blair. The real weakness, however, suggested by this development is the abandonment of a considered, strategic approach to repositioning the party, in favour of short-term profile raising.

In the early days the more pronounced rhetoric of compassionate Conservatism grew out of the efforts to address the reasons for the defeat. One way to admit to the failings of the Conservative government without rubbishing its achievements was to concede that, in order to introduce necessary reforms, the party had seemed overly concerned with economics. Now was the time for it to look at 'quality of life' issues, so Hague would talk about family life and a broader social agenda. On the advice of his team he made inclusive gestures like visiting the Notting Hill Carnival and sending a message of support to the Gay Pride. Such gestures suggested the Conservatives were softening and reaching out to a wider constituency, although not all were comfortable with explicit references to compassionate Conservatism, given its inference that 'ordinary Conservatism' was uncaring. Some observers concluded wrongly that compassionate Conservatism was a return to old-style Tory paternalism. In reality, however, Hague's efforts to wrest the One Nation mantle back from Tony Blair involved explaining why the policies of the right are inherently compassionate. 'I'd like to tell you about an open Conservatism, that is tolerant, that believes freedom is about much more than economics, that believes freedom doesn't stop at the shop counter. I'd like to tell you about a democratic, popular

Conservatism, that listens, that has compassion at its core,' he told the Blackpool audience in 1997 in the speech that was for many their introduction to their new leader.

It was not until some time later that Hague associated himself with an explicitly named 'Compassionate Conservatism'. In early 1999 he went on a fact-finding mission to Texas, where he met Governor George W. Bush, the Republican Presidential candidate who had deliberately branded his successful strain of folksy conservatism 'compassionate'. Bush had boosted his party's success through a popular programme of public spending targeted at core services and sold it in language aimed at including the whole social mix of his state.

On the same trip Hague also encountered Canadian common sense, a theme which was to fit his personality well. In substance Bush's strain of Compassionate Conservatism is much closer to Hague's Common Sense agenda than Hague's own early forays into rebranding the British Conservatives. For Bush, in an American setting, there is no contradiction in advocating a type of compassion that includes the death penalty, opposition to abortion and replacing the work of the state with free market alternatives, including religious charities. In the British context these views are not so mainstream, particularly in the political class, although they are the views of Hague. His Anglicised version of a similar agenda which has emerged since spring 2000 is more appropriately conveyed as Common Sense.

In 1997 many who had deserted Hague's party for New Labour required a specific apology. For them the party had to swallow a double whammy: it had sounded obsessed with economics and yet it had also managed to lose its reputation for economic competence. Speaking about the decision to take Britain into the European Exchange Rate Mechanism, Hague said: 'The time has come to be brutally candid about those events. Looking back I believe going into the ERM was a great mistake and I am sorry we did it.' It was an apology that made Norman Lamont and John Major wince: both considered it too simplistic, but it was one which Hague was set to repeat in several keynote speeches.

Hague himself has rejected as a cliché the analysis that would categorise him as either 'economically dry and socially wet' or 'liberal in economics and libertarian on social issues'. Unlike others who have been keen to brand the nuances of their beliefs, most notably Michael Portillo, Hague says defiantly: 'I am a Conservative.' By that he means he is a classic centre-right politician who believes in small government and low taxation but has strong convictions about traditional bonds of family, nation and history. In substance his views differed little from those of many of his former cabinet colleagues whose tone in government had contributed to the perception of an uncaring party. Conference speeches that had sought to make political capital by invoking stories of benefit-defrauding single mothers, the malign conspiracy of Brussels, and the bravery of the SAS had given the impression of a mean-spirited, chauvinist party. By contrast Hague had from the start of his leadership campaign adopted a more measured and inclusive tone. That, as much as any issues of substance, created an impression that he stood for a different kind of Conservatism.

Hague had learnt from New Labour the importance of finding a new language, but unlike Tony Blair his preoccupation with it was to find better ways of revealing, rather than concealing, the true nature of his party. Hague's fresh Conservative Party would immediately seem more compassionate by admitting to its past failings and discussing a range of issues beyond the economy. In a keynote speech on the family (to the Social Market Foundation in January 1998) he identified the way in which Conservatives had allowed themselves to seem remote and fundamentalist. 'We were worried that any attempt to draw connections between, for example, unemployment and criminality would look like a threat to individual moral responsibility ...We ought to be capable of both keeping a hold of individuals' responsibility for shaping their own lives whilst at the same time acknowledging that there are also wider truths which are borne out by statistical evidence.'

In the same speech Hague repeated his second policy: apology. In flagging up a feature for the next election manifesto, Hague said the Conservative government had been wrong to phase out married tax allowance. As a commitment to bolstering the family and proving the Conservatives are more than 'the economics party', this benefit would return under a Hague administration.

Although Hague should be given credit for his real effort to discuss the reasons for and the implications of his party's fall from power and popularity, such contemplation is not the stuff of newspaper headlines. Coupled with that, the party's exercise in 'Listening to Britain' struck some as further evidence of self-indulgent introspection in place of effective opposition.

Since June 1998 Peter Lilley had been Hague's deputy leader in charge of a policy review. The first stage of that review was 'Listening to Britain', another idea inspired by the USA, where in the aftermath of defeat the Republicans set about 'Listening to America' and found ideas that contributed to their return to success in mid-term elections. Every member of Hague's shadow cabinet was involved in the national programme of meetings, some with specific interest groups, and others with a general audience. It was partly a public relations exercise to demonstrate a newly humbled approach, and partly a genuine attempt to gauge the priorities of voters. As the party was too broke to afford much in the way of focus group research, 'Listening to Britain' constituted a nationwide focus group. The responses suggested that Hague was correct in looking to broaden the agenda and that if the party was to make a comeback it had to address the wide-spread perception that it did not care about public services.

This concern about public services went to the core of Hague's problems. Thus far his leadership had been short-termist. Although he had set a tone for measured contemplation, he had dealt with issues as they arose rather than determining a fixed strategy. Hague's strategy, as far as he had had one, was sensibly to concentrate on party reforms and dealing with the Europe issue: beyond that it was still to be thought through. In policy terms the outcome of 'Listening to Britain' offered the Conservatives an agenda on which they could move forward by developing practical solutions to bread-and-butter issues like education, health and transport.

But the potential solution was also fraught with problems. How far could or should the Conservatives champion new market solutions? Hague and his deputy were cautious, anxious that Labour could once again portray the Conservatives as dangerous privatisers. The dilemma was to reach crisis point almost two years into Hague's leadership when, exacerbated by an internal breakdown in communications, both appeared to repudiate Thatcherism.

On 20 April 1999, Peter Lilley, in charge of the policy review, presented the annual R.A. Butler lecture. He argued that Conservatives recognised the limitations of the free market in supplying social goods and welfare. Elsewhere in London, William Hague was addressing a dinner celebrating the twentieth anniversary of Margaret Thatcher's election as Prime Minister. On close inspection Lilley's speech was hardly a Damascene conversion to socialism, but its tone and its timing were haphaz-ardly provocative. Hague was forced to defend his deputy leader's line that evening and for days to come. It caused consternation in the ranks. Where MPs had questioned Hague's image and his management style, now they were questioning his beliefs. What was he all about? The unknown leadership contender who had risen to the top with the last-minute intervention of Lady Thatcher seemed to be repeating the treachery of her downfall: he had risen to prominence on her handbag straps and now he was unceremoniously dropping her.

In policy terms Lilley's speech was a natural, if clumsy, extension of the themes Hague had been considering during the first eighteen months of his leadership, an effort to prove the party had been listening and was ready to move on from its recent legacy of infighting; and its aim to reassure people that the public services were safe with the Conservatives accorded with the findings of private research.

In the autumn of 1998 the party had splashed out on a burst of polling. The conclusions were grim, confirming the suspicions of Cooper and Finkelstein that although many on the front bench had tired of apology, the message was nowhere near getting through to the public.

Andrew Cooper, who had been the Deputy Director of the Research Department during Major's government, had moved on to become Director of Political Operations: his expertise is opinion analysis and strategic advice. Like others in Central Office, Cooper had been impressed and inspired by an insider's account of Labour's transformation. As king of the focus group, Philip Gould had played a vital role in shaping the changes which had made New Labour electable, and his book *Unfinished Revolution* had detailed the disciplined steps that Labour had made to update its thinking, its operation and its aims, demonstrating that Labour's transition to power had been possible only as a result of a long, determined and focused strategy.

Hague too was an avid reader of Gould. When he later set up a Strategy Group of close advisers and senior members of the shadow cabinet, Hague gave each of them a copy of Gould's book with the inscription, 'Know thine enemy'. The book only served to highlight how lacking the Tories were in applying similar thinking, and the research that Cooper undertook in autumn 1998 provided further proof, showing that the bad impressions the Conservatives had created in government were as deeply held as ever. The party had long since stopped listening to the concerns of real people. It had lost touch with the 'kitchen table' issues.

Cooper had made no secret of his concerns about the inability of the shadow cabinet to fix a message and stay on it. Archie Norman, who had worked with him on the reforms of Central Office, was impressed by Cooper but feared his persistently critical tone would work against him, so challenged Cooper to work on the logic of his research and come up with some positive recommendations. Hence the next phase in the Conservatives' journey through opposition, the arrival at 'Kitchen Table Conservatism'.

The phrase had derived from an interview with Democrat Congressman Richard Gephardt who had blamed his party's bad showing in mid-term elections on the failure to address the issues that Americans discussed around the kitchen table. Cooper had coined the expression for use in an internal policy paper: it was never intended for public attention, although it was later offered to the press and portrayed as a relaunch, one step on from 'Compassionate Conservatism'.

The Kitchen Table Conservatives paper was completed late 1998 and copied only to Hague, Norman and Michael Ancram (who had succeeded Lord Parkinson as Party Chairman at the conference in Bournemouth). It made uncomfortable reading: the party had made no real headway since its defeat; Hague had made little impression outside party supporters; Conservatives had not demonstrated that they understood the reason for their defeat and thus still seemed arrogant and complacent. The fundamental problem was that the party did not have a strategy 'and has not had one for at least four years and arguably for the best part of a decade'.

Cooper's proposed strategy arose from three questions the Conservatives had to ask of themselves: 'Where are we now? Where do we want to be? And how are we going to get there?' Looking on from the outside, political pundits guessed that the Tories had a limited aim: relying on Euroscepticism to reconnect with their core vote, winning back the 750,000 supporters lost to the Referendum Party in 1997, and using that as a base for some sort of revival at a 2001 election. In fact, even that aim had never been articulated in Central Office.

The answer to the first of Cooper's questions was supplied by the research in the paper (as well as by countless other objective tests of public opinion). Together with Hague's head of policy, Danny Finkelstein, Cooper suggested answers for the other two. The party had to build on Hague's start in developing and using a new language that was rooted in the real world, rather than the 'beltway' of Westminster. It had to continue to rebuild trust in the economy. It had to neutralise its vulnerabilities on the key 'kitchen table' concerns about public services, and it had to identify and pursue new ideas for the future. Hague's leadership had to be shown to be strong, perhaps by demonstrating '10,000 volt' shocks. Such high-profile initiatives would include moves like calling the Euro ballot or, as proposed in the document, taking on the party traditionalists at the Carlton Club in a public challenge to drop their opposition to female members. For the longer term, the party had to decide what it stood for and where it was headed, both in its own right and in contrast to Labour. Tactically all of the party's activities had to be geared to this programme. It required a fundamental change, 'being prepared to rethink our entire agenda, not just continuing on auto pilot' and a ruthless and efficient use of professional campaigning techniques.

Although Hague disliked the expression 'Kitchen Table Conservatives', fearing it could seem trite, he was initially excited by the ideas in the paper. Having been offered a strategy on a plate, he told Cooper that he agreed with nearly all of it. (He was never specific about where he disagreed.) Archie Norman and Michael Ancram were impressed and supportive. It seemed as though the party's leaders, freed from the burden of internal reforms, were now ready to step up the fightback.

At a November meeting in the Opposition offices Hague gathered his closest colleagues, Archie Norman, Michael Ancram, PPS David Lidington, Lord Cranborne, Lord Strathclyde, press secretary Gregor Mackay and George Osborne. Copies of the original paper were circulated. There was little discussion, no debate. Hague simply told the group: 'This is our strategy.'

The progress towards implementing the strategy, however, was to be starkly interrupted by 'events'. When Hague gathered his top team for the November meeting, Lord Cranborne was his leader in the House of Lords, Lord Strathclyde his chief whip. Within days one had replaced the other in a sacking that did more to undermine Hague's leadership, and to prove the 'kitchen table' case for a more strategic approach, than any single event yet had.

With Hague's approval Lord Cranborne had been liaising with the Government about its plans for Lords reform. Although the shadow cabinet and the Commons benches had not reached a consensus about the appropriate Conservative solution for a new upper house, there was agreement on tactics. Without an agreed policy, the party was at least sure that it must not sign up to the first stage of removal of hereditary peers before seeing what New Labour were proposing in their place. The delaying tactic stalled the need to develop a policy that might have helped the Government or required Hague to challenge the most historic of interests in his party.

As Conservative leader in the Lords, Robert Cranborne owed a debt of loyalty to his party leader, but it proved to have a weaker hold on his affections than historic and family ties. Although Hague had been banging the Conservative drum from an unusually young age, in comparison with Cranborne he was a mere *arriviste*. A direct descendant of the Cecil family, which had given the country one prime minister and generations of contribution to the ruling élite, Cranborne had inherited the responsibilities of history. In the weeks since the beginning of the new session Cranborne had found his conscience increasingly troubled. Among his ancestor's bequests was the Salisbury Convention, an agreement that had effectively prolonged the existence of the hereditary principle by binding peers in a commitment not to disrupt the electorally mandated programme of a new government. The policy of the shadow cabinet to obstruct the passage of the European Elections Bill sat uneasily with Cranborne. It had been one of the Conservatives' most successful parliamentary campaigns under Hague's leadership. The bill passed easily in the Commons was repeatedly sent back by the Lords, where Labour were in a minority. Technically Conservative peers could reassure themselves that the Salisbury Convention had not been designed to deal with constitutional issues, but Cranborne and others felt uneasy about waging a continued campaign of disruption.

In his dealings with the Government, Cranborne had won, in June 1998, what he believed was an extraordinary concession: Tony Blair was prepared to water down his manifesto commitment to abolish the hereditary peerage, and the Government was offering to allow 10 per cent of hereditary peers survival of their first-stage cull. Cranborne and his close Lords lieutenants thought it likely that the second stage of reforms would be so long in the making that it allowed them time to negotiate a possible permanent reprieve. It was certainly a potentially embarrassing climbdown by Tony Blair, one from which the Conservatives could make considerable political capital.

However, it was not a plan that impressed the shadow cabinet. Blair's deal had too many strings. It required the compliance of Conservative peers in the passage of future changes to the upper house. Constitutional spokesman Liam Fox, shadow home secretary Norman Fowler and Michael Howard were strongly opposed to the proposal, objecting to it both in principle and for its arbitrary nature. Hague was more cautious. He was did not want to shoot a potentially advantageous fox, yet he was unwilling to be bumped into an agreement by Cranborne. So keen was Cranborne to secure the deal that he told Hague he was willing to complete the negotiations and then to stand aside in advance of their completion allowing Hague to take all the credit. Cranborne told Hague he was prepared to offer him an envelope containing his undated resignation, to be made public whenever Hague felt it politically advantageous to announce the deal. 'I'll go when it's necessary,' Cranborne told Hague. He was told that was not necessary and was instructed to carry on negotiating but not to agree to anything. Hague wanted to keep his options open.

With all the dramatic flourish of a true parliamentary power clash, the issue erupted on Wednesday 2 December 1998. In the morning Hague had had one of his most exacting sessions of judo, the physical combat an appropriate preparation for a day of politically bruising encounters. Later, preparing for Prime Minister's Questions, Hague caught wind of plans to double-cross him. The convenor of the Lords' crossbenchers was calling a press conference for 3.15 that day. Hague suspected what was afoot, although he didn't then know the extent of the treachery. The press conference was to unveil details of an agreement between the Tory peers and the Government, an agreement that Lord Cranborne had made without Hague's approval and that he was intending to put to the Association of Conservative Peers at

a meeting later that afternoon. Plans for PMQs were rapidly changed. Instead of attacking the Government on European tax harmonisation, Hague would seek to embarrass Blair by revealing that he was prepared to sell out on his commitment to end the hereditary principle. Unfortunately for Hague his intelligence on the day was not as informative as it needed to be, and in the event he was bested by Blair, who had the advantage of knowing the full extent of Cranborne's collusion.

It was a particularly bitter upset for Hague to be outdone by Blair in the one arena he had made his own. Even when Blair had been at his most popular in the country, Hague had reigned supreme in the chamber of the House of Commons. But not on this occasion: he had been done over by Cranborne and outdone by Blair, in a fiasco that he could have avoided had he followed advice made much earlier.

Cranborne was well liked by colleagues but had a slippery reputation. Apart from his historic loyalties no one was quite sure where he stood. Whether or not Hague thought the best of him, he was entitled not to expect the worst. Not all his advisers were so optimistic. Even at the beginning of the parliamentary session several weeks before the row blew up, there were enough clues seriously to worry some in Hague's team. Policy head Danny Finkelstein and Press Secretary Gregor Mackay advised Hague that he should head off potential problems with an exposé of the Government's plans during his response to the Queen's Speech. The day before the opening of Parliament, Mackay and George Osborne suggested another tactic for gaining the initiative. They wanted to leak the Government's proposals to the press. That way the unveiling of the Government's programme would be over-shadowed by press headlines announcing New Labour duplicity. Where his advisers smelled a rat, Hague was rather more chival-rous and not sufficiently cold-blooded. He refused to consider the leak strategy without first discussing it with Lord Cranborne.

Cranborne advised him against. On hearing that Hague was allowing Cranborne to continue, Hague's advisers became even more worried. They were convinced that the Leader in the Lords had a different agenda to Hague's and that it would lead to a direct clash between the two parliamentary wings of the Conservative Party.

The line that Conservative Central Office pushed and that most members of the Commons were prepared to voice was that Hague's eventual sacking of Lord Cranborne showed the smack of firm leadership. After Prime Minister's Questions Hague went immediately to the Lords with his PPS David Lidington, Michael Ancram and James Arbuthnot. As Hague swept into the meeting for the Association of Conservative Peers, Cranborne was on his feet addressing his colleagues. It turned into a bruising public encounter. Cranborne had planned his tactics carefully, as he was determined to win the argument. 'You never hold a meeting unless you know in advance what the outcome will be.' Many people in the room were convinced that Cranborne had struck the best deal possible. In a deliberate strategy to prove the seniority of the Upper House he had laid plans to humiliate Hague, having arranged for a host of former cabinet ministers and Conservative luminaries to speak in defence of his deal.

Hague believed they were being misled by their leader. He challenged Cranborne to come clean about the extent to which Conservative peers would be muzzled by his deal. The atmosphere was tense and antagonistic. It was clear to any observer that both men considered there were no grounds for compromise. At the close of the meeting Hague and Cranborne, accompanied by Lords chief whip Thomas Strathclyde, crossed the corridor into the Leader of the Opposition's office. Lord Carrington was also dispatched to try to broker a peace, but even his experience as a negotiator in the former Yugoslavia could not soften the atmosphere. Cranborne, seeing traces of farce in the prospect of being sacked by a man to whom he had already offered his resignation, turned his back to Hague in an effort to compose himself, but it was laughter and not anger he was trying to disguise. As he crossed the corridor he had caught the eye of his old friend Strathclyde, and the two had dissolved into swallowed giggles.

'Robert, you have been utterly duplicitous,' Hague told Cranborne.

'Yes. Will you accept my resignation, or would you prefer to sack me?' Cranborne offered, emasculating his leader's ultimate sanction.

'I would and you are sacked,' came the reply. It had all happened before Lord Carrington had been able to get a word in.

Adrenalin still rushing, Hague returned to the Commons and his colleagues in the shadow cabinet, who had been waiting patiently for close on an hour. Hague immediately informed them of Cranborne's sacking. There was a stunned silence. Gillian Shephard, a close friend of Cranborne's, broke the silence by questioning whether they could afford to lose people of his calibre, although she later admitted that Hague was left with little alternative. After absorbing the shock the rest of the shadow cabinet were supportive.

However, among some of the snobbier elements of the 1922 executive there were doubts about the appropriateness of a comprehensive school boy sacking the descendant of a prime minister, but the Committee as a whole gave Hague a tub-thumping welcome that evening. Most MPs believed but regretted that Hague had had no choice but to sack Cranborne. Privately many also reckoned it was not so much the smack of firm leadership but a last-ditch option. Hague too realised that his authority was under question.

When he returned to the Lords later that evening he knew he was fighting for his leadership. Unless he was able to fix a replacement for Lord Cranborne it was quite possible, as had been hinted at the meeting of the ACP, that the whole of the front bench would resign, leaving him forced to consider his own position. The obvious choice was the Lords chief whip, Lord Strathclyde – but as a close ally of Cranborne, Strathclyde was reluctant to take his place, not least because he had also been involved in brokering the deal with the government. Short of options, Hague was prepared to appoint him as long as the party did not concede its duty to oppose further details of the government's reform programme.

Despite the anger at Cranborne's dismissal, Hague had won some grudging respect at the meeting of Conservative peers. Baroness Young, then chairman of the ACP, was struck by his composure and calm presentation of his case. Hague had to use all the powers of persuasion he had, warning Strathclyde that the party simply could not function without the resumption of collective responsibility. Hague remains grateful for the intervention of Baroness Young, who forced Strathclyde to recognise his duty to the party as a whole. Young effectively saved Hague's leadership by securing Strathclyde as leader in the Lords and minimising the potential for further resignations from the front bench.

When several members of the Lords front bench went ahead and resigned the following day and newspapers were full of stinging criticism about Hague letting Blair off the hook, doubts took hold. It hardly seemed like firm leadership to have allowed the Lords to pursue their own agenda; it hardly seemed like firm leadership to lose so many off the front bench. Cranborne had behaved in his own words like an 'ill trained spaniel', but that he had been able to do so suggests that Hague should not have left him off the leash. At McKinsey, Hague had set briefs and devolved responsibility for their details. The 'hands off' approach to management has remained a constant which goes some way to explaining all of the problems that have beset Hague's leadership, and was most explicitly exposed by former frontbencher John Maples in an open letter to Hague two years later.

The Lords debacle had graphically illustrated the Tories' need to develop an agenda which would engage public attention beyond inevitable 'events'. It was time to go back to the kitchen table.

Hague wanted the whole of his team to grasp the logic of 'Kitchen Table Conservatism', so Cooper and Finkelstein were told to prepare a presentation for the shadow cabinet. Under the ever-watchful gaze of William Pitt, whose portrait dominates the oak panelled room, the lights were dimmed for a high-tech presentation. There in stark terms was the state of the party that all those seated around its highest table were responsible for and presided over. The words on the screen were taken from Hague's 1997 Conservative Party Conference speech: 'Our parliamentary party came to be seen as divided, arrogant, selfish and conceited. Our party as a whole was regarded as out of touch and irrelevant so we need to change our attitudes, our organisation, our culture.'

The presentation went on to explain the rest of the thesis – that from then on all those in the room had to lead the charge to be 'kitchen table Conservatives', conceding their 1997 defeat and moving on to issues of public concern, expressed in clear, principled and distinctive terms.

Opinion was divided. John Redwood, deeply suspicious of anything to do with focus groups, was unimpressed. The only person who really seemed to grasp the full implications was Gary Streeter. 'It means we will have to do everything differently,' he said.

Hague himself was even more convinced, telling his colleagues: 'I will judge the progress of the party and individuals against the application of this strategy.'

Cooper and Finkelstein were dispatched on a mission to

spread the message, and there followed a concentrated programme of presentations to groups of MPs, to councillors and to staff. Press coverage heightened the profile of the project. Cooper developed six rules that summed up the core values of the approach. Posters outlining each of these were put up around the Party's 'war room'.

The battle to win the hearts of ordinary people around their kitchen tables was on, and Hague himself made the clearest explanation of the approach in his speech to the party's spring conference in March: 'I am not asking the party to spend the next three years mumbling apologies. I am not asking the party to abandon the fundamental principles in which it believes. . . Instead I am asking the party to do something very simple, very human. Admit that for all our successes we made some mistakes. Admit that listening to the new priorities of the British people has changed our perspectives. Admit those simple, human things and move on.'

Hague had told his shadow cabinet that their career progression would depend on proven commitment to the strategy, but there was still confusion as to how exactly he himself would come to personify this new, improved vision. In the annals of failed political leaders, one particularly haunted Hague's advisers. The presidential ambitions of Teddy Kennedy had been irreparably damaged by his inability to answer a simple question in a television interview: 'Why do you want to be President?' What kind of answer would Hague give to an equivalent question? Research was showing that Hague's approval ratings had improved over the turn of the year as he had taken a tougher line over prisoner releases in Northern Ireland. When focus groups had been shown clips of Hague opposing Blair at PMQs, his approval ratings improved dramatically, from very negative to very positive. In January 1999 the advice of Finkelstein and Ceri Evans to break the cross-party consensus on the Northern Ireland peace process matched his own instincts and those of almost all senior Conservatives. It clearly followed that a tougher line would go down well in the party and have wider political benefits. It was successful and fulfilled one piece of 'kitchen table' advice to have him champion strong, distinctive issues. His advisers were anxious to build on the momentum of that success, and to encourage Hague gave him a video to play at home – a clip taken from a focus group in which Hague was strongly rated for his tough approach on Northern Ireland.

As part of the concerted effort to move the party out of the doldrums, Hague was pushed to put time aside for reflection. In February he toured North America to learn how Compassionate Conservatism and Common Sense Conservatism had helped turn round the fortunes of sister parties. Back at home he came under critical inspection.

Forced to put aside his own distaste for what he considers the indulgence of introspection and self analysis, Hague took time out to think about and confirm the foundation stones of his own Conservatism. He summoned up a vivid mix of his parents' views, part Republican individualist, part Conservative tradition-alist, proudly Eurosceptic and very positively Atlanticist. He has a visceral dislike of metropolitan élitism and a disregard for unearned privilege; he is not conventionally religious (having sometimes described himself as 'anti-religious') but opposes abortion and favours the death penalty; he is not a regular churchgoer but recognises the social value of shared observance; he has absorbed but finessed his father's gut patriotism and earthy reaction; he is motivated by his mother's sense of duty and devotion to the family; he believes he represents mainstream opinion and is utterly scornful of anything he considers 'politi-cally correct'. Everything that Tony Blair has fashioned himself to be, Hague is not.

Hague clarified his own objectives: he wanted to be Prime

Minister to champion his kind of common sense approach, emote less and deliver more, protect the nation, defend the family and run an efficient economy.

After contemplation, action. A second presentation was prepared for Hague to deliver to the shadow cabinet in the run-up to the May local elections. Cooper told him that the changes outlined in the kitchen table document had to be accelerated and that more than ever the single most important act for the party was to 'concede and move on'. Almost two years after his election, Tony Blair was still able to avoid discussing his own record in office by reminding people about the past Conservative Government. Danny Finkelstein had devised a line for Hague to deflect that tactic, so that when the Prime Minister mentioned Major's time in office Hague would counter, 'Every time I talk about the future, you talk about the past.' Cooper and Finkelstein argued that the party's ability even to start building a new agenda was hampered by its obsession with the past: their point was that no matter how disenchanted the public might become with New Labour, it would never regret throwing out the Conservatives in 1997.

As Hague's deputy in charge of policy development, Peter Lilley felt it was his responsibility to develop a line that would eliminate the negatives of past associations and accentuate the positives of a forward-looking agenda. He knew from Listen to Britain and the Kitchen Table research that health and education were the two areas on which the Conservatives were not trusted.

Lilley had particularly felt the blow of the Conservatives' defeat. A clever, assiduous minister, he had relished the work of government and operated well with the back-up of advisers and civil servants. Without the disciplines of office he had found it more difficult to apply himself, especially in the 'hands off' regime led by Hague. When Lilley decided to make a speech stressing the

Conservative Party's continued commitment to publicly funded health and education, it seemed completely consistent with current and historic thinking. After all, Prime Minister Thatcher had stressed that the NHS was safe in her hands and William Hague was a vocal defendant of state schools. As deputy leader, Lilley was responsible for vetting the speeches of other shadow cabinet members, but there was no one more senior assigned to vet his own.

The weekend before he was due to deliver the R.A Butler Lecture, Lilley phoned Hague at home in Yorkshire. The two men discussed the content of the speech. Neither considered it contro-versial, and both had underestimated the unintended but provocative implications of its delivery on the twentieth anniver-sary of Margaret Thatcher's election.

Earlier that week Lilley had circulated draft copies to senior members of the shadow cabinet, especially to those whose briefs it covered. The shadow health team, Ann Widdecombe and Alan Duncan, had been developing policies of their own: such had been the autonomy of individual members of the Shadow Cabinet that Widdecombe had herself dictated the pace of health policy on her own terms. At the Conservative Party Conference in 1998 she had wowed the audience with her unscripted speech, choosing to speak off the cuff so that she could effectively bounce the policy on. She had made reassuring noises by committing the party to maintaining 'current' spending on health to buy her the right to talk openly about the need for initiatives to break down the 'Berlin Wall' between the private and public sector, and she and her deputy Alan Duncan had been developing policies that would involve a more explicit role for private health insurance. Duncan had given a keynote speech arguing that case and received good reviews from the national press. On Lilley's request the speech had been softened, but it was the most bold expres-sion of the limitations of the NHS that the party had yet made.

Now they felt Lilley was in danger of undermining that message, if not completely reversing the direction of their policy. As well as the health team, shadow social security secretary Iain Duncan Smith and Francis Maude suggested some changes to tone down the speech. Michael Howard also advised a rewording. Widdecombe expected to be consulted again before the speech was finalised, but Lilley considered the speech cleared after his discussion with Hague and was coming under pressure to brief the press in advance of its delivery.

By the time Widdecombe returned from her constituency, rumours were circulating among Westminster journalists of a speech that would repudiate Thatcherism. She was alarmed but argued initially that, on substance, it was consistent with her message on health. Though the speech was not due to be delivered until the following evening, the damage had already been done. Journalists explained that the briefing they had received was clear and unapologetic: the speech was a U-turn away from Thatcherism.

No one accepts responsibility for authorising such a line; certainly Hague's lobby briefer Nick Wood knew that line would ensure coverage – but at what cost? The briefing indeed caught the imagination of the press, and it was clear what the next day's headlines would be.

An extremely acrimonious shadow cabinet meeting followed. Widdecombe demanded to know 'where the train was going'. Ironically, her most ardent backer was Michael Howard, angrier than he had ever been. The mess had confirmed his doubts about the whole 'concede and move on' strategy. It seemed as though the party was apologising for far more than its arrogant image and in the process risked losing its identity.

Finkelstein and Cooper were also dismayed. Their intention had been to focus the party on the future, not for it to make humiliating and confusing apologies for its past achievements.

Lilley had taken their message too much to heart, but it was really the briefing that ensured that an embarrassment became a crisis.

By the time the speech was delivered its substance was far less important than the impression it had created. Hague was extremely irritated about having to defend the speech in his own address to the Thatcher dinner and in articles, speeches and interviews for the next few weeks. Rather than reassuring the public that the Conservatives had no plans to privatise the NHS, it once again summoned up the impression of a confused and divided party still arguing out the debates of the 1980s.

It was a public relations disaster that again severely undermined Hague's leadership.

The press wanted to know the extent to which he had sanctioned the speech. An early draft was leaked to *The Times* by Michael Simmonds, the Membership Director, outraged at its implications. Simmonds's position at Central Office became untenable after an investigation into e-mails revealed him as the leaker, but that prompt action could not disguise the administrative faults that had contributed to the mess. Morale among MPs hit another all-time low. Some Thatcherites were contemptuous of Hague on ideological grounds, others just thought he was incapable of running a professional machine. It was a shock to discover that the man whose CV suggested great management skills seemed to be failing the party on just those grounds.

Once again Hague was aware of the fragility of his position. The conflict between his gut instincts and his intellectual interest in developing a more progressive agenda was an inherent weakness, restricting his ability to define clear objectives. Rumours around the House of Commons suggested angry MPs favoured Francis Maude as a possible replacement, but Hague's position was at least bolstered by the absence of any charismatic alternatives on the right. He realised that he had not paid sufficient attention to Lilley's speech, but felt that his deputy managed to make matters worse after the event by issuing increasingly confusing explanations of it. The party went on to make a respectable showing at the local elections, but Hague felt the debacle had prevented the Conservatives from winning several hundred more seats. His own ratings were down and even Alan Duncan, his oldest friend in politics, privately warned him that 'most sections of the electorate have already written you off as a potential prime minister'.

Duncan was no longer part of Hague's inner circle. Now even he, a former aide, empathised with other concerned critics who had constantly complained it was too difficult to get past Hague's private office to offer him counsel. Duncan resorted to a private memo to Hague urging him to articulate a strategy that would motivate his party, and more importantly to consider developing radical policy alternatives to New Labour. 'Everything is arbitrary, amateurish, confusing and lacking in intellectual discipline.' He wrote: 'We do have a lot to learn from New Labour but we are a long way from reaching their standard and there is little understanding about how to go about it'. When Duncan made his policy frustrations public in an interview with the *New Statesman* urging Hague to address the battle of ideas, his chances of promotion were curtailed. Hague particularly resented the timing of this criticism as it deflected from positive local election results. He felt there was political capital in being seen to reprimand Duncan, but he did not realise that Duncan's article had been cheered by those MPs increasingly worried about his lack of direction. Some Conservatives remained suspicious of the wealthy former oil trader. Others – and, on this occasion, Hague – considered him too much of a policy maverick.

Duncan's book *Saturn's Children* had made an intellectual case for legalising drugs, and for many Conservatives that alone was enough to damn him. Although Duncan's best-mate status had already been usurped by Seb Coe, Hague was genuinely irritated with his old friend. There was an angry phone call and then the reprieve in Yorkshire when Hague agreed to discuss Duncan's thesis. It required a change of priorities, a willingness to risk losing short-term electoral improvement in order to search out a long-term role for the party in a battle of ideas.

Lilley's fate was more final. He left the shadow cabinet in a reshuffle that also saw the voluntary departure of Michael Howard, Gillian Shephard and Norman Fowler. Lilley had told Hague that he was expecting to go, and Hague felt that Lilley's credibility had been irreparably damaged and he no longer had any faith in his ability to deliver the policy review.

The departure of so many of the faces associated with the Major government came soon after the positive results of the European elections. It marked an essential reprieve for Hague. Many of his doubters were prepared to give him credit for winning the elections and for establishing his own team in good time for a 2001 general election.

Behind the scenes there were also important changes which have played a significant part in the development of Hague's emerging brand of popular Conservatism. Hague beefed up the role of the strategy group, a sub-committee of senior members of the shadow cabinet, in an attempt to prevent future mismanagement. He introduced a set of subject committees within the shadow cabinet, covering home affairs, foreign affairs and the economy, more thoroughly to vet statements and policy proposals. Tim Collins MP, a former Director of Communications at Central Office, was brought back to develop a more effective system of liaison between departments. The job of managing the policy review was passed to Andrew Lansley MP, a former director of the Conservative Research Department, who had brought system and discipline to the planning of the European election campaign.

For the first time since Hague had become leader he worked to a day-by-day grid (known internally as the 'Stalingrid') that had been devised by Lansley, who like Collins had cut his teeth during tough times in the party's recent history. Like Hague both are middle-class, state school educated meritocrats with right-of-centre convictions on the economy, law and order and Europe. Their influence over the character of policy is obvious and insiders recognise that Lansley has overtaken Finkelstein as Hague's most important policy adviser.

In September 1999 the shadow cabinet got together to discuss plans for their party conference in Blackpool. No one there was quite sure what to call the document that would reveal their most considered statement of policy so far. When Peter Lilley had started the project its working title was the 'Agenda for Britain'. Other similarly bland thoughts were discussed, perhaps 'Forward with Britain', maybe 'Beyond the Millennium'.

Hague was frustrated. None of these titles seemed to sum up the essence of his or the Conservatives' approach. Suddenly Ann Widdecombe, who had become his deputy, had a breakthrough. 'What about "Common Sense Revolution"?'

Surprisingly the thought had not occurred to Hague, even though earlier that year he had met the Canadian Conservatives who had devised the phrase. He knew immediately that Widdecombe's thought was inspired.

The 'Common Sense Revolution' formed the backbone to Hague's most successful conference thus far. Buoyed up by the Prime Minister's conference rant against the 'forces of Conservatism' the previous week, Hague believed that he now had something positive to offer those Conservatives that Tony Blair had offended.

Lansley, Finkelstein and a former civil servant Paul Raynes had devised a package of specific guarantees to replicate the five pledges that Labour had used so successfully in the run-up to the 1997 election. Beyond that the 'Common Sense Revolution' was a term that, without being too explicit, at last captured the essence of Hague's Conservatism. It was gutsy, straightforward and practical. Only three weeks before the conference a group of interested Conservatives and sympathetic journalists had crowded into the party's most traditional home, the Carlton Club, to hear a private preview of the document, but even the splendour of the surroundings could not distract from their disappointment. Neither Lansley nor Raynes had been able to inspire with any specific insight into their common sense vision. Lilley had left the policy review in such an undeveloped state that much of the work was still being done in the days leading up to its launch at the party conference, so it was a surprise when Hague and his team unveiled a document that was broadly well received by the party and the press – although in one area, taxation, the disadvantage of producing policies in haste soon became apparent.

The Common Sense Revolution developed the traditional Conservative belief in small government into a set of policies that defined a Tory version of devolution, devolving decision-making to parents, patients and communities – more common sense than revolutionary, but Hague likes to suggest that he is leading a grass roots rebellion against the contrived Third Way of Blairism.

As an umbrella heading the Common Sense Revolution has worked effectively, allowing Hague to pull together subsequent policy announcements under a common theme of passing power away from the centre directly to the people. If the common sense theme contrasts well with some of the more contrived elements of New Labourism, the 'revolution' is as much a move on from the tendency of Thatcher's government to centralise as it is a reaction against Blair. In that sense the document turned an important corner for Hague, beginning to offer a new version of Conservatism for a new set of problems.

Chapter Eleven

A Taxing Problem

We need to start by winning the argument for low taxes all over again. We need a revolution in our approach to tax that makes a virtue of honesty and transparency. We need to break through people's understandable cynicism that every politician puts up taxes – some openly, some by stealth, some despite good intentions. So we offer a Tax Guarantee that a Conservative government would cut the overall burden of tax over the lifetime of the next parliament and so put an end to stealth taxes.

William Hague, 'The Moral Case for Low Taxation',

speech to Politeia, 15 March 2000

When Michael Portillo returned to the House of Commons at the Kensington by-election the month after the 1999 Conservative Party Conference, commentators predicted a new set of problems for Hague.

But the problem that Portillo soon identified, a flaw in the Common Sense Tax Guarantee, was not the one they had in mind. The charismatic, remodelled former darling of the right was thought to be the obvious contender for leadership in any future challenge. There was still a group of Portillistas in the House, although many had to admit that in terms of policy there seemed to be little between Hague and their man – and Hague had effectively neutered their ability to organise by making the chief parliamentary Portillista, John Whittingdale, his own PPS. Elsewhere their influence had also dispersed. Central Office had lost Michael Simmonds and Andrew Cooper (whose job had gradually become redundant as Kitchen Table Conservatism morphed into the Common Sense Revolution under Lansley's direction).

When Portillo was appointed shadow chancellor in February 2000, replacing Francis Maude, he was prevented from inheriting his predecessor's chief of staff in what developed into a hysterical row, and David Prior, Archie Norman's successor as Chief Executive, had to deal with the argument that threatened to result in the departure of the Communications Director and the shadow foreign secretary.

Robbie Gibb had worked loyally for Francis Maude and for Hague, whom he had supported through the leadership contest, but his well-known enthusiasm for Portillo suggested to some, particularly Amanda Platell, that he might use the post to undermine the leader. Hague had ruled against Gibb, but with no proof that he had been disloyal referred the decision to Prior, who concluded that there was no case against Gibb. But Platell threatened to resign if Gibb was allowed to work for Portillo. When Hague told advisers that Gibb was 'just staff' and thus dispensable it precipitated a furious row with Maude, now shadow foreign secretary, who threatened to stand down from the shadow cabinet. The row was only defused when Gibb, barred from joining Portillo's team, departed for the private sector and Maude accepted that his own departure from the top team could precipitate a crisis for Hague's leadership. An immediate crisis was averted, but the row has had a lasting effect, severely undermining both Maude's and Portillo's already low regard for Platell and her assistant Nick Wood.

Ironically Gibb's replacement in the shadow chancellor's office was Malcolm Gooderham, a former member of the

Research Department, whose Portillista credentials were well known to many except Platell. Portillo, however, did inherit something from Maude's shadow chancellorship: the 'Tax Guarantee'.

In their eagerness to give the Common Sense Revolution some impact, Hague, Lansley and Maude chose to risk the potential problems of their Tax Guarantee. Lansley had worked on the Tories' last successful general election campaign, in which the 1992 'tax bombshell' attack on Labour had helped secure victory for the Tories. The iconic status of low taxation as a defining characteristic of Conservatism cannot be overestimated in Tories who grew up with Margaret Thatcher, and Hague, who is so inspired by the battles of the 1980s, has sought to reclaim the low tax cause with his high-profile advocacy of the moral case for such policies.

Under Major's government the Tories had lost their reputation for economic competence and for being the low tax party, and Labour had been able to capitalise on that by pledging not to raise income tax, creating the impression that they, not the Conservatives, were now the low tax party.

The frustration for the Conservatives was that, although they stuck to their pledge on income tax, Labour did start raising taxes almost as soon as they came to power. Gibb had devised the phrase 'stealth taxes' to try to get the message across to the public that taxes had gone up, and when devising the Tax Guarantee Maude was insistent that the wording should contrast the Tories' intentions with Labour's record. The document stated: 'We pledge that taxes will fall as a share of the nation's income over the term of the next parliament under a Conservative government. By stating that tax will fall as a share of GDP the guarantee ensures a government cannot put up taxes by stealth.' So concerned were the Common Sense architects to stress this point that they overlooked the impracticality of their pledge, a flaw that rendered it less a guarantee than a statement of intent. In the event of a recession, business receipts fall and the proportion of GDP taken in taxes could also fall, forcing the Government to make expenditure cuts or to borrow to cover the cost of the rising proportion of state spending. Even without specific tax cuts during a recession, the Tax Guarantee raised the spectre of cutting state spending on social security, health or education.

Labour was delighted with this Tory own goal, and Millbank Tower election planners relished the prospect of running a campaign that forced Hague to reveal where he would make cuts.

In a deft move, Hague was quick to bring Portillo into the shadow cabinet. There was a risk that Hague was offering his most obvious rival a platform from which to rebuild his own constituency in the party, but now he was tied by shadow cabinet responsibility. The role of shadow chancellor for Portillo was crucial to Hague's calculations. He was giving Portillo the most difficult job in his team, opposing impressive Chancellor Brown, who was running a successful economy. It would be hard for Portillo to make an impact, and if he did it would be to the good of the whole party, and thus Hague's leadership. In terms of protecting his position in any post-election challenge, it was generally considered a sensible tactic in what was otherwise a contentious reshuffle. John Maples was more surprised than many of his colleagues that he was the first victim: Hague thought Maples had not pulled his weight as shadow foreign secretary. As Maples later explained in his critical open letter to *The Times*, he had not responded well to Hague's devolved management style but thought Hague's reasons for sacking him were weak. In the privacy of the Leader's office Hague told Maples he was just unlucky: 'Someone has to go to make room for Michael; it's either you or Francis and I'm afraid it's you.' Unlike John Redwood, Maples – an urbane liberal who was a Treasury minister under John Major – had no power base within the parliamentary party.

Redwood, whose dismissal Hague also explained as just a manoeuvre to allow room for a new face, has a band of vocal supporters to which he had added new fans impressed with his effective shadowing of Margaret Beckett (Trade) and John Prescott (Environment). Their irritation at his removal was matched by their concerns about Hague's judgement, since Redwood's replacement was Archie Norman. For all of Redwood's 'Vulcan' tendencies, he had proved himself the Tories' best Commons weapon against Labour. Norman, by contrast, had little standing as a parliamentarian. Redwood had suffered from taking the logic of Hague's *laissez faire* management too far. The previous summer he had developed a controversial plan for injecting private money into the London Underground and wanted to launch it without Hague's approval: he was prevented from doing so only by Hague's holiday stand-in, Ann Widdecombe. The episode enhanced Widdecombe's position but suggested that Redwood was a little too independent.

Media advisers had always been gunning for Redwood because of his associations with the Tories' turbulent past, but his supporters believed Hague's agenda should not be dictated by concerns about image.

At a dinner of the right-wing 92 Group soon after the reshuffle, Hague was left in no doubt about the displeasure of many of his parliamentary colleagues. The atmosphere was tense and angry. The first criticism was voiced by John Bercow, who politely but firmly suggested that Hague had made the wrong decision. Others followed but as Bercow was a member of the front-bench team his intervention was the most serious. Hague accepted he had underestimated Redwood's strengths, and a few months later he reshuffled him back into the team with anti-Labour spinning responsibilities.

Hague's gamble in bringing Portillo to the top table quickly seemed to have paid off. Within a few days of becoming shadow chancellor, Portillo had conceded two points to Labour: he announced the Conservatives would not seek to overturn the minimum wage, and that they would support an independent Bank of England. Clever Hague: Portillo was doing the party's necessary dirty work in 'conceding and moving on' in economic policy, but he was confusing his own supporters. Right-wingers wondered what their previous hero was all about. Now they feared that Portillo's newly defined social liberalism was dampening his economic prospectus. It seemed that Hague had no need to fear that Portillo would outflank him on the right, although Portillo's new clothes were opening up the possibility of a rather different challenge in the future.

Portillo's priority was and is maintaining a unified front, although his most ardent supporters still hope that he will eventually overtake Hague. Watchful for his long-term prospects, Portillo's closest political allies warned him about the dangers of having to defend the Tax Guarantee. Portillo was initially unwilling to rock the boat even in a private challenge to Hague's policy, but the warnings were vociferous. Even before he was made shadow chancellor, Portillo's natural preference for tax cuts was being challenged by his newly informed doubt about the Tax Guarantee, so when Hague offered him the job he explained that he would use his own set of words to justify it. On the advice of Gooderham, Portillo's version of the Tax Guarantee was to present it as an aspiration, something the Tories would do as long as the economy offered up the right circumstances. The unofficial rewording was met with a stern response from Hague's office, stressing that Hague, not Portillo, was in charge of policy direction. Hague approved of the Guarantee and was reluctant to change it, although he was becoming increasingly aware that the policy had many critics within his party.

John Major had written an article suggesting weaknesses in the Tax Guarantee; though in private he thought the scheme mad. Doubts were also spreading among MPs, who feared the likely Labour assault, and the authoritative BBC political programme *On the Record* set about making a film exposing the unease. When journalists telephoned MPs on a Friday in early March, several admitted that the centrepiece policy was just wrong. Stephen Dorrell, a former Treasury minister, agreed to give a critical interview. When news of the programme reached the Central Office news operation a silencing operation worthy of New Labour swung into action. When journalists called back on Monday MPs had revised their opinions, and Dorrell gave an interview so anodyne that it could not be used.

Hague was forced to admit that the policy could prove a campaign liability, although he wanted to hang on to the spirit of the Guarantee. Portillo had vowed not to rock the boat but the pressure on him to effect a change was pushing him to press Hague for a change. Once Hague had accepted his shadow chancellor's argument he had to wait for the best opportunity to alter the policy, but realised that nothing could be done immediately.

Even in March 2000 the party was still struggling to make headway in the polls, and Hague wanted his party's standing to improve before making the change. He had plans for a series of moves that he believed would give the Conservatives, and his leadership, a new lease of life. Aside from the Tax Guarantee, the Common Sense Revolution had had a favourable launch but had made little impact with voters. Of all the five guarantees, the only one that had made an impression was the doomed Tax Guarantee. Hague believed that the pre-Christmas campaigns against 'bogus asylum seekers' that Ann Widdecombe had fronted and his own defence of section 28 had popular appeal, and had also noted the outcry at the case of Norfolk farmer Tony Martin, found guilty of murder after shooting a burglar. These were issues that Hague intended to make his own before changing the Tax Guarantee.

His calculation was astute. Having put the Government on the defensive over the summer, July and the Queen Mother's birthday offered Hague the opportunity to change the Tax Guarantee.

The press operation was carefully planned and reflected Hague's priorities rather than those of his shadow chancellor. Portillo had argued that if the party was really to benefit from making the change it should be blatant about it, while Hague preferred a more subtle approach which also matched his own ambivalence about their actions. Even at this stage Hague hoped that he would be able to justify the change as an improved guarantee, rather than as a policy dropped, and wanted to sugar the pill of an embarrassing climb down by offering new policy alongside.

Hague prevailed. The announcement was planned for 11 July, the day of an official service to mark the Queen Mother's centenary birthday, and royal pictures were likely to dominate the next day's papers and distract attention from Hague's retraction. An exclusive deal was struck with the *Daily Telegraph*, which ran an interview with Hague, an article by Portillo and a front page news story announcing the Tories' intention to restore the married couple's tax allowance. Further down the article it explained that Hague had decided to rethink the Tax Guarantee, stressing that increases in spending on health and other vital services would take priority over tax cuts in the event of an economic crisis. In other words, Hague's original guarantee was as Portillo had explained, merely an aspiration. If Hague had pulled off such a U-turn earlier in his leadership he would have been pilloried by the press, but in the context of his recent newsworthy campaigns he was finally being taken more seriously. The move was welcomed as a sensible and brave change of heart, with Hague taking the credit for Portillo's judgement.

Chapter Twelve

UPPING THE ANTI

We are outflanked on patriotism and crime; we are suffering from disconnection; we have been assailed for spin and broken promise . . . we have appeared soft on crime, not pro-family, lacking in gut patriotic instincts.

Philip Gould, leaked private memo to Tony Blair

Not that Hague would have been bothered, but in the minimalist Tuscan dining rooms of Islington and the morally indignant salons of Hampstead his populist crusade was curdling the goat's cheese gazpacho. In the eyes of his hated 'liberal élite' Hague's common sense was really the politics of the lowest common denominator.

Since December 1999 Hague's uncompromising line on asylum, crime and section 28 had brought him a new lease of life with the Conservative press and was making New Labour uneasy.

Margaret Thatcher had introduced section 28 of the Local Government Act in 1986 to prevent local government spending public money on promoting homosexuality. Critics had always argued that the law was discriminatory and fostered prejudice, but supporters maintained that it was rightly up to parents to teach children about the nuances of sex education. Opposing Labour's pledge to overturn the law had become a *cause célèbre* for campaigners for traditional values. The Government could hardly endorse Hague, but as a leaked memo from Blair polling guru, Philip Gould, revealed in summer 2000 they recognised that Hague was eating back into their middle England support. It was a particularly sweet irony for all those who had made Gould a cult figure in Central Office.

However, some Conservative supporters shared a liberal-minded distaste at the emerging Hague model 2000. Shaun Woodward's defection to Labour in December 1999 and businessman Ivan Massow's similar move in August 2000 were damaging. As a former Communications Director at Smith Square, Woodward had contributed to the Tories' general election success in 1992. In both cases the facts behind their actions are less significant than the impression it builds of a narrow, intolerant party. Hague thinks both departed for issues of personal advancement rather than of conscience. He had offered Woodward amendments to section 28 to address the specific issue of school bullying, and insists that he had never offered Massow a peerage as the press has claimed. Did their departure reveal the party was lurching to the right under Hague? No, but it confirmed that their cause is not a priority for Hague, and that he had effectively abandoned his earlier attempts to reposition the party.

It also highlighted the inconsistencies of his own record.

As a junior minister, Hague had taken the bold move for a Conservative MP of voting in favour of equalising the homosexual and heterosexual age of consent at sixteen; as leader of the party he absented himself from a similar free vote under Blair's government. If not a complete change of heart, this is a sign that since becoming leader Hague is increasingly aware of the value of appealing to the more traditional sections of his own party, who themselves represent the potent values of his own background.

The section 28 campaign has been spearheaded in the House of Lords by Baroness Young, to whom Hague still owes a debt of gratitude for her role in resolving the Cranborne row. Young showed Hague evidence emerging from the investigation into child abuse that he had set up as Secretary of State for Wales, suggesting that certain convictions could not have been achieved if there had been an equal age of consent at sixteen. If people chose to interpret his recent stance on that and section 28 as homophobic, so be it. Hague has a clear conscience: he has always had gay friends and close colleagues, and his record of appointments shows he does not discriminate on grounds of sexuality; however, as a cultural conservative he finds it hard to embrace the more flamboyant aspects of gay culture, has told friends that 'objecting to homosexuality is like objecting to rain'. That may stop short of being an unreserved endorsement of a different culture, but in a move recognising his own inadequacy for such a role he has brought Steven Norris into the Central Office team to devise an inclusiveness drive.

The election for mayor of London highlighted conflicting views in the Tory body politic and pointed to fertile territory from which a future challenge to Hague could emerge. Norris, a social liberal, decided on a deliberate policy to offend the sensibilities of the *Daily Telegraph* with his opposition to section 28 and his apparent lack of concern about gay sex in public places. Hague tolerated Norris's position as an appropriate agenda for a metropolitan audience, although he is not completely comfortable with it. In trying to encourage the forces of reform within his party, while apparently favouring the forces of reaction, Hague undermines his ability to represent either, and has possibly sown the seeds for an alternative power base within Central Office.

On asylum, Hague's argument in the run-up to the local elections 2000 that certain areas were facing a 'flood' of illegitimate asylum seekers brought him accusations of racism. Again, there were Conservatives who felt uneasy at their leader's rhetoric, and again Hague made some attempt to reassure them that he is more than a populist. A close reading of 'Common Sense on Asylum', his keynote speech to the Social Market Foundation in May 2000, reveals a thoughtful, considered argument which studiously avoids inflammatory prose. Advisers in Central Office say the word 'flooding' appeared in their election literature by mistake and should have been excluded in the final drafts. But Hague has consistently defended his use of the word, both in media interviews and in the House. Privately he is also adamant that he is right to use the word 'flood', and he seems to relish the fact it is not 'politically correct'.

The real encouragement for this straight-talking Hague was the response he received on his 'Keep the Pound' tour. After a faltering beginning in St Albans when he arrived late, the flatbed lorry tour refreshed his taste for popular campaigning. From the back of a lorry in town centres he feels he has tested the temperature of public opinion on issues other than Europe. Early outings suggested crime and asylum were serious concerns. In Bolton a man in the crowd accused Hague of racism. Seb Coe recalls that the heckler was shouted down. When Hague appeared on BBC's *Question Time*, he was again accused of racism but had no compunction in defending himself and his right to argue that taking action against 'bogus' asylum seekers was practical politics, not racism.

On the case of the Norfolk farmer Tony Martin, Hague again offended liberal opinion and faced the charge of opportunism when he suggested a change in the law to protect people defending their own property. Hague believed that he was representing a widespread dismay at Martin's conviction for murder rather than manslaughter, but to many it seemed reasonable that Martin, who had killed with an illegal automatic weapon, had been found guilty of murder. Certainly Hague has become more adept at timing his interventions, choosing the moment of maximum impact to issue statements, but on the Martin case a charge of insincere opportunism does not stick. Of all his populist campaigns the Martin case most closely chimes with his own convictions. The idea that an Englishman's home is his castle is the stuff of Hague's upbringing. It coincides absolutely with the strain of American Republicanism that informs his beliefs. Hague would be more than happy to campaign under a banner of being tough on crime, even tougher on criminals. An authoritarian concern with law and order issues has been a consistent strain in his beliefs since childhood. When Hague later suggested tougher laws to deal with paedophiles in the light of the tragic murder of schoolgirl Sarah Payne, most comment was favourable. Surprisingly, given that the Government had maintained a disciplined silence, he was not judged to be exploiting the case but to be responding sensibly to an issue that had provoked deep public anxiety. His suggestion that persistent paedophiles face mandatory life sentences was matched with a strong condemnation of vigilantism.

The more confident, high-profile Hague of 2000 has confused some observers. Whether he had found his new voice through political expediency or articulating his convictions, it did not seem to match his earlier rhetoric of compassion and inclusion. Had Hague changed? Which phase told us more about the real Hague?

Hague's remarkable career progression reflects the old adage that nothing succeeds like success. His academic and professional career prove that he is exceptionally clever and focused; his ministerial career revealed that he is an efficient pragmatist and a shrewd tactician, a politician who will respond to each issue in the circumstances of the moment rather than applying an overarching philosophy. He encountered problems only after becoming leader, and has started to make any sort of public impact only with his stand on the pound and these populist campaigns.

But for Hague this phase is about more than shoring up his
core vote, although early polls suggested it could have that effect.
The enhanced confidence of the Conservative leader came from
more than scoring political points. It shows Hague had found his
stride with campaigns that flow from his own convictions. For a
man who had faced constant pillorying for three years, his reception on these issues was a valuable personal boon and offered him
new platforms that he was eager to embrace. In April 2000 he
was given a rapturous welcome by thousands of evangelical
Christians at their annual 'Spring Harvest'. Although Hague has
never been at all religious, he was more than happy to discuss the
common ground of his family values message with this devout
audience.

Against this background of apparent validation, Hague was
less worried than he had been about the elements of his personal
philosophy that had sent conflicting messages. Hague felt reassured that the voice he had found which most accurately reflected
his gut instincts had succeeded, where previous efforts had not,
in lifting the Tories out of the doldrums. The impression he had
once given of being a 'touchy feely' politician has passed. Hague
nevertheless continues to advocate his own version of compassionate Conservatism, as he did when addressing the
International Democratic Union at the Republican Party
Convention in Philadelphia in August 2000. It is just that
Hague's compassion is more akin to 'tough love', and his inclusiveness welcomes anyone into the party but makes no
concessions in his treatment of any one group.

The summer of 2000 has revealed more about the man the
Conservative Party prematurely chose as its leader, but not
enough yet about whether he has long-term plans for its recovery.
Anxious Conservative activists reassure themselves that straight-
talking Hague could yet become the people's choice, but to break

out of this narrow constituency and win broader support he must convince people that his party amounts to more than a vehicle for reactive campaigning, more than a news-driven protest group.

As Hague prepared for what is likely to be his final party conference before his first general election as leader, he faced the depressing prospect that the boost provided by his populist campaigns had only been a temporary distraction from the Conservatives' persistently weak position. Late summer opinion polls had confirmed that despite their declining popularity New Labour's poll rating remains high. The gloss has come off New Labour, in part due to Hague's energetic criticisms, but most people intend to vote for them none the less. In August only 29 per cent of people polled by MORI said that they would vote Conservative in an immediate general election, putting the party back below its 'flatline' persistent rating of around 30 per cent throughout Hague's leadership. It was a bitter blow to Hague, who had believed he had turned a corner.

Three conferences ago he had made his debut as leader. Commentators of all hues had written him off as the Michael Foot of the Conservative Party, but unlike Foot he had successfully minimised the key ideological rift in his party. His policies on Europe had won the Conservatives their first national election in seven years in May 1999. With so low a turn-out it was no indicator of a general election recovery, but the European elections had consolidated his hold on the leadership and a year later he had beaten Labour into their worst local elections results for years. May 2000 had been a mixed message for the Conservatives, however, with the loss of the Romsey by-election to the better organised but increasingly anonymous Liberal Democrats.

To those who said he was delivering his party into the hands of zealots, he could argue that what they had called extremism had found a degree of popular approval that Old Labour's excesses had never achieved, and that New Labour's advisers envied.

To those who had said he would not last, he had proved himself resilient and determined.

To those who had predicted a new golden age for Labour, Hague could say: 'I told you that New Labour would bring fascination, admiration, disappointment and then contempt, and in summer 2000 we saw the second phase begin to make way for the third.'

To anxious supporters who had said he needed to broaden his agenda and offer positive reasons to vote Conservative, he could point to 'Believing in Britain', an effort to motivate party members with a vote on a prototype manifesto, even though he knew it might bear little relation to the final version. To his controversial but distinctive stance on crime, asylum and the family he had added positives such as 'common sense' on schools, hospitals, pensions and tax – but in competition for column inches these made nowhere near the impact of his coaxed admission of 'fourteen pints' teenage machismo. 'Believing in Britain' has been the start of what Conservative strategists call 'painting the sky blue' – that is, suggesting why things could be better under a Conservative government. The theme is positive and confident: to make Britain the best place in the world in which to live and to do business. Hague's method is to stress decentralisation, low regulation and the common sense agenda on social issues. The aim was high, but it had diluted the impact of the original common sense guarantees (one already discarded) and lacked the immediacy and saleability of New Labour's pre-1997 pledges.

As Hague launched this pre-election phase he knew that he had at first underestimated the dire position of his party after their 1997 defeat, that he had seriously struggled to find a new role for it, and that his critics still doubted he had. He knew he had to use this conference to enthuse his troops, so he prepared to talk about bold new policies devolving power to parents, patients and taxpayers, although no one could predict which might be adopted by the chameleon-like Government. He prepared to stir the party faithful with his defence of the Pound, and he relished the prospect of challenging Blair to respond to the EU's increasingly federalist agenda, to be highlighted at the Nice summit in December. Characteristically he did not dwell on the state of the economy, which he knows is the single factor most likely to ensure Labour a second term.

So in the run-up to the 2000 conference Hague can reassure himself that he is not a Tory version of Michael Foot. But is he destined to be the Conservatives' Kinnock, a party moderniser who establishes the foundations of recovery but lacks the credibility to win sufficient public support? Like Kinnock, Hague will fight his first general election as leader against a charismatic, iconic leader. Hague takes comfort in the fact that voters' loyalties have grow increasingly fickle and he maintains that he can (not that he will) win.

Conservative MPs set a less exacting measure for his survival. To continue as leader Hague must cut the Labour majority at the next general election well into double figures and put the Conservatives in sight of victory at the election after that. Hague has never, even to his closest advisers, articulated a two-term strategy, yet if he manages to emerge as Kinnock after his first general election, a stronger leader of a stronger party – that will qualify as a success, but only as long as his popularity increases. If MPs believe another candidate would have broader appeal, they will be ruthless in deposing Hague. His own changes to the party rules have made his position slightly more secure, and new Conservative MPs entering the House after the next election will start off loyal, in part owing their success to Hague and relying on him for future advancement. However, as Hague has increasingly defined his politics he has opened up the possibility of a tectonic shift on the Tory benches. For now he has successfully claimed the mantle of the right, but if his 'common sense' fails to broaden the appeal of the Conservatives, MPs may look to an alternative right-winger or a centrist. In contrast to the blunt, traditionalist Hague stands reconstituted Portillo, Eurosceptic but socially progressive.

As Chairman of the International Democratic Union, a fellowship of right-wing parties launched by Ronald Reagan and Margaret Thatcher, Hague has watched the progress of sister parties that have come back from the dead. The Spanish Prime Minister José Maria Aznar inherited his party in his thirties and against all odds has won two general election victories for the right. He told Hague of the three stages to success:

First: show your party who is boss. Hague believed he fulfilled that by reforming the Tories and establishing a firm line on Europe which gives the country a real choice at the next election.

Second: become a credible opposition.

Third: establish your party as an alternative government. Hague soon proved he could beat Blair at the dispatch box, but this is not a skill that makes much impact outside Westminster. Throughout 2000 he has put New Labour on the defensive, but not on issues that will decide the outcome of a general election.

Against early expectations but almost by default, Hague has taken his party into Aznar's second stage but 'Believing in Britain' will not be enough to secure transition to the third. Hague has effectively highlighted the government's still superficial problems but he has yet to show that he can fashion a Conservatism that enough voters will actively choose as a convincing alternative to New Labour. He has still to articulate a distinctive role for the Conservatives if Britain were to join the Euro, to convince a sceptical audience that he understands that a return to success requires attention to ideas as well as to tactics, and to enthuse potential supporters with a contemporary vision of a modern Conservative Party. This must be the next stage of his project if he is ever to fulfil his life's ambition and become Prime Minister in his own right.

Index